T0097417

MARSHAL
ZHUKOV'S
GREATEST
BATTLES

MARSHAL GEORGI K. ZHUKOV

*New Introduction
and Biographical Record by
DAVID M. GLANTZ*

*Edited with a Preface
and Explanatory Comments by
HARRISON E. SALISBURY*

*Translated from the Russian by
THEODORE SHABAD*

MARSHAL ZHUKOV'S GREATEST BATTLES

BY

GEORGI K. ZHUKOV

Publisher's Note: The portions of the Marshal Zhukov articles here translated into English are based upon the Russian text appearing in *Voyenno-Istoricheskii Zhurnal*, published by the Ministry of Defense in Moscow in June 1965, August, September, and October 1966, and August and September 1967; and in *Stalingradskaya Epopeya* published by the Military Publishing House in Moscow in 1968. The original articles are in the public domain.

First Cooper Square Press edition 2002

This Cooper Square Press paperback edition of *Marshal Zhukov's Greatest Battles* is an unabridged republication of the edition first published in New York in 1969, with the addition of a new introduction and a biographical record. It is reprinted by arrangement with HarperCollins Publishers, Inc.

Maps by Jean Paul Tremblay

Published by Cooper Square Press
A Member of the Rowman & Littlefield Publishing Group
200 Park Avenue South, Suite 1109
New York, New York 10003-1503
www.coopersquarepress.com

Distributed by National Book Network

Library of Congress Cataloging-in-Publication Data Available.

ISBN 978-0-8154-1098-0

Contents

Introduction to the Cooper Square Press Edition

The heroic figure of Marshal Georgi Konstantinovich Zhukov, the Red Army's "Greatest Captain" of the Soviet Union's Great Patriotic War, strides like a colossus across the pages of Russian history. He is portrayed as the Red Army's most illustrious military commander and as the architect of the Soviet Union's signal victory over Hitler's vaunted *Wehrmacht* in the most terrible war that mankind has endured. Today, the ignominious demise of the Soviet Union in 1991 has propelled Zhukov's stature to even more grandiose proportions. The country's unexpected, precipitous fall and the associated revelations of Communism's crimes, which savaged the reputations of entire generations of Soviet political and military heroes, left a yawning vacuum that the famous Zhukov now fills. He has become the sole remaining icon of Russia's twentieth century past.

Zhukov's historical stature and military reputation reflects the tortuous history of the state that he served so loyally. As the perceptive Harrison E. Salisbury noted in his 1969 introduction to *Marshal Zhukov's Greatest Battles*:

History in Russia should be published in loose-leaf books so that pages can be extracted and new ones inserted. Zhukov had been a hero during the war. He became an "unperson" with the war's end. He re-emerged as a hero upon Stalin's death. He vanished from the printed page in 1957. With Khrushchev's fall he came back into print. . . . Comparison of the Zhukov accounts reveals discrepancies, changes, omissions, and inclusions, which reflect not the Marshal's views, but the imposition of higher Communist Party censorship.

In Soviet historiography—and to a lesser extent elsewhere—the victors record the history of the struggles in which they prevail. This has meant accentuating victories and understating, or in some cases, utterly ignoring defeats as the times dictate. Furthermore, in the case of totalitarian states such as the Soviet Union, historians must write and interpret history within the context of current internal political relationships. Accordingly, the interpretation of past victories and defeats, as well as the reputations of wartime military and political leaders, depends largely on whom power rests at any given time and how those in power were associated with those victories and defeats. In short, political sensibilities have forced Soviet military historians to emphasize, obscure, or re-interpret major portions of the war to protect the reputation of the Soviet state or its current leaders.

In Stalin's day, recorded history was only a pale reflection of the war's real course, replete with a litany of the Red Army's victories and a fawning exposé of the dominant role the *Generalissimo* played in their achievement. After Stalin's death in 1953, historical candor ebbed and flowed in consonance with who was in—or out—of power and who was in—or out—of favor. This process was punctuated in the early 1960s and late 1980s by sharp bursts of historical *glasnost* (publicity), first mandated by Khrushchev during his program of de-Stalinization and later by Gorbachev, as he attempted in vain to revitalize the decaying Soviet state. Despite these periods of increased openness and greater candor, Soviet history has remained fettered by censorship. Today, more than ten years since the demise of the Soviet Union and the birth of "democratic" Russia, forty percent of actual Soviet wartime military operations remain obscure or totally forgotten. Given the incomplete operational record and Russian congenital preoccupation with maintaining or denigrating reputations as political need dictates, the reputations of the Soviet army's wartime military commanders require fundamental revision. Since his is the leading star in the galaxy of senior wartime commanders, Marshal Zhukov's reputation requires reevaluation before this historical cleansing process can begin.

As was the case with all senior Red Army generals, Zhukov's wartime reputation reflected postwar political realities. After the war's end, an ever-suspicious Stalin relegated Zhukov to relative obscurity by exiling him to command the Odessa and Ural military districts from 1946 through 1953. At the same time, Stalin ordered historians to expunge Zhukov's name from all written records of the war. After Stalin's death in 1953, Zhukov's reputation rebounded as Stalin's successors rehabilitated him as a counterweight to their former dictator. His reputation as a wartime commander soared, and he became Minister of Defense largely as reward for the constructive role that he played in Khrushchev's rise to power. After 1957, however, the vagaries of Soviet history struck once again, as a suspicious Khrushchev relegated Zhukov to obscurity. The tortuous twists and turns of Soviet history continued as he reemerged triumphant after Khrushchev's ouster from power in 1964. Zhukov's reputation grew steadily in the 1970s and 1980s, finally reaching god-like proportions in the final days of the Soviet Union and in the first decade of the fledgling Russian Federation's existence. Despite Zhukov's ultimate victory, like the war during which he served, the full measure of his service and, by extension, his reputation, remains imperfectly understood.

Marshal Zhukov's Greatest Battles is a compilation of articles published during the late 1960s in the Soviet Ministry of Defense's *Military-Historical Journal* [*Voenno-istoricheskii zhurnal*]. The book establishes the modern baseline for Zhukov's wartime military service and contributions by focusing on the four major battles (Moscow, Stalingrad, Kursk, and Berlin) that gave rise to his reputation. During the same year Zhukov published his memoirs, *Reminiscences and Recollections* [*Vospominaniia i razmyshlenia*], in which he filled in the details of his entire military career and wartime record.[1] Before his death in 1974 Zhukov also contributed to other anthologies covering most of the major operations in which he took part. Since his death numerous biographies have recorded his life and military exploits.[2]

It is now clear, however, that major gaps, omissions, and misinterpretations exist in Zhukov's account of the war and his personal involvement in it. Since disparities exist in virtually every Soviet historical work, they are clearly the fault of censors rather than of Zhukov himself. While the Russians have released the unexpurgated versions of many commanders' memoirs since 1991, they have yet to do so for Zhukov—if such a version exists at all.[3] Sufficient documentary evidence now exists to begin the arduous process of reassessing the Red Army's combat record and the roles and performances of its commanders during the war. While revealing the immense scope and complexity of the reassessment process,

[1] G. Zhukov, *Reminiscence and Recollections* (Moscow: Progress, 1974) (a translation of his 1969 memoirs).

[2] Among the favorable biographies, see V. V. Karpov, *Marshal Zhukov: Ego sobratninki i protivniki v dni voiny i mira* [*Marshal Zhukov: His Colleagues and Enemies in Peace and War*] (Moscow: Voenizdat, 1992); and M. A. Gareev, *Marshal Zhukov: Velikie unikal'nost' polkovodcheskogo iskusstva* [*Marshal Zhukov: The Great Uniqueness of the Commander's Art*] (Moscow: Vostochnyi universitet, 1996). More critical treatments include, Boris Sokolov, *Neizvestnyi Zhukov: Portret bez retyshi* [*The Unknown Zhukov: An Unretouched Portrait*] (Minsk: "Rodiola-plius," 2000) and A. N. Mertsalov and L. A. Mertsalova, *Inoi Zhukov* [*Another Zhukov*] (Moscow: Private Publication, 1996).

[3] For example, see K. K. Rokossovsky, *Soldatskii dolg* [*A Soldiers Duty*] (Moscow: "Golos," 2000) and I. S. Konev, *Zapiski komanduiushchego frontom* [*Notes of a Front Commander*] (Moscow: "Golos," 2000). Both contain fresh information, including derogatory materials on Zhukov.

what follows is also far from complete. In this case, the new information on Zhukov's wartime service represents, in microcosm, the reevaluation process to which the war as a whole must be subjected. The remarks that follow apply broadly to Zhukov's collective memoirs as well as to all biographies about his service. Discrepancies regarding Zhukov's military career extend back to his service in the prewar years. For example, his memoirs—and virtually every Soviet account of the famous clash between his 1st Army Group and the Japanese Army at Khalkhin Gol in August 1939—proclaim the brilliance of his victory. While Zhukov was indeed triumphant at Khalkhin Gol, Soviet historians overemphasized and exploited the victory as a sharp counterpoint to the Red Army's embarrassing performances in Poland and Finland in 1939 and 1940. It is now clear that Zhukov achieved his first celebrated victory at immense human cost, which may have even resulted in a General Staff censure.[4]

While serving as Chief of the Red Army General Staff and as Deputy People's Commissar of Defense during the chaotic initial weeks of the German assault code-named Operation Barbarossa, Zhukov was instrumental in planning and coordinating counteroffensives and counterstrokes mandated by the Soviet 1941 Defense Plan. As described in his memoirs, in late June 1941, he coordinated the Southwestern Front's counterstroke with multiple mechanized corps against the vanguard of German Army Group South. After this failed, he was instrumental in coordinating major counterstrokes in July and August 1941 against German forces in virtually every sector of the front, from Sol'tsy and Staraia Russa in the north to Vladimir-Volynskii and Korosten' in the south. So ex-

[4] For example, see Petro G. Grigorenko, *Memoirs* (New York: W. W. Norton, 1982). At Khalkhin Gol Zhukov's 1st Army Group suffered 15,925 casualties, including 7,974 dead, captured, or missing out of 57,000 men engaged in the operation. This source, and a few others, mention the censure but claim Zhukov removed the incriminating evidence after he became Chief of the General Staff in January 1941.

tensive were these operations that they formed an as-yet-unacknowl-edged, full-fledged counteroffensive.[5]

In late July and early August, Zhukov directed several major Red Army counterstrokes in the Smolensk region in a failed attempt to halt the precipitous German advance east of the Dnepr River. After the Germans captured Smolensk in early August, he coordinated yet another concerted offensive by the Western, Reserve, and Briansk Fronts against German Army Group Center in late August and September, while, at the same time, commanding the Reserve Front. Because it failed with heavy losses, Soviet historians have ignored the grandiose scope of the Smolensk counteroffensive, instead focusing on Zhukov's successful defeat of German forces in the El'nia bridgehead.[6] In his memoirs Zhukov notes correctly that his violent attacks at El'nia convinced Hitler to temporarily abandon the *Wehrmacht*'s advance on Moscow and instead to turn south to destroy German forces defending Kiev. However, the failed Smolensk counteroffensive so debilitated the three defending Soviet *fronts* that they quickly collapsed when, on October 2, 1941 German forces began their advance on Moscow in Operation Typhoon.

Serving as Stalin's and the *Stavka*'s (Headquarters of the Supreme High Command) "fireman," Zhukov halted the German advance on Leningrad in September 1941 before being recalled to Moscow in early October to organize that city's response in the

---

[5] Soviet and Russian sources fail to mention the coordinated nature of these operations, preferring instead to treat each in isolation.

[6] David M. Glantz, *Forgotten Battles of the German-Soviet War (1941–1945), Vol. I: The Summer-Fall Campaign (22 June–4 December 1941)* (Carlisle, PA: Self-published, 1999). Zhukov's signature is on the order mandating many of these counterstrokes and counteroffensives. For recently released *Stavka* and *front* orders, see V. A. Zolotarev, ed., *"Stavka VGK: Dokumenty i materialy 1941 god"* [*Stavka of the Supreme High Command: Documents and materials*], *Russkii arkhiv*, No. 16 5 (1) (Moscow: "Terra," 1996). Subsequent volumes contain *Stavka* and front orders from 1942–1945.

wake of the collapse of Soviet forces west of the city.[7] At Leningrad in September and at Moscow in October and November, Zhukov displayed that unique combination of tenacity, ruthlessness with subordinates, and disregard for human loss that would characterize his performance throughout the remainder of the war. Having helped to save Moscow in those months, Zhukov organized the Red Army's strategic counteroffensive at Moscow in early December. By mid-January, it had grown into a full-fledged winter campaign that encompassed virtually the entire Soviet-German front. Although Zhukov later castigated Stalin for attacking too often in too many locations, it now appears that Zhukov himself insisted on the broad-front approach. He did so based on the assumption that overwhelming pressure applied on German forces in multiple sectors would inevitably produce German collapse. This approach established a pattern to which Zhukov would adhere throughout the remainder of the war.

Zhukov's close association with the Western Front and western (Moscow) strategic axis would endure from his appointment as Western Front commander in October 1941 through the summer of 1943. This was not surprising, since both Stalin and Zhukov considered the western axis to be the most critical sector of the front during this period. Recently released archival materials— and the course of combat on the front as a whole—sharply contradict much of what Zhukov wrote about this period in his postwar testimony.

While planning for operations during the spring and summer of 1942, Zhukov notes correctly that he urged Stalin repeatedly to concentrate operations (both defensive and offensive) along the western axis and that he objected to Stalin's decision to conduct offensives at Khar'kov and in the Crimea in May 1942. While this statement absolves Zhukov of blame for the Red Army's disasters

---

[7] The *Stavka*, headed by Stalin, served as a virtual "war cabinet" by directing all aspects of planning and conducting the war.

that ensued in May, it also indicates that Zhukov did indeed share blame with Stalin for mistakenly assessing German strategic intentions in the summer of 1942. In late June, when the Germans began their drive toward Stalingrad and the Caucasus in Operation Blau, Zhukov remained with the Western Front. His whereabouts underscored his perception of, and preoccupation with, the significance of the western axis. As the *Wehrmacht* plunged deep into southern Russia, Zhukov launched major offensives in July against German forces at Zhizdra and Bolkhov, north of Orel, and in August and September against German forces in the Rzhev-Viaz'ma salient. While Zhukov and Soviet historians have described the twin offensives as mere diversions designed to draw German attention and reserves away from the more critical Stalingrad axis to the south, it is now clear that the operations were far more ambitious. As Zhukov lets slip with regard to the August offensive near the Rzhev-Viaz'ma salient:

> If we had had one or two more armies at our disposal, we could have defeated the enemy, in conjunction with the Kalinin Front, not only in the Rzhev area but in the entire Rzhev-Vyazma salient, and could thus have improved our operational situation on the entire front west of Moscow, but our forces were extremely limited at the time.[8]

In fact, his August 1942 Rzhev-Sychevka offensive was far stronger than Zhukov indicated, and served as a dress rehearsal for an even more massive offensive planned for several months later. Certainly, as Deputy Commander-in-Chief and *Stavka* representative, Zhukov played a major role in planning the famous Stalingrad counteroffensive, Operation Uranus. However, his account of military operations during the fall of 1942 and of his role in them was disingenuous at best and outright falsification at worst. Archival documents now indicate that Zhukov planned and conducted Operation Mars, a companion piece to Operation Ura-

---

[8] *Marshal Zhukov's Greatest Battles*, p. 131.

nus and a clear follow-up to his August and September Rzhev-Sychevka offensive. Furthermore, the scope and intent of Operation Mars was comparable to—if not more important strategically—than Operation Uranus, which his *Stavka* colleague Marshal A. M. Vasilevsky coordinated. Zhukov states the following about his involvement with Operation Mars (without ever using its code name), beginning with a meeting with Stalin on either November 12 or 13:

> Vasilevsky and I drew Stalin's attention to the fact that as soon as the enemy was in trouble at Stalingrad and in the Northern Caucasus, the German command would be compelled to move relief forces from other sectors, especially from the Vyazma area, west of Moscow. To prevent this, we proposed an offensive north of Vyazma against the German salient around Rzhev. Such an operation could be launched by troops of the Kalinin and Western Fronts.
>
> "That would be a good idea," Stalin said. "But which of you would handle it?"
>
> Vasilevsky and I had agreed on that point beforehand, and therefore I said, "The Stalingrad operation is essentially all prepared. Vasilevsky could take over the coordination of operations around Stalingrad, and I could handle preparations for the counteroffensive on the Kalinin and Western fronts."
>
> On November 17 I was summoned back to Supreme Headquarters to work out the operations plan for the Kalinin and Western fronts.
>
> On November 28 I was at Kalinin Front headquarters discussing the proposed offensive west of Moscow.
>
> To prevent the Germans from shifting forces from Army Group Center, Supreme Headquarters had decided to launch an offensive on the Western and Kalinin fronts against the Rzhev salient (as I stated earlier). Planning and preparations for the offensive were completed in the period from November 20 to December 8 [for an attack on December 10–11].[9]

Zhukov describes Operation Mars in five short paragraphs, noting only that, while it failed, it did prevent the German command

[9] *Marshal Zhukov's Greatest Battles*, p. 170–173, 177, 180–182.

from shifting forces southward to the Stalingrad region. Archival materials now reveal that planning for Operation Mars began in early October (rather than November 12–13), and that the operation was to commence on October 28, but poor weather delayed its start to November 25. Further, Zhukov was with the Kalinin Front from October 21 to October 29 (rather than on November 28), ostensibly planning the operation, and on two other occasions from November 19 to December 6 and from December 9 to December 29 to supervise its conduct. Rather than beginning on December 10–11, Operation Mars began on November 25 and did not end until December 23.[10]

After the failure of Operation Mars, in January 1943 Stalin dispatched Zhukov to Leningrad with orders to raise the German blockade of the city. There, Zhukov planned and supervised the conduct of Operation Spark (*Iskra*), an offensive designed to penetrate German defenses east of the city and to restore communications between the forces besieged in Leningrad and the rest of the country. While Zhukov's brief account of Operation Spark is accurate, it fails to note the vast scope and ambitious intent of the ensuing Red Army offensive. In reality, Operation Spark was merely the first phase of a far larger and vastly more ambitious plan that Zhukov had convinced the *Stavka* to adopt. In short, in late January 1943, adhering to his broad-front strategy, Zhukov argued that the Red Army had to exploit its dramatic victories in southern Russia by mounting multiple major offensives along the Western and Northwestern strategic axes.

Beginning in early February, on Zhukov's recommendation,

---

[10] For Zhukov's wartime assignments see, S. I. Iseev, "*Vekhi frontovogo puti: Khronika deiatel'nosti Marshala Sovetskogo Soiuza G. K. Zhukova v period Velikoi Otechestvennoi voiny 1941–1945 gg.* [Landmarks of a Front Journey: A Chronicle of the Activities of Marshal of the Soviet Union G. K. Zhukov in the Great Patriotic War 1941–1945] in Voenno-istoricheskii zhurnal [Military-HistoricalJournal], No. 10 (October 1991), p. 22–34. For details on Operation Mars, see David M. Glantz, *Zhukov's Greatest Defeat: The Red Army's Epic Disaster in Operation Mars* (Lawrence, KS: The University Press of Kansas, 1999).

the *Stavka* expanded the scope of Vasilevsky's offensive in southern Russia toward Khar'kov and into the Donbas region by adding a series of new strategic objectives. First, the *Stavka* added Kursk to the list of objectives and then, in succession, the Orel region, the Rzhev-Viaz'ma salient, the Smolensk region, and finally all of Leningrad's *oblast'* (region). To accomplish such ambitious aims, the *Stavka* formed the new Central Front in mid-February (under General Rokossovsky's command) and the powerful "Special Group Khozin" under Northwestern Front command. Rokossovsky's Central Front was to advance on Briansk and Smolensk in conjunction with a Kalinin-Western and Briansk Fronts offensive on Rzhev, Viaz'ma, and Orel. Together, the four fronts were to destroy German Army Group Center and to advance through Smolensk into Belorussia. Khozin's Special Group, under Zhukov's direct personal supervision, was to advance on Pskov and Narva to destroy Army Group North and to liberate Leningrad. Zhukov's and the *Stavka*'s ultimate objective in February and March 1943 was nothing short of driving the *Wehrmacht* into the Baltic region and across the Dnepr River into Belorussia and the Ukraine. Signifying the importance of the offensive and Zhukov's key role in it, the *Stavka* assigned Zhukov responsibility for supervising the liberation of the Leningrad region in an offensive codenamed Operation Polar Star.

Operation Polar Star and the other associated offensives failed spectacularly, which most likely explains their omission from Zhukov's memoirs, for a variety of reasons.[11] First, the *Stavka*'s plan, which adopted Zhukov's approach of applying maximum pressure on German defenses across an exceedingly broad front was overly ambitious and in no way accorded with the Red Army's actual capabilities. Second, poor weather and regrouping problems thwarted the Soviet offensive timetable. Third, the Germans preemptively withdrew from the threatened Demiansk and Rzhev salients,

---

[11] Zhukov includes a short description of his role in operations at Leningrad at the end of the final chapter of the first volume in his memoirs.

shortening their front and disrupting Soviet offensive plans. Finally, German Field Marshal von Manstein's counteroffensive in the Donbas and Khar'kov regions disrupted the Soviet offensive, leaving the Kursk bulge as a telltale legacy of Soviet over-ambition. Understandably, Zhukov fails to note any of these operations in his various memoirs.[12]

Nor does Zhukov spend much time recounting his actions in the Northern Caucasus region in April and May 1943, instead focusing primarily on his involvement in preparing and conducting the Kursk defense and offensive in the summer of 1943. In fact, Stalin dispatched Zhukov to the North Caucasus Front to break the German stranglehold on the Taman' region and on the vital Black Sea port of Novorossiisk. Once again, Zhukov organized an offensive against German defenses around Krymskaia in characteristic fashion, by relying on well-organized but costly frontal attacks on German defensive positions. After heavy Red Army losses and minimal gains the offensive failed, and Zhukov returned to the Kursk region in May.[13]

Zhukov served as *Stavka* representative to the *fronts* participating in the Kursk defense from May through July 1943. During this period, while preparing the Red Army's defense of the Kursk bulge, Zhukov also helped to plan offensive operations in conjunction with the Kursk defense as well as major counteroffensives scheduled to begin once the expected German attack faltered. These aggressive plans included major operations (later described as diversions) by the Southwestern and Southern Fronts along the Northern Donets and Mius Rivers and, more importantly, major

[12] For complete coverage of "Operation Polar Star" see David M. Glantz, *Forgotten Battles of the German-Soviet War (1941–1945), Vol. IV: The Winter Campaign (19 November 1942–21 March 1943)* (Carlisle, PA: Self-published, 1999).

[13] For details on the battles in the Krymskaia region see, David M. Glantz, *Forgotten Battles of the German-Soviet War (!941–1945), vol. V, part 1: The Summer-Fall Campaign (1 July-31 December 1943)* (Carlisle, PA: Self-published, 2000).

offensives by the Western, Briansk, and Central Fronts against German Army Group Center's forces at Orel, Briansk, and Smolensk. The latter marked a return to Zhukov's earlier fixation on destroying German Army Group Center. After the German offensive against the Kursk bulge failed, Red Army forces conducted Zhukov's Orel offensive (codenamed Operation Kutuzov) and, soon after, the Belgorod-Khar'kov offensive (Operation Rumiantsev).[14]

The ensuing Red Army summer-fall campaign bore the clear hallmarks of a series of Zhukov-style offensive operations. It began in July 1943 with the Orel offensive; by August, massive Red Army offensives rippled continuously along the entire Soviet-German front, from Nevel' to the Black Sea. During this period the *Stavka's* immediate goal of reaching the Sozh and Dnepr Rivers expanded into full-scale offensives across those water barriers into Belorussia and the Ukraine. Contrary to conventional histories, the Red Army once again adopted Zhukov's broad-front strategy in these operations. Zhukov himself remained along the southwestern axis from August through December 1943, and coordinated the operations of the Central (Belorussian), Voronezh (1st Ukrainian), and Steppe (2d Ukrainian) Fronts.[15] After Soviet forces reached the Dnepr River from Gomel to south of Kiev in September 1943, Zhukov orchestrated a series of massive offensives to establish strategic bridgeheads west of the Dnepr River in southern Belorussia and northeastern Ukraine.

In his memoir Zhukov seriously understates the scope and violence of the October 1943 operations along, and west of, the Dnepr:

> Between October 12 and December 23, the troops of the Voronezh Front carried through the Kiev strategic operation.

---

[14] Zhukov remained with the Briansk and Western Fronts from 9–13 July, and, after their operation commenced on 12 July, returned to the two *fronts* from 28 July through 1 August

[15] The Central and Voronezh Fronts were re-designated the Belorussian and 1st Ukrainian Fronts on 20 October 1943. At the same time, the Steppe, Southwestern, and Southern Fronts became the 2d, 3d, and 4th Ukrainian Fronts.

It had initially been planned to smash the Kiev grouping and regain Kiev by a main blow from the Bukrin bridgehead [south of the city]. This plan later had to be abandoned as the enemy concentrated the main forces of the Kiev grouping at that point. This direction was stated for subsidiary action, while the main blow was shifted to the Lyutezh bridgehead, north of Kiev, where the Nazis had weakened their northern sector.

He then recounts in detail the regrouping of Red Army forces to the Lyutezh bridgehead north of Kiev and the spectacularly successful offensive that captured Kiev and established a major bridgehead west of the Dnepr.

Throughout his account of the fighting for Kiev, Zhukov fails to mention the Central (Belorussian) and Voronezh Fronts' violent and costly offensives that raged for almost a month west of the Dnepr River. These included multiple offensives by the Central Front's 13th and 60th Armies near Chernobyl' and Gornostaipol', by the Voronezh Front's 38th Army at Liutezh, and the bloody repulse of five Voronezh Front armies (including the 3rd Guards Tank Army) at the Bukrin bridgehead south of Kiev.[16] Zhukov neglects to mention the *Stavka*'s revulsion over these repeated bloody defeats. Nor does he note that the plan approved by the *Stavka* to shift the Voronezh Front's forces to the Liutezh bridgehead was likely formulated by General Vatutin, the 1st Ukrainian Front commander, rather than by Zhukov himself. At the same time, Zhukov echoes the same mistaken claims by other Soviet historians that offensive operations in fall 1943 and winter 1944 were limited primarily to the Ukraine. In fact, the Red Army conducted powerful and sustained offensives into Belorussia, most of which achieved only limited gains.[17]

---

[16] The 38th Army's (and 5th Guards Tank Corps') attack from the Liutezh bridgehead penetrated into Kiev's western outskirts before being repulsed.

[17] The clear exception was the Kalinin (1st Baltic) Front's thrust at Nevel', north of Vitebsk, and the deep penetration by Rokossovsky's Central (Belorussian) Front southwest of Gomel'.

After the successful conclusion of the Kiev strategic offensive in December, Zhukov remained with the 1st and 2nd Ukrainian Fronts throughout the winter of 1943–44, coordinating their Zhitomir-Berdichev and Korsun'-Shevchenkovskii offensives. At the same time, he monitored and provided advice on offensive operations in Belorussia and along the lower Dnepr River, many details of which have been forgotten or concealed. Throughout, the Red Army operated on the basis of his broad-front strategy, maintaining unrelenting pressure on defending German forces.[18]

In early March, after its commander, General Vatutin, had perished at the hands of Ukrainian partisans, Zhukov took personal command of the 1st Ukrainian Front. During March and April 1944, he led that *front* in its dramatic advance to the Carpathian Mountains in the western Ukraine, encircling the German First Panzer Army in the process.[19] Although much has yet to be revealed about this offensive, it is known that the beleaguered German army managed to escape into southern Poland in mid-April 1944.

In early May 1944, in circumstances that remain unclear, Zhukov may have been involved in yet another major forgotten operation. Between May 2 and 12, 1944, the Soviet 2nd and 3rd Ukrainian Fronts conducted a major offensive to liberate Iassy and Kishinev and to gain a strategic foothold in northern Rumania. The twin offensives, which involved three Soviet tank armies, failed leaving only memories of what the Germans termed the Targul-Frumos Operation. Zhukov may have been instrumental in directing both operations.[20]

---

[18] For a description of largely forgotten operations in Belorussia and along the lower Dnepr in fall 1943 see, David M. Glantz, *Forgotten Battles of the German-Soviet War (1941–1945), vol. V, parts 1 and 2: The Summer-Fall Campaign (1 July–31 December 1943)* (Carlisle, PA: Self-published, 2000).

[19] The Soviets termed the offensive the Proskurov-Chernovtsy operation and the Germans call it Kamenets-Podolsk.

[20] Soviet historians have erased virtually all references to this operation, even though the German Fuhrungsakademie has long included it in its instruction. For a German account, see F. M. on Senger und Etterlin, Der Gegenschlag [The encounter

During late spring and early summer 1944, Zhukov took active part in planning the summer strategic offensive, which began against his old nemesis, Army Group Center, in Belorussia. During the course of the summer, the offensive expanded to consume German forces in Poland and Rumania. Here, Zhukov's memoirs track well with events, as Red Army forces defeated, in succession, German Army Group Center and Army Groups Northern and Southern Ukraine. His involvement in these operations included service with the 1st Belorussian Front during its controversial advance on Warsaw in August 1944. Zhukov's account, however, avoids any comments on the ensuing heated debate over why the Red Army failed to capture Warsaw and to rescue the Polish Home Army during its ill-fated uprising.

After the heavy fighting along the Narew and Vistula Rivers in the fall of 1944, during which Zhukov coordinated the operations of multiple Red Army *fronts*, on November 30 Stalin gave Zhukov command of the 1st Belorussian Front, which he led during its January 1945 advance across Poland toward Berlin. Zhukov's account of the planning and conduct of the so-called Vistula-Oder operation, which propelled Soviet forces westward to the Oder River in early February 1945, is straightforward and candid. He describes accurately his *front*'s spectacular advance across Poland and the historical controversy that ensued over Stalin's early February decision to halt the offensive along the Oder River line, only thirty miles from Berlin. Likewise, his account of the Berlin offensive is accurate, though it tantalizingly skirts direct mention of the political factors that entered into Stalin's decision to attack on April 16, 1945:

> The original idea and plan for the Berlin operation were further developed at Supreme Headquarters throughout the entire period of

---

battle] (Neckargemund: Scharnhorst Buchkameradsschaft, 1959). Soviet archival materials now confirm that the offensive was of even larger scale than described in German sources. In essence, this operation should be termed the 1st Iassy-Kishinev offensive.

the Vistula-Oder operation. At first Supreme Headquarters thought of starting the operation with three *fronts* simultaneously, but it was developed that the Second Byelorussian Front, which after the East Prussian operation had to move its forces from the Danzig-Gdynia area to the lower reaches of the Oder, would not have been ready to force the Oder before April 20.

In view of the existing military and political situation, Supreme Headquarters decided to launch the Berlin operation with two *fronts* not later than April 16.

What Zhukov leaves unsaid was that Allied forces had reached the Elbe River west of Berlin by April 16 and were poised to strike toward Berlin from the west, thereby prompting Stalin's decision to hasten his offensive.[21] In his account of that titanic battle, which spelled doom for Hitler's Third Reich, Zhukov also obscures the difficulties his forces encountered during their costly advance on the German capital, as well as the heated postwar controversy over the relative performance of his and other forces participating in the Berlin offensive.[22]

The vagaries of how the Soviets wrote the history of their great Patriotic War demands fundamental reassessment of the wartime careers and performance of Zhukov as well as of other senior Red Army commanders. After all, however great the "Great Captains" have been, they are indeed men, and are not free from human faults and frailties. Candidly acknowledging those features makes these figures more human and hence more credible.

When assessing Zhukov's long and illustrious career, several distinct attributes emerge. First and foremost, his iron will and strong stomach made him tenacious on offense and defense and unsparing of himself and his subordinates. Recent archival evidence

[21] In fact, unbeknownst to Stalin, the Americans received an order to halt their advance on 16 April.

[22] This applies, in particular, to the account by Marshal Konev, the commander of the neighboring 1st Ukrainian Front, who star rose in the immediate postwar years, while Zhukov's went into decline.

serves only to reinforce Harrison Salisbury's judgment that "Zhukov never fought a battle in which he was sparing of the lives of men. Only by expenditure of life, he believed, could the military goals be achieved." In this sense, Zhukov resembled the American general Ulysses S. Grant, a superb strategist and practitioner of operational art who, nevertheless, displayed frequent tactical errors. Just as bloody military defeats at Cold Harbor and Spotsylvania in 1864 during the American Civil War did little to diminish Grant's fame, so also Zhukov's failures should not diminish the fact that he was one of the preeminent architects of Soviet victory over Hitler's vaunted *Wehrmacht.*

> DAVID M. GLANTZ
> Carlisle, Pennsylvania
> January 2002

DAVID M. GLANTZ, author of *Zhukov's Greatest Defeat,* and (with Johnathan M. House) *When Titans Clashed,* and *The Battle of Kursk,* is editor of *The Journal of Slavic Military Studies.* He lives in Carlisle, Pennsylvania, near Harrisburg.

Biographical Record of Zhukov, Marshal of the Soviet Union

Born November 19 (December 1), 1896 in Strel'kovka, Kaluga Province

Joined the Tsarist Army (August 1915) and served as an enlisted soldier and non-commissioned officer in the 5th Reserve Cavalry Regiment (August 1915–August 1916) and 10th Cavalry Regiment (August 1916–December 1917) during World War I

Joined the Red Army's 4th Regiment, 1st Moscow Cavalry Division (October 1918)

Fought as a soldier and platoon and squadron commander in the 1st Moscow Cavalry Division on the Eastern, Western, and Southern Fronts during the Russian Civil War (1918–1920). Joined the Bolshevik Party on March 1, 1919

Attended and graduated from the 1st Riazan' Cavalry Course (January–August 1920)
Sergeant Major, cavalry squadron, composite regiment, 2d Moscow Brigade (July–August 1920)

Commander, 2d Platoon, 1st Cavalry Regiment, 14th Detached Cavalry Brigade (August–September 1920)

Commander, 2d Squadron, 1st Cavalry Regiment, 14th Detached Cavalry Brigade (September 1920–June 1922)

Squadron commander, 38th Cavalry Regiment, and Deputy Commander, 40th Cavalry Regiment, 7th Samara Cavalry Division (June 1922–March 1923)

Commander, 39th Buzuluk Cavalry Regiment, 7th Samara Cavalry Division (May 1923–1924)

Attended and graduated from the Course for the Improvement of Cavalry Officers, Leningrad Higher Cavalry School (1924–1925)

Commander, 39th Melekess-Pugachevsk Cavalry Regiment, 7th Samara Cavalry Division (1925–May 1930)

Commander, 2d Cavalry Brigade, 7th Samara Cavalry Division (May 1930–February 1931)

Attended and graduated from the Senior Command Cadre Course in Moscow (December 1929–March 1930)

Assistant Inspector of Red Army Cavalry (February–March 1931)

Commander, 4th Cavalry Division, 3d Cavalry Corps, Belorussian Special Military District (March 1931–July 1937)

Commander, 3d Cavalry Corps, Belorussian Special Military District (July 1937–February 1938)

Commander, 6th Cavalry Corps, Belorussian Special Military District (February–June 1938)

Deputy Commander, Belorussian Special Military District (June 1938–July 1939)

Commander, 1st Army Group of Soviet Forces, Mongolia (July 1939–June 1940)

Commander, Kiev Special Military District (June 1940–January 1941)

Chief of Staff, Red Army, and Deputy Peoples' Commissar of Defense (January–June 1941)

Member, *Stavka VGK* (1941–1945)

1st Deputy Peoples' Commissar of Defense and Deputy Supreme High Commander (August 1942–1945)

Stavka VGK representative/coordinator, Southwestern Front (June 1941)

Commander, Reserve Front (July–September 1941)

Commander, Leningrad Front (September–October 1941)

Commander, Western Front (October 1941–August 1942)

Commander, Western Direction Main Command (February–May 1942)

Stavka VGK representative/coordinator, Reserve Front (October 1941)

Stavka VGK representative/coordinator Western and Kalinin Fronts (November–December 1942)

Stavka VGK representative/coordinator Leningrad and Volkhov Fronts (January 1943)

Stavka VGK representative/coordinator, Northwestern Front (February–March 1943)

Stavka VGK representative/coordinator, Voronezh and Steppe Fronts (April 1943)

Stavka VGK representative/coordinator, North Caucasus Front (April–May 1943)

Stavka VGK representative/coordinator Voronezh, Central, and Western Fronts (May–June 1943)

Stavka VGK representative/coordinator, Southwestern Front (June 1943)

Stavka VGK representative/coordinator, Briansk, Central, and Western Fronts (June–July 1943)

Stavka VGK representative/coordinator, Steppe and Voronezh Fronts (August–September 1943)

Stavka VGK representative/coordinator, Central and Voronezh Fronts (September–December 1943)

Stavka VGK representative/coordinator, 1st and 2d Ukrainian Fronts (January–March 1944)

Commander, 1st Ukrainian Front (March–May 1944)

Stavka VGK representative/coordinator, 1st and 2d Belorussian and 1st Ukrainian Fronts (June–August 1944)

Stavka VGK representative/coordinator, 3d Ukrainian Front (September 1944)

Stavka VGK representative/coordinator, 1st and 2d Belorussian and 1st Ukrainian Fronts (September–November 1944)

Commander, 1st Belorussian Front (November 1944–May 1945)

Commander-in-Chief, Group of Soviet Occupation Forces, Germany, and Chief, Soviet

Military Administration (June 1945–March 1946)

Commander-in-Chief, Soviet Army Ground Forces and Deputy minister of the Armed Forces (March–July 1946)

Commander, Odessa and Ural Military Districts (July 1946–March 1953)

First Deputy Minister of Defense (March 1953–February 1955)

Minister of Defense (February 1955–October 1957)

Died June 18, 1974

Maps

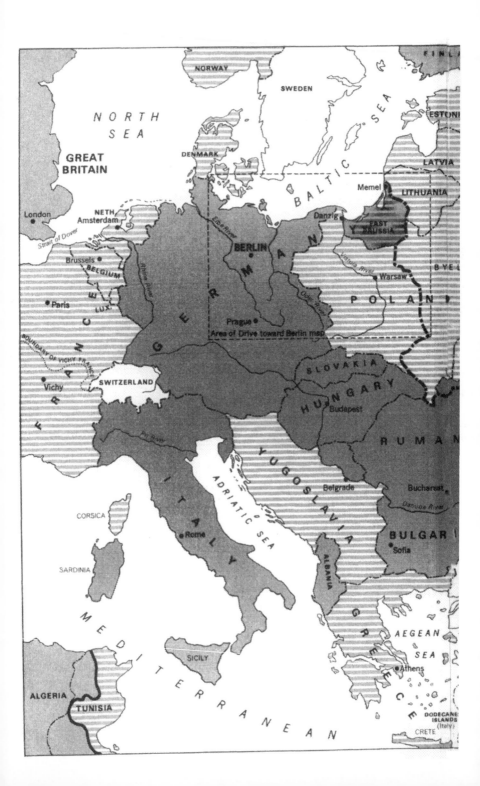

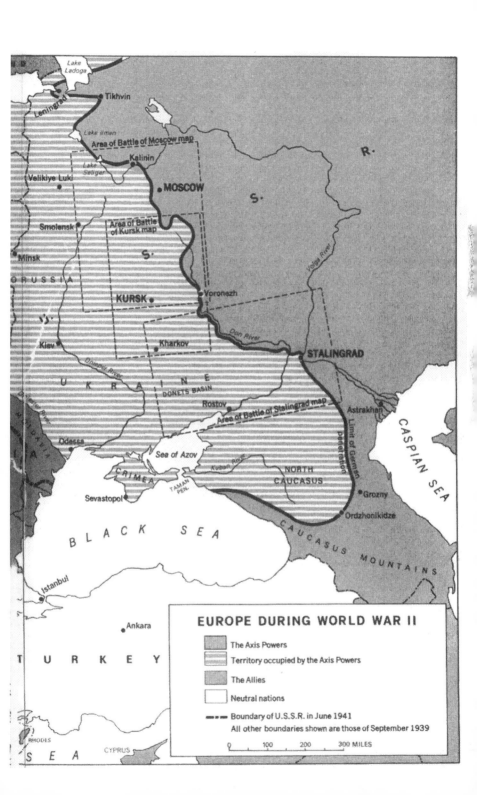

EUROPE DURING WORLD WAR II

- The Axis Powers
- Territory occupied by the Axis Powers
- The Allies
- Neutral nations
- ▬ ▬ ▬ Boundary of U.S.S.R. in June 1941

All other boundaries shown are those of September 1939

0   100   200   300 MILES

Lake Ladoga
Tikhvin
Leningrad
Lake Ilmen
Area of Battle of Moscow map
Kalinin
Lake Seliger
Velikiye Luki
MOSCOW
Smolensk
Area of Battle of Kursk map
Minsk
W. RUSSIA
KURSK
Voronezh
Kiev
Kharkov
Dnieper River
Don River
STALINGRAD
Volga River
UKRAINE
DONETS BASIN
Rostov
Area of Battle of Stalingrad map
Astrakhan
Odessa
Sea of Azov
Kuban River
Limit of German penetration
CASPIAN SEA
MOLDAVIA
CRIMEA
TAMAN PEN.
NORTH CAUCASUS
Grozny
Sevastopol
Ordzhonikidze
BLACK   SEA
CAUCASUS   MOUNTAINS
Istanbul
Ankara
TURKEY
RHODES
CYPRUS
SEA

Preface

In the late evening of June 21, 1941, Georgi Konstantinovich Zhukov sat at a desk in the Defense Commissar's office on Frunze Street in Moscow, furiously scribbling telegrams to the principal commanders of the Red Army.

It had been a tense day and the evening was humid and close despite thundershowers a bit earlier. Zhukov, at forty-five, a solid, heavy-set, rather darkly handsome man, wore the shoulder insignia of a full general in the Red Army. He was now, as he had been for several months, Chief of Staff of the Soviet High Command, No. 2 to his friend and long-time associate, Marshal Semyon Timoshenko, the People's Commissar of Defense.

On that evening of June 21 Zhukov and Timoshenko were working in Timoshenko's office, personally filling out telegraph blanks. The pile of telegrams grew higher and higher as the clock slowly ticked away, but not until thirty minutes after midnight, thirty minutes into the morning of June 22, 1941, was an orderly summoned to rush the messages to the dispatchers for transmission to all military commands on Russia's western, northern and southern frontiers.

Orders to draft the telegrams had been given at a troubled meeting of the Politburo which Josef Stalin had hurriedly called in his Kremlin office a few hours earlier to consider mounting evidence that the Nazis were preparing to attack the Soviet Union.

The sense of the Politburo meeting had been confused because Stalin still refused to believe that war was about to begin. The Soviet dictator continued to suggest that the *real* danger was of a provocation, an attack, possibly by individual Nazi generals who wished to create a *casus belli*, to make an excuse for a war between Russia and Germany. Nor had Stalin been able to erase from his mind a deep, festering suspicion that, by some means or other, that old fox, Winston Churchill, was trying to trick him into war with Germany.

The fact that Stalin's military and intelligence chiefs were able to present him with detailed plans, precise data on the hour of the intended German attack, the numbers of divisions emplaced on the western frontiers, the objectives of the main German thrusts—none of this counterbalanced in Stalin's mind a sickly fear that Russia somehow might be provoked into taking action which would make war with Germany inescapable. Not even information brought across the lines by German deserters, warning that the hour of attack had been fixed for 4 A.M., seemed to make an impression on Stalin. The deserters, he thought, could be part of the big trick.

What General Zhukov thought of all this—if, indeed, he was even asked for an opinion at the Kremlin meeting—is not known. Now as a good soldier he was writing out telegrams which expressed the essence of Stalin's position. The telegrams warned Russia's commanders of the possibility of a sudden attack from the German side on either June 22 or 23. They said that the action might begin with a "provocation." The Soviet armed forces were ordered to avoid any action that could be interpreted by the Germans as provocation but at the same time to take up defensive positions, occupy advanced field fortifications, camouflage aircraft, disperse planes to field locations, place all troops on the alert, man antiaircraft defenses, prepare to black out cities and institute civil defense precautions. All of this was to be done before dawn of June 22 and in the greatest secrecy lest even the carrying out of defense maneuvers be seized upon by the Nazis as an excuse for making war.

Long before many of the telegrams could be delivered the German attack had begun, at 3:30 A.M. Even in those commands where the instructions arrived before the actual start of war the interlude was far too short to permit the assumption of an effective defense posture.

The truth was that one of the great military disasters of our time was in the making on the night of June 21-22, 1941—the colossal tactical surprise which Hitler's armies achieved over the Russians. Within hours the Soviet Air Force would lie burnt, wrecked, destroyed on the ground, its commanders facing the firing squad or cheating the executioner by suicide. The flower of the Red Army would be staggering east, some units decimated, many without arms, others virtually exterminated. Hundreds of thousands of troops would find themselves fatally trapped and encircled, scores or even hundreds of miles behind the spearheads of the advancing Nazi panzers. Within a few weeks German armies would stand at the gates of Leningrad, Kiev and Moscow, and the fate of the Soviet state would hang in the balance.

As the clock ticked away that long spring evening, it brought Stalin and his Russia minute by minute closer to disaster. By the same token it propelled Zhukov into perhaps the most striking military career of the century.

The names of many military men may be better known in the West—England's Montgomery, Germany's Rommel and Guderian, de Gaulle of France, America's Eisenhower, MacArthur and Patton.

But when history has completed its painful task of evaluation, when the grain of achievement is sifted from the chaff of notoriety, it seems certain that the name which will stand above all others as the master of the art of mass warfare in the twentieth century will be that of this broad-beamed, fierce, determined man who turned the tide of battle against the Nazis, against Hitler, not once but time after time after time.

Not that Zhukov is without his critics, particularly in his own country. The passions, ambitions and rivalries born in the titanic battles of Russia have left deep marks. The struggle of the Soviet armies against the German forces was succeeded by the struggle of the Soviet marshals against each other. These men, powerful, egocentric, domineering, central figures in battles in which they commanded as many men as are to be found in a great metropolitan city, superfigures who held hundreds of thousands of lives at their disposal, seldom see the events of World War II in an even light. You will look in vain in their memoirs for objective or dispassionate accounts of what happened. They are combative, argumentative men carrying on polemics not only with those German generals who have written of the war but against each other, against Stalin, against Stalin's associates and Stalin's successors. They are quick to blame, slow to acknowledge error.

In these polemics no greater controversies have arisen than those which have swirled around the name of Zhukov, a humble name in Russian, the root of which is *zhuk*—meaning beetle or cockroach.

In the inevitably acrimonious debate over responsibility for the colossal blunders which came so close to giving Hitler victory over Russia, there was a savage search for scapegoats. Stalin, of course, was the man upon whom responsibility rested since, as absolute dictator, the decisions and errors were his. His hated, feared police chiefs and his bumbling cronies, Voroshilov and Budenny, have shared the opprobrium. However, some

Soviet critics, particularly those who wanted to protect the sacrosanct figure of Stalin, sought to shift the blame to Zhukov and Timoshenko. These men headed the defense establishment on the eve of war. They should have taken precautions. They should have insisted on Stalin's putting the Red Army on the alert. So ran the indictment.

In actual fact, as the record shows, there was not a chance of turning Stalin from his fatal course. Zhukov had been serving as Chief of Staff just six months when war broke out. He was named to the post on January 14, 1941, in a manner typical of the way in which Stalin ran his country. Over Christmas and New Year's the Kremlin had conducted a military conference which wound up with high-level war games, based on a postulated German attack. Suddenly (on two hours' notice) Stalin summoned his top commanders to the Kremlin and ordered the Chief of Staff, Kirill Meretskov, to deliver a report on the exercise. Flustered and unprepared, Meretskov botched his report. Discussion was supposed to follow. Instead, Stalin curtly intervened:

"Comrade Timoshenko has requested that Comrade Zhukov be named Chief of the General Staff. Do you all agree?"

There were no objections. Without explanation Meretskov was out, Zhukov was in. Even at that point Zhukov was not exactly an unknown. But he was a comparatively junior officer, almost as junior an officer in the Soviet hierarchy as was Dwight D. Eisenhower when General George Marshall jumped him over hundreds of seniors and put him on the path to becoming America's No. 1 World War II commander.

The parallels in the careers of the two men were to strike both of them later when each found himself his nation's supreme commander at war's end in Berlin.

In 1941 Zhukov's career had reached the take-off point. All his life he had been a professional soldier. In fact, he may descend from a line of Russian professional soldiers dating back to Tartar times. He was born into a poor peasant family in the village of Strelkovka about sixty miles east of Moscow, but Strelkovka was no ordinary hamlet. The name of the village derives from the *streltsi,* the archers of Ivan the Terrible who set up settlements on the approaches to Moscow to protect the Russian capital against Tartar assault.

Zhukov's military life began early. At twelve he had been apprenticed to the fur trade in Moscow, but when World War I broke out, he joined the crack Novgorod Dragoons, winning two Orders of St. George, the highest czarist military decoration, for bravery before the Revolution came and he signed up for the Red Army in October, 1918.

Zhukov's career and that of the Soviet regime are practically coterminous. He became a Bolshevik Party member in 1919 and fought against the Whites at Tsaritsyn, where Stalin made the military reputation which his courtiers later were so vastly to inflate. Zhukov was wounded in the Tsaritsyn battles but not seriously. Here he first came in contact with Timoshenko when his cavalry unit was attached to Timoshenko's 2nd Cavalry Brigade, which, in turn, was part of Budenny's famous First Cavalry Army. Zhukov had been a noncommissioned officer in the Czar's army. He rose to squadron commander under Timoshenko.

With the end of the Civil War Zhukov began his education in Red Army schools and was still serving under Timoshenko in the 3rd Cavalry Corps, attached to the Byelorussian Military District, when he was detached for study at the Frunze Military Academy in 1928–31.

In the early thirties Zhukov shifted from cavalry to tanks. He had been one of the Red Army officers who had gone to Germany secretly before the rise of Hitler to study with General Hans von Seeckt, and he was one of the officers sent to Spain to observe German, Italian and Russian armored tactics under battlefield conditions. Later, he went to China with the Soviet military mission attached to Chiang Kai-shek and had a look at the techniques of the Japanese Kwantung Army. All of this made excellent preparation for Zhukov's great chance, now dramatically taking shape on the night of June 21–22. The years 1936–38 had been the time of the great Stalin purges. In 1938 the blow fell on the Red Army. Stalin wiped out its leadership cadre, beginning with the commander in chief, Marshal Tukhachevsky, and continuing through the officer corps. One-half or more of the 75,000 officers in the Red Army were liquidated—shot, arrested, sent to prison or concentration camp.

The void had to be filled. The men of Zhukov's generation—those who had survived—found themselves propelled into top positions.

In 1938 the Russians and the Japanese had fought a bloody but undeclared war at Lake Khasan on the Manchurian–Maritime Provinces frontier about seventy-five miles southwest of Vladivostok. The engagement ended inconclusively. Then in 1939 more serious fighting developed along the Manchurian-Mongolian frontier. The trouble started in January with a minor border clash but steadily grew more intense. By May major Japanese forces were engaged against combined Soviet-Mongolian units in the vicinity of Khalkhin-Gol on the eastern approaches of Mongolia. The fighting spread as the Japanese engaged larger and larger units, until in July a small-scale war was in progress in which the Soviets were being very hard pressed.

At this point Georgi Zhukov made his appearance. He took over the Soviet First Army Group and for the first time demonstrated what came to be his outstanding military characteristics. Zhukov assumed command in early July. He held a defensive posture against the Japanese for weeks while carefully, methodically, building up his forces until he mustered a three-to-two superiority in manpower, a two-to-one ratio in artillery and planes and a four-to-one advantage in armor. By the time he was ready to attack, Zhukov had mustered 35 infantry battalions and 20 cavalry squadrons against the 25 infantry battalions and 17 cavalry squadrons of the Japanese Sixth Army. Zhukov also had nearly 500 tanks, 346 armored cars and 500 planes. He attacked at 5:45 A.M. August 20, 1939. By August 31 he had driven the Japanese back in disorder across the Mongol-Manchurian frontier. The British military historian John Erickson describes this action accurately as "a brilliant but costly operation." Zhukov had been lavish in expenditure of manpower. He had been painstaking in building up a massive superiority. But the pay-off was impressive. He drove the Japanese out of Soviet territory with crushing losses. It was a lesson which cut deep. The memory of the terrible Soviet firepower stayed with the Japanese military. It played an important role in discouraging the Japanese High Command from intervention in the Far East during the dangerous days when Russia was so heavily engaged against the Nazis in the west. It may well have played a decisive role in the Japanese decision to sign a nonaggression pact with the Russians just weeks before Hitler's attack on the Soviet Union.

Talking with General W. Bedell Smith, Eisenhower's Chief of Staff, at the end of World War II, Zhukov was modest about his victory over the Japanese. "The Japanese are not good against armor," he said. "It took about ten days to beat them."

As for his expenditure of manpower, his willingness to take human losses, Zhukov offered no excuses. It was part of war. He made his attitude clear in a talk with General Eisenhower.

"If we come to a mine field, our infantry attack exactly as if it were not there," he said. "The losses we get from personnel mines we consider only equal to those we would have gotten from machine guns and artillery if the Germans had chosen to defend the area with strong bodies of troops instead of mine fields."

This was the philosophy of a man determined to attain his military objective. It might cost many human lives. But if the position had to be taken, if the battle had to be won, if the enemy had to be smashed, one must be prepared to pay the price. This was the philosophy which Zhukov took with him into World War II. And it followed him from one great engagement to another. Zhukov never fought a battle in which he was sparing of the lives of men. Only by expenditure of life, he believed, could the military goals be achieved.

Khalkhin-Gol made Zhukov's name one to be reckoned with. He came back from Mongolia to assume the post of deputy commander of the Ukrainian Military District, commanded by his old friend and close associate, Marshal Timoshenko. When in January, 1940, Timoshenko was hurriedly ordered to Leningrad to take command of the thus far disastrous winter war against Finland, he naturally took Zhukov along as Chief of Staff.

Once the winter war was won Stalin conducted an exhaustive post-mortem. It did not get to the root of all Soviet military troubles (most of them were related to political misjudgments by Stalin himself and to a lesser extent by his Leningrad lieutenant, Andrei A. Zhdanov), but it did bring about a shuffle in Soviet commands which put Marshal Timoshenko into the Defense Commissariat, replacing Stalin's inept crony, Marshal Voroshilov. It also resulted in a new distribution of command posts, which placed many able young officers in key spots, including Zhukov in Timoshenko's old post at Kiev.

Zhukov's assignment to Kiev marked another milestone in his career. It placed him in association with Nikita S. Khrushchev, then the Ukrainian Communist Party chief—a man who later would play a major role in Zhukov's life, as would Zhukov in Khrushchev's.

In 1940 each was a relative unknown, a newcomer, a younger

man very much on the move. The year 1940 was a curious and unreal year in the Soviet Union. It was the year when Stalin's dream of Hitler becoming bogged down in the West—of Hitler and the Western powers draining each other's strength (to Russia's advantage)—began to come apart. Hitler with bold strokes occupied Denmark and Norway and crunched France in a classic blitzkrieg. By autumn he stood at the Channel. London and other English cities burned and crumbled under the bombs of the Luftwaffe. All was quiet in the east. But would it so remain? Stalin showed no sign of concern, although in November he sent Foreign Minister Molotov to Berlin to negotiate with Hitler—a baffling, bullying meeting which probably confirmed Hitler in his intention (already virtually fixed) that he must now attack Russia.

In the Soviet Union there was no hint, public or private, of any rift, no warning of danger, no sign that the Nazi-Soviet pact had not guaranteed "peace in our time" for Stalin and his co-partner, Hitler.

It was against this background that Zhukov made his first public declaration—a speech which later became rather famous. He delivered it on December 11, 1940, in Kiev at a special Party-military meeting in which Khrushchev participated. Zhukov leveled a strong attack on the traditional Red Army system of "political commissars" with all its implications of divided control. The system had been abolished a few months earlier by decree of his friend Timoshenko, but there was still much to be done, Zhukov stressed, if better and traditional military discipline was to be established. He criticized the older officers of the High Command and went on to warn sternly against any tricks of foreign enemies, however they might be disguised. The Red Army must stand guard on the western frontiers at this moment of international peril and conflict.

There was no doubt but that the thrust of his remarks was directed at possible war with Germany—and this at a time when Soviet commanders were being reprimanded and even subjected to political repression for any statement which suggested that the Nazi-Soviet pact did not firmly safeguard Soviet security.

A few days later Zhukov with the other top Soviet Army commanders went to Moscow for the military conferences and war games which were to wind up with his appointment, once again, as Chief of Staff to his friend Timoshenko. No longer was Zhukov on the periphery. Now he was at the center of the Soviet defense organization, Chief of Staff to the High Command.

It is difficult to imagine that Zhukov was not concerned by what he found when he entered the Defense Commissariat in January, 1941. Intelligence reports were flowing in about Germany's preparations for attack. Zhukov was too experienced an officer to be complacent about the state and disposition of Soviet defenses in case Hitler struck. But there was little he or anyone could do so long as Stalin was possessed of his conviction that war would not come—or at least not before 1942. The record shows that Zhukov initiated a series of measures which would have put the Red Army in excellent shape to hold off Hitler—in 1942. But like the rest of the Red Army command he was paralyzed so far as urgent immediate steps were concerned so long as Stalin insisted that nothing be done which might upset Hitler or encourage elements in Germany who were looking for an excuse to attack Russia.

In fact, acting upon direct orders from Stalin, Zhukov angrily countermanded instructions given by General M. P. Kirponos, his successor in Kiev, who sought a few days before the start of war in June, 1941, to move his advance units into forward fortifications. And Zhukov compelled General F. I. Kuznetsov, commander of the Special Baltic Military District, to cancel orders to Baltic cities for blackout precautions.

Now on the night of June 21–22 events overtook Russia, overtook Stalin, overtook Zhukov.

The outbreak of war threw Russia into chaos. Stalin fell into a nervous collapse from which he did not emerge for some time. It was several weeks before his hand began to be felt again at the throttle of the Soviet machine.

Zhukov was caught up in the whirl of Communist political leadership in which no one really knew how to act without Stalin. Timoshenko was named to head a new High Command, of which Zhukov was Chief of Staff and Stalin only an ordinary member. This did not last long. In July Stalin took over again as the head of a State Defense Committee, and men like Timoshenko and Zhukov were rushed from one crisis point to another in an endless and seemingly vain effort to halt the onrush of the German panzers.

It was at this time that Zhukov began to emerge as the master of disaster, as the general who was sent in when all else failed, whose terrible temper, iron will and savage determination, which wore men down (and condemned not a few to the firing squad), somehow succeeded in bringing the German war machine to a grinding halt and in setting the stage for a counter-blow.

Zhukov's name became attached to every great battle of Russia's Western Front. He won the first victory of Russian arms over the Germans in the merciless Battle of Yelnya, fifty miles southeast of Smolensk and 220 miles west of Moscow, in the last days of August and the early days of September, 1941.

The great battles fought by Zhukov included the Battle of Moscow (October, 1941–January, 1942), the Battle of Stalingrad (August, 1942–February, 1943), the Battle of Kursk-Orel (spring–summer, 1943) and the Battle of Berlin (spring, 1945).

Each of these engagements had its own characteristics. But each was in the Zhukov pattern. Each time he directed enormous masses of troops—as many as twenty armies or more. Each engagement involved upwards of a million men on each side. Each was marked by enormous casualties. Each was characterized by extremely careful staff work, lavish expenditure of artillery, maximum use of armor and deployment of masses of infantry. Each inflicted on the Germans the kind of casualties which leave a lasting mark not only on an army but on a nation.

There was nothing nice, nothing gentle, nothing refined about Zhukov's tactics. There are no warm passages in the memoirs of Russian military figures about kind deeds, thoughtful encouragement, friendly comfort given by Zhukov. But there is story after story of his terrible threats: Fulfill the order or face the firing squad! Obey or die! Zhukov's style was simple. No one who had to deal with him was ever in doubt of the consequences of failure. Carry out the order by morning or you will be shot for treason in the Palace Square—this was Zhukov's warning to one commander. He indicted another general for "passive resistance" when the officer refused to carry out an order (Zhukov did not happen to be the man's commander). A favorite Zhukov tactic was to issue a sharp and often impossible order by telephone and hang up before the commander could offer argument or comment.

Marshal Konstantin K. Rokossovsky served with Zhukov from the early 1920's. He knew Zhukov as well as any Soviet military figure and deeply respected him. After the war he characterized Zhukov in these terms:

"Zhukov was always a man of strong will and decisiveness, brilliant and gifted, demanding, firm and purposeful. All these qualities, unquestionably, are necessary in a great military leader and they were inherent in Zhukov. It is true that sometimes his toughness exceeded what was permissible. For example, in the heat of the fighting around Moscow Zhukov sometimes displayed unjustified sharpness."

As the war went on, Zhukov acquired enormous authority. He was hailed as a national hero for his victory in the Battle of Moscow, sharing the tributes with his close wartime associate, Marshal Rokossovsky. Zhukov was known as the *"spasitel"*— the savior—of Moscow. In this period he had Stalin's confidence and may even have acquired a certain domination over the dictator, although, as is evident from his battle histories, this did not mean that he was able necessarily to get his way in either tactics or strategy.

Zhukov's way of fighting a battle—and it may have been a way dictated as much by necessity as design—was to let the enemy extend himself, to wait until the last moment of the German offensive momentum, and then to grind the Nazis down in terrible bloody exchanges as they drove in for their objective. Meanwhile, despite fearful Russian losses and the dangerous German penetration, Zhukov cautiously, carefully and painstakingly massed reserve armies which he refused to commit to action, no matter what the peril at the front. Then, at the moment when the German strength was spent he would unleash his counterblow with dramatic rapidity—often within forty-eight hours of a German pause and before the Nazis were able to establish a reliable defense.

Zhukov hurled his reserve forces on the German flanks, striking for an envelopment or a pincers movement. It did not always work. He tried for an envelopment in his first big battle— the Yelnya engagement. The Germans managed to escape entrapment—by a whisker. He repeated the tactic in each great battle thereafter. He knew the military classics from Caesar to Clausewitz. He was a literate, even a cultured, man. But he deliberately presented himself as rude, profane, abusive, domineering.

The engagements in which Zhukov won his reputation were so massive that, inevitably, many outstanding Soviet military men were involved—either under Zhukov's command or in coordinated and associated movements. There was then, and there continued for years to be, a raging competition for military glory in these engagements. Deep lines of political cleavage and quarrels also underlay the military disputes. Not only military glory was involved; political intrigue, intra-Party quarrels, high-level Kremlin politics were at issue.

The principal military rivals of Zhukov were his fellow marshals, Ivan S. Konev, Rodion Malinovsky, V. I. Chuikov, A. I. Yeremenko, Semyon Timoshenko, and to a lesser extent men like K. K. Rokossovsky, V. D. Sokolovsky, and the staff chiefs, A. M. Vasilevsky, Boris Shaposhnikov and, later on, S. M. Shtemenko. Rivals of a different category were Stalin's cronies, men like Voroshilov and Budenny, and police generals such as L. Z. Mekhlis and G. I. Kulik.

Yet at the end of the war Zhukov's prestige was so enormous that he shared the podium with Stalin at the great Moscow victory parade in June, 1945, and entertained as his guest his fellow commander and friend, General Dwight D. Eisenhower. The two men were not merely military associates, fellow members of the Kommendatura in Berlin. They had genuine empathy. Both were popular figures, heroes in their countries, nonpolitical men, men with a rather simplistic view of life. Eisenhower came to Moscow as Zhukov's guest. He invited Zhukov to visit America as his guest. Zhukov accepted. To many it seemed that Zhukov's prestige was such that he might well be Stalin's first minister and probable successor. It seemed that in any event the influence of Zhukov and of the other great Soviet generals would be such that they would dominate postwar Soviet political life.

Acting on this theory, the United States hastened to send Eisenhower's Chief of Staff, General W. Bedell Smith, to Moscow, as Ambassador. He was almost as good a friend of Zhukov's as was Eisenhower.

The calculations failed. They did not take into account Stalin and the nature of Kremlin politics. Zhukov never had a chance to make his visit to the United States as Ike's guest. Indeed, he never even met his old friend Ambassador Smith in Moscow. Before Smith could take up his post Zhukov had vanished from the scene. A year or two later he was found in Odessa, patiently (or not so patiently) carrying out his duties as commander of the Odessa Military District. He had been rusticated. Stalin was taking no chances on Zhukov's becoming a Red Napoleon. Eisenhower might become President, but Zhukov would get no chance at the general secretaryship of the Communist Party. Whatever their rivalries and disagreements, Stalin's associates in the Politburo shared his views. They wanted no military candidates upsetting the already murderous and intricate rivalry for the succession.

It was years before Zhukov moved back into the public eye —not until after Stalin's death. A year or so before Stalin died Zhukov was permitted to attend a meeting of the Warsaw powers. But not until Stalin was dead did he emerge from the shadows. When he did, he came on fast. He stood in the honor guard at Stalin's bier together with the surviving Politburo members, and he became Deputy Minister of Defense in the first post-Stalin government.

Then came a dramatic event. On June 30, 1953, the other members of the Soviet Government arrested Lavrenti P. Beria, the chief of secret police, and all of the top police aides. It was a daring maneuver, carried out with military precision. It was Zhukov who provided the military forces which enabled the Soviet civilian leadership swiftly, surgically, to swoop down upon the powerful police apparatus. And it was Zhukov who publicly prodded his civilian colleagues at the November, 1953, holiday reception to act against Beria, who had not at that point yet been brought to trial. Zhukov offered a toast to "justice" in the presence of the leading foreign ambassadors. The Politburo acted soon afterward. Beria and his aides were brought to trial and shot. Justice was done.

With the rise of Nikita Khrushchev, Zhukov became Minister of Defense. He took the salute on May Day and November 7 in Red Square. He spoke for the government on national defense. The relationship of Khrushchev and Zhukov, first established in 1940 in prewar Kiev, grew closer. In June, 1957, Khrushchev's colleagues in the Politburo joined in a plot to oust him. Khrushchev fought back and won—with the aid of Zhukov, who put air force planes at his disposal to fly to Moscow members of the Party Central Committee. Their support gave Khrushchev victory over the combined forces of Georgi Malenkov, Vyacheslav Molotov, Nikolai Bulganin and—as it turned out—a majority of the Politburo. Zhukov now emerged as the strong man of the Khrushchev regime. It began to appear that Stalin and his associates had been right at the end of the war when they feared that Zhukov might take political leadership in Russia.

Zhukov's role in the arrest and ouster of Beria and his role in keeping Khrushchev in power in 1957 demonstrated that he did, indeed, possess political power—political power greater than that of Khrushchev. The lesson was not lost on Khrushchev. If he had kept his job only through Zhukov's aid, then the day might come when Zhukov would decide to oust *him*— and Zhukov had the power to do it. Khrushchev got the message. At the first opportunity—an October, 1957, visit by Zhukov to Albania—Khrushchev set the stage. When Zhukov landed at Moscow airport on his return, he was put under guard. A few hours later he was out of a job.

For seven years Zhukov endured rustication again. He lived in a pleasant villa outside Moscow. He puttered with his memoirs. He fished. His enemies—political and military—had a field day. A succession of histories poured from Soviet presses. Some of them managed to write the whole story of the Battle of Moscow without mentioning his name. The Battle of Stalingrad was revised to eliminate his role in it. The accounts of the Battle of Berlin presented Zhukov as a cautious, indecisive meddler—or simply failed to speak of him at all. His role at Leningrad was forgotten. His victory at Yelnya vanished.

History in Russia should be published in loose-leaf books so that pages can be extracted and new ones inserted. Zhukov had been a hero during the war. He became an "unperson" with the war's end. He re-emerged as a hero upon Stalin's death. He vanished from the printed page in 1957.

With Khrushchev's fall he came back into print. He began to tell his own story, his own version of the great battles on which his reputation rested. In the telling he repaid some old scores. He answered some of his critics and he laid the groundwork for new fireworks with the revelation of conversations with Stalin, of arguments over strategy, of errors made by Stalin and by other members of the Soviet High Command. He challenged the German generals, and he challenged many of the Soviet military historians.

Whatever else may be said of Zhukov, he was not leaving the world stage without one more dogged, determined Zhukov-like effort to put the record straight, to tell what really happened behind the scenes in the Kremlin and on the battlefield in the terrible days when the fate of Russia and the fate of Germany hung in the balance.

The memoir which Zhukov wrote was, inevitably, not only a personal but a political document. He set forth his own position, sought to answer critics and undercut his military and governmental rivals and opponents. At the same time, the memoir had to pass the censorship of the Soviet Government. It was exhaustively reviewed by the political administration of the Soviet armed forces, which was not necessarily sympathetic to Zhukov. There were excisions, suppressions, additions to and changes from what Zhukov originally wrote. The chapters on his great battles appeared at different times, in different publications, and under varying conditions of censorship, varying emphases in the Party propaganda line.

The first of the Zhukov battle accounts to be published was an account of the Battle of Berlin. It was published in June, 1965, in the technical Soviet military organ, *Voyenno-Istoricheskii Zhurnal,* and was specifically designed as a reply to devastating attacks on Zhukov which had been published under the

Khrushchev regime and very probably inspired by Khrushchev. A year later Zhukov published in the same technical journal a detailed account of the Battle of Moscow. He then supplemented this account in chapters which were included in collections of essays by commanders who participated in the Moscow fighting, published a year later. In 1967 he published, again in *Voyenno-Istoricheskii Zhurnal,* his version of the Battle of Kursk-Orel, the greatest tank engagement which has ever been fought and probably the bloodiest single engagement on Russia's Western Front. Some Soviet and foreign critics believe the battle was somewhat mismanaged on both the German and Soviet sides. Finally, in 1968 he published a lengthy exposition of his role in the Battle of Stalingrad in a volume on Stalingrad edited by the excellent Soviet military historian A. M. Samsonov. Here Zhukov established for the first time publicly his dominant role in the strategic and tactical conception of the great Soviet offensive which closed the iron circle around the unfortunate von Paulus and some 600,000 Nazi troops.

Comparison of the Zhukov accounts reveals discrepancies, changes, omissions and inclusions which reflect not the Marshal's views but the imposition of higher Communist Party censorship. A number of these have been noted in the commentary on the present text.

Marshal Zhukov's accounts of the four final battles of World War II in which he played a leading role comprise about half the contents of his complete memoir, which has appeared in the Soviet Union and is scheduled for publication in the West sometime in 1970.

HARRISON E. SALISBURY

New York
April, 1969

The Battle of

MOSCOW

OCTOBER, 1941—JANUARY, 1942

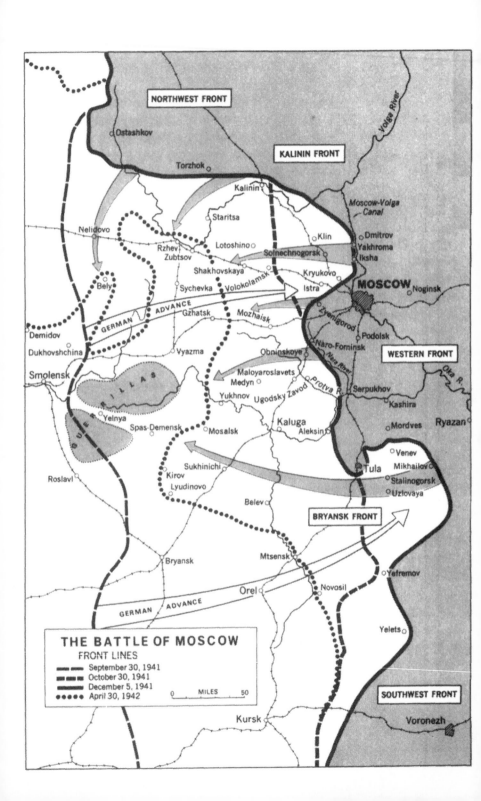

NORTHWEST FRONT

KALININ FRONT

Volga River

Ostashkov

Torzhok

Kalinin

Moscow-Volga Canal

Staritsa

Nelidovo

Lotoshino

Klin

Dmitrov

Rzhev
Zubtsov

Solnechnogorsk

Yakhroma
Iksha

Shakhovskaya

Kryukovo

Bely

Sychevka

Volokolamsk

Istra

MOSCOW

Noginsk

GERMAN ADVANCE

Gzhatsk

Mozhaisk

Zvenigorod

Demidov

Vyazma

Obninskoye

Naro-Fominsk

Nava River

Podolsk

WESTERN FRONT

Oka R.

Dukhovshchina

Smolensk

GUERILLAS

Maloyaroslavets
Medyn

Yukhnov

Ugodsky Zavod

Protva R.

Serpukhov

Kashira

Yelnya

Spas-Demensk

Mosalsk

Kaluga

Aleksin

Mordves

Ryazan

Roslavl

Sukhinichi

Kirov

Lyudinovo

Belev

Tula

Venev

Mikhailov

Stalinogorsk

Uzlovaya

BRYANSK FRONT

Bryansk

Mtsensk

Yefremov

Orel

Novosil

GERMAN ADVANCE

Yelets

THE BATTLE OF MOSCOW
FRONT LINES

- —— September 30, 1941
- —■— October 30, 1941
- —│— December 5, 1941
- •••• April 30, 1942

0   MILES   50

SOUTHWEST FRONT

Kursk

Voronezh

Editor's Note

The story of the first weeks of war in Russia, from Hitler's attack on June 22 into August, is one of unrelieved horror. Everywhere the Nazis swept forward. Everywhere the Red Army fell back. In some places it was a rout, in others a more orderly retreat. But everywhere the air was filled with tragedy, menace and apprehension.

Stalin gradually got control of himself during July, and with his return to leadership there were major changes at Supreme Headquarters. He sent Zhukov to the front on special missions. Timoshenko went, too, taking command of the Western Front, and then, after the utter disaster in September in which Marshal Budenny lost Kiev (probably because of Stalin's stubborn orders to hang on) and nearly two-thirds of a million troops, Timoshenko was put in charge of the collapsing Southwest Front.

On July 30 Zhukov was named commander of the so-called Reserve Front. The Reserve Front was a peculiar feature of Soviet military tactics, a front that was set up some distance behind the active front. The theory was that if the actual front collapsed the Reserve Front would be in position to halt the further advance of the Germans. If the Nazis were held up at the regular front, the reserve army could swing up and deliver a crushing counterblow.

The Reserve Front which Zhukov took over was established about a hundred miles east of Smolensk in the Rzhev-Vyazma area. Smolensk was the key to the western approaches to Moscow: if Smolensk fell, it would be Zhukov's task to halt the onrushing German panzers on the direct highway to Moscow. There had been fierce fighting there since mid-July.

Zhukov had six armies under his command on the Reserve

Front. He did not go into a static defense and await the arrival of the Germans. He pushed forward and early in August went into action near Yelnya. Heavy, grinding fighting, typical of the Zhukov style, ensued. It went on for twenty-six days. The Germans were brought to a halt. Yelnya returned to Soviet hands. The slashing Nazi advance on the Central Front was temporarily bogged down. The battle ended September 5, and on September 10 Stalin ordered the front onto the defense.

Zhukov's success at Yelnya, shared by Rokossovsky and Rokossovsky's Sixteenth Army, was the only bright spot in the picture. The terrible Kiev encirclement was closing. Northward the Germans seemed about to capture Leningrad. The most tense moment of the war was at hand.

Zhukov probably preferred to continue his westward drive at Yelnya. Instead, he was summoned to the Kremlin and dispatched on September 12 to Leningrad, now encircled by the Germans. Stalin had come to believe that his old Civil War associate, Marshal Voroshilov, and Party Secretary Zhdanov either were about to deliver Leningrad to the Nazis or were so incompetent that the Germans would capture the northern capital.

Zhukov flew off to Leningrad in a towering rage. When he got to headquarters at Smolny Institute, he hardly spoke to the shattered Marshal Voroshilov. He called Moscow on the high-security telephone and gave Stalin a message that he had taken charge and would pursue operations less lethargically than his predecessor. Voroshilov, broken, left Leningrad thinking he might face the firing squad. Luckily for him, he did not.

Zhukov plunged into his task with savagery. He ousted commanders right and left. He ordered officers and troops not to retreat a step farther. If they did, they went to the firing squad. His anger and ferocity caused the toughest generals to pale. But he halted the Germans. Actually, he came to Leningrad at the high tide of the attack. The Germans had less than a week's leeway before they would start shifting their heavy armor and crack units southward for the climactic assault on Moscow. The Russians did not know this. In his first week at Leningrad Zhukov's brutal orders and fiery energy brought the German attacks to a standstill. The moment he detected slackening in the German attack he ordered his battered troops to shift to the offensive. Wave after wave of assaults swept up to the German positions. They gained little. The Soviet forces did not have the strength. But Zhukov was merciless. He ordered his men to attack again and again, heedless of weariness, heedless of casualties.

While Zhukov was bringing the Germans to a halt at Leningrad, a situation of incredible danger was opening up on the Moscow Front.

The German drive for Moscow was launched September 30 on the so-called Bryansk Front, about 150 miles southwest of Moscow. This front was commanded by General A. I. Yeremenko. The Germans struck at the link between Yeremenko's troops and those of the Western Front commanded by General Ivan S. Konev. Konev had Nikolai Bulganin (the future Defense Minister, Premier and erstwhile colleague of Nikita Khrushchev) as his Military Council member and the brilliant General Vasily D. Sokolovsky as his Chief of Staff. It was probably the best command group in the Soviet Army. On October 2 the Nazi offensive widened to include all three fronts west of Moscow, the Western, the Reserve (now commanded by Marshal Budenny) and the Bryansk. The Russians had twelve armies in the front lines, with four in reserve. They had concentrated about 40 percent of their troops and artillery and 35 percent of their tanks and planes to meet the expected offensive.

But once again (as Zhukov sharply notes) the High Command and the field commanders were caught off-guard. Their attention was directed to a Nazi breakthrough in the Orel sector which brought that city into German hands. German armor was heading for Tula, the ancient Russian arms center, sixty-five miles south of Moscow.

The night of October 4–5 was possibly the most alarming of the war. Moscow lost contact with the Western Front and had no definite information as to what was going on. At 9 A.M. October 5 word was received that the Germans had broken through between the hinge of the Forty-third and Twenty-fourth armies, just south of Yelnya and east of Roslavl, and were moving east on the Warsaw highway toward Moscow. This report was dismissed as a product of panic.

About noon a reconnaissance flier of the 120th Fighter Squadron reported that he had spotted a fifteen-mile-long Nazi armored column moving up the Warsaw highway from Spas-Demensk toward Yukhnov, a scant hundred miles southwest of Moscow. No one in Moscow could believe the Nazis were so close to the capital. Two more reconnaissance flights were sent out. Stalin was advised only after the first report had been verified. There were no Soviet troops in the path of the Nazi panzers. He immediately ordered a scratch force assembled to hold off the Germans for "five to seven days" while major reserves were brought up. Typically, Stalin's secret police chief, Beria, declined to believe the information and threatened the air reconnaissance men with court-martial and execution. The intelligence was correct. The Nazis had broken through once again. The Moscow front was falling apart. But because of Beria's intervention it was eight hours before any troops moved out to the Warsaw highway, and not until the next day was an air strike launched at the Nazi panzers.

It was at this moment that Stalin telephoned Zhukov (as he describes) on the evening of October 6 and ordered him into Moscow to see what could be done to save the capital. Zhukov arrived in Moscow October 7. On October 10 he was named commander of the Western Front, responsible in effect for all the defenses west of the Soviet capital. Konev and Yeremenko (on both of whom, as well as on Stalin, Zhukov placed blame for the critical situation) were subordinated to him. The battle on which the fate of Russia was to depend was joined.

H.E.S.

1

The Eve of Battle

The beginning of October, 1941, I was in Leningrad, commanding the troops of the Leningrad Front. Those days were difficult for all of us who had been through the September fighting for Leningrad. But our forces were succeeding in thwarting the enemy's plans. Because of the unparalleled steadfastness and mass heroism of Soviet soldiers, sailors and noncommissioned officers and the endurance of commanders and political officers, the enemy was encountering an unsurmountable defense on the approaches to the city.

By the end of September pressure was noticeably relaxed on all sectors and the front line had become stabilized. But this is not the place to tell the story of the Leningrad fighting nor of the attempted seizure of the city named for the great Lenin. I mention it only to emphasize that all of us, from the Military Council of the front down to the city's ordinary defenders, in those days lived with but a single thought: to stop the enemy no matter what. Everyone did all he could in his assigned post.

The front's Military Council at that time consisted of Comrades A. A. Zhdanov, A. A. Kuznetsov, T. F. Shtykov, Ya. M. Kapustin and N. V. Solovyev. And, it should be noted, they worked together harmoniously and effectively. Each one of them made a great contribution to the common cause, fighting the enemy and defending Leningrad, which was threatened with mortal danger in those September days of 1941. Unfortunately, not one of these comrades is now alive.[1]

Despite the burden of our own immediate problems, we were just as interested in the situation on other sectors of the long Soviet-German front. As a member of Supreme Headquarters, I received information from the General Staff that enabled me to judge the gravity of the danger threatening the homeland.

As we know, the German forces achieved substantial successes in the first two and a half months of the war. They seized Byelorussia, Moldavia, a large part of the Ukraine, Lithuania, Latvia and Estonia; they blockaded Leningrad and, by the end of September, had moved large forces up to the distant approaches of Moscow with a view to seizing the capital.

The enemy achieved these successes at the cost of tremendous losses of the best elements of his army and air force. And the deeper the Nazi forces advanced into our country, the stronger the resistance of the Soviet troops became.

The German command gave priority to the capture of the Crimea and the Donets Basin. Anticipating an attack against the flank of its Army Group Center by our forces on the Southwest Front, the enemy briefly halted the drive toward Moscow and shifted substantial forces from Army Group Center (in-

[1] Zhdanov was Communist Party Secretary in Leningrad, and the others were his deputy secretaries. Zhdanov died August 31, 1948. The official announcement attributed his death to a heart attack. There has been speculation that the death may have been due to poisoning. All of his deputies, except for Shtykov, were shot in the so-called "Leningrad Affair," one of Stalin's purges, which was launched immediately after Zhdanov's death.   H.E.S.

cluding Guderian's tank army) to strike at the flank and rear of the Southwest Front.

In September, just before the battle on the distant approaches to Moscow, the enemy inflicted a heavy defeat on our forces in the southwest.[2] Intoxicated by its success in the Ukraine, Hitler's High Command overestimated the capabilities of its armies and made major operational and strategic miscalculations in its plan for the offensive against Moscow. The enemy thought that the Soviet forces were weakened, demoralized and incapable of defending their capital.

The State Defense Committee, the Soviet Government and our Party took decisive steps to overcome the serious situation confronting our country, especially relative to Moscow.

In October the enemy began an offensive that was supposed to end with the capture of the capital of our Motherland. We had prepared three fronts on the distant approaches to Moscow: the Western Front, the Reserve Front and the Bryansk Front.

The Western Front (Colonel General Ivan S. Konev in command; Nikolai A. Bulganin as a member of the Military Council; Lieutenant General Vasily D. Sokolovsky as Chief of Staff) consisted of six reinforced armies and front reserves astride the principal approaches to Moscow from Lake Seliger to the town of Yelnya. Its task was to keep the enemy from breaking through toward Moscow.

The Reserve Front (Marshal Semyon M. Budenny in command; Sergei N. Kruglov as a member of the Military Council; Lieutenant General A. F. Anisov as Chief of Staff) with its forces (the Thirty-first, Thirty-second, Thirty-third and Forty-ninth armies) took up defensive positions behind the Western Front along the line Ostashkov–Selizharovo–Olenino–Spas-Demensk–Kirov. These four armies were intended to fend off the enemy in case he broke through the defenses of the Western

[2] This was the capture of Kiev and the smashing of the Soviet forces defending the Ukraine. H.E.S.

Front; they were the second operational echelon of our defense. Two other armies, the Twenty-fourth and the Forty-third, were in defensive positions next to the Western Front between Yelnya and Frolovka.

The Bryansk Front (Colonel General Alexei I. Yeremenko in command; P. I. Mazepov, a divisional commissar, as a member of the Military Council; Major General G. F. Zakharov as Chief of Staff) consisted of three armies and an operational group in defensive positions on the east bank of the Desna River from Frolovka to Putivl. Its assignment was to stop the enemy from breaking through toward Bryansk and Orel.

The combined strength of the three fronts at the end of September was 800,000 men, 770 tanks and 9,150 guns, not counting reinforcements and rear units. Most of the strength was concentrated on the Western Front.

The Nazi Army Group Center, as we now know, had more than a million men, 1,700 tanks and self-propelled guns and more than 19,000 guns and mortars. It was supported by the powerful Second Air Fleet under Field Marshal Kesselring. By his directive of September 16, Hitler gave Army Group Center the task of breaking through the Soviet defenses, surrounding and destroying the main forces of the Western, Reserve and Bryansk fronts and then, pursuing the remaining forces, of seizing Moscow by enveloping it from north and south.

At the end of September our intelligence reported that the enemy was preparing a major offensive against Moscow. The Supreme Command issued appropriate warnings to the front commanders and asked them to prepare a firm defense. The general plan of the Supreme Command was to inflict the heaviest possible losses on the enemy and to prevent a breakthrough.

The construction of vast fortifications began on the immediate and distant approaches to Moscow. The city itself prepared for defense. Workers of Moscow and the oblasts [provinces] of

Moscow, Kaluga, Tula and Kalinin worked day and night constructing fortifications in the city's streets and on the outskirts. Army engineers prepared to lay mine fields and to install a wide variety of obstacles. Moscow's air defenses were prepared with particular care. On order of the Moscow City Committee of the Communist Party, hundreds of voluntary teams were formed and trained in air defense and first aid. A strict blackout was introduced in the city and its environs, and key military objectives and many other buildings were camouflaged.

Twelve divisions of People's Volunteers, formed earlier on orders of the Party's Central Committee, were already stationed on the approaches to the city. Five more divisions were completing their training, and the Moscow City Committee had begun to form additional volunteer units.

The Moscow Party organization subordinated all its activities to the defense of Moscow. The city and its environs were transformed into a fortified camp.

The enemy began his offensive against the Bryansk Front on September 30 and against the Western and Reserve fronts on October 2. The attacks were heaviest north of Dukhovshchina and east of Roslavl against the Thirtieth and Nineteenth armies of the Western Front and against the Forty-third Army of the Bryansk Front. The German forces succeeded in breaking through our defenses. The enemy's shock groups raced ahead and enveloped the entire Vyazma grouping of the Western and Reserve fronts from north and south.

The situation was also extremely serious on the Bryansk Front, where the Third and Thirteenth armies were threatened with encirclement. Without encountering any significant opposition, part of Guderian's army swept toward Orel, which had been left unguarded. Orel fell on October 3. The Bryansk Front collapsed; its troops, suffering heavily, retreated toward the east and southeast, creating a threatening situation in the direction of Tula.

On orders of Western Front Commander General Konev, an operational group under Lieutenant General I. V. Boldin counterattacked the advancing northern forces of the enemy, but without success. By late October 6 a substantial part of the forces of the Western Front (parts of the Nineteenth Army of Lieutenant General M. F. Lukin, the Sixteenth Army of Lieutenant General Konstantin K. Rokossovsky, the Twentieth Army of Lieutenant General F. A. Yershakov, and General Boldin's operational group) and of the Reserve Front (the Thirty-second Army of Major General S. V. Vishnevsky and the Twenty-fourth Army of Major General K. I. Rakutin) had been surrounded west of Vyazma.

On October 6 the enemy threatened to break through along the Minsk-Moscow highway toward Mozhaisk and along the Warsaw highway toward Maloyaroslavets. At that time fortifications on the Mozhaisk defense line and on the immediate approaches to Moscow had not yet been completed and the defense line was unmanned.

The grave possibility of an enemy breakthrough hung over Moscow.

The State Defense Committee, the Party's Central Committee and the Supreme Command took measures to halt the enemy advance. Troops had to be stationed promptly along the defense lines, especially the Mozhaisk line. These movements began on October 7, when 14 rifle divisions, 16 tank brigades, more than 40 artillery regiments and other units were transferred from the Supreme Headquarters reserve and adjoining fronts. These forces were clearly inadequate for a reliable defense, but they were all that Supreme Headquarters could spare at the time since the transfer of troops from the Far East and other distant areas had been delayed.

On the evening of October 6 I had a telephone call from Josef V. Stalin, the Supreme Commander in Chief, who inquired about the situation around Leningrad. I reported that the enemy had ceased his attacks. According to prisoners, enemy forces near Leningrad had suffered heavy losses and were taking up defensive positions. The Germans were shelling and bombing the city. Our aerial reconnaissance had observed an important movement of motorized and tank columns southward from Leningrad. The German command seemed to be transferring these forces in the direction of Moscow.

Stalin listened to the report, remained silent for a while, and then said that the situation had become critical in the Moscow sector, especially on the Western Front.

"Appoint Chief of Staff General Khozin acting commander of the Leningrad Front and take a plane to Moscow," he ordered.

I passed the orders of the Supreme Commander in Chief along to M. S. Khozin,[3] said good-bye to members of the Military Council and flew to Moscow. Our plane landed at the Central Airport at dusk on October 7. I went immediately to the Kremlin.

Stalin was in his apartment. He was suffering from a case of influenza and was not feeling well. He greeted me with a nod, pointed to a map and said, "Look, we're in really serious trouble on the Western Front, yet I can't seem to get a detailed report about what's going on."

He asked me to leave at once for front headquarters. I was to examine the situation thoroughly and telephone him at any time during the night.

"I'll be waiting for your call," he said, ending the conversation.

Fifteen minutes later I was in the office of the Chief of the General Staff for briefing. Marshal Boris M. Shaposhnikov looked quite exhausted. He said Stalin had already telephoned

[3] Actually, Zhukov turned over his command to his deputy, General Ivan I. Fedyuninsky. General Khozin assumed command in Leningrad about a month later.   H.E.S.

and instructed him to give me a map of the Western sectors.

"The map will be here right away," Marshal Shaposhnikov said. "Western Front headquarters is now where the Reserve Front had its headquarters in August, when you were conducting your operation against the Yelnya salient."

The map was to show the situation as of noon on October 7. While we were waiting, Shaposhnikov ordered tea served. He said he was very tired.

After telling me about the critical situation at the fronts, he added that work on the construction of defense lines in the Mozhaisk area and nearer to Moscow was still under way and that there were almost no troops in the area. The State Defense Committee, the Party's Central Committee and the Supreme Command were taking steps to halt the enemy's advance. Troops were to be stationed hurriedly on the new defense lines, especially in the Mozhaisk area.

As soon as my map was ready, I left for Western Front headquarters. En route I studied the situation and the operations of the two sides with the aid of a flashlight. I was getting drowsy. To keep from falling asleep, I had the car stopped and jogged for some two or three hundred yards. I reached front headquarters late at night. The officer on duty reported that the Military Council was meeting in the commander's office. General Konev, Bulganin and General Sokolovsky were meeting with Lieutenant General G. K. Malandin, the front's operations chief, in semidarkness in a room lighted by a few stearin candles. But it was clear that all of them were worn out. I said that I had come on orders of the Supreme Commander in Chief and that I was to study the situation and report to him by telephone.

"I just spoke with Stalin," Bulganin said, "but I could not tell him anything specific because we don't know ourselves what is happening to the troops that have been encircled west of Vyazma."

General Malandin, in answer to my questions, was able to

add some details to the information I already had about the events of October 2 to 7. The substance of his account was this:

The enemy, having regrouped his forces on the Moscow approaches, exceeded the combined strength of the Western, Reserve and Bryansk fronts by 40 percent in infantry, 120 percent in tanks, 90 percent in guns and mortars and 160 percent in planes. Our defenses had been unable to withstand the concentrated attacks. By October 7 there was no longer a continuous front in the west, and the large gaps could not be closed because the command had run out of reserves.

Actually, toward the end of September, Soviet intelligence had obtained information about major concentrations of enemy forces on the Moscow approaches, suggesting that the Nazi command was preparing a major offensive toward Moscow. In a directive dated September 27, Supreme Headquarters had warned front commanders that an offensive might begin within the next few days.

Consequently, the enemy offensive was no surprise in the sense that the German attacks had been at the beginning of the war. In fact, the Moscow fronts had sufficient manpower and arms to repel the enemy. A successful defense required only a proper evaluation of the situation, a determination of the principal direction of the enemy attacks and a timely concentration of forces for counteraction in those sectors. Unfortunately, this had not been done, and our forces were unable to withstand the concentrated blows of the enemy.

I telephoned Stalin at 2:30 in the morning. He was still working. I reported the situation on the Western Front and said, "The principal danger now is that the road to Moscow is almost entirely unprotected. The fortifications along the Mozhaisk line are too weak to halt a breakthrough by German armor. We must concentrate forces on the Mozhaisk defense line as soon as possible from wherever we can."

Stalin asked about the location of the Sixteenth, Nineteenth and Twentieth armies and the Boldin group of the Western Front, and the Twenty-fourth and Thirty-second armies of the Reserve Front.

I replied that they were encircled west and northwest of Vyazma.

"What do you plan to do?"

"I was about to visit Marshal Budenny [the Reserve Front commander]."

"Do you know where his headquarters is?"

"No, but I'll look around near Maloyaroslavets."

"Good. Call me when you get there."

It was drizzling, a dense fog hugged the ground, and visibility was poor. At dawn on October 8, as we were approaching the railroad station of Obninskoye, about seventy miles from Moscow, we saw two signalmen laying a cable over a bridge across the Protva River. When asked where the cable was going, they replied curtly.

"Where it's supposed to go, that's where," said one of them, a huge soldier, who seemed to be suffering from a head cold.

The soldiers evidently knew their business and had no intention of giving information to unknown persons. I identified myself and said I was looking for headquarters of the Reserve Front and Marshal Budenny. The big signalman said we had passed it and must return to the forest on a hill to the left of the bridge and then inquire for further directions.

Ten minutes later I was in the office of Army Commissar First Rank L. Z. Mekhlis, together with General Anisov, the front's Chief of Staff. Mekhlis was berating someone over the telephone. When he had finished, I announced the purpose of my visit. I explained that I had come as a member of Supreme Headquarters on orders of Stalin to study the situation. I asked where the front commander was. Budenny had visited the Forty-third Army the previous day, but his present whereabouts was unknown. Headquarters was worried that something might have happened to him, and signal officers sent in search of him had not yet returned. Neither Mekhlis nor Anisov could tell me anything specific about the position of either the Reserve Front troops or the enemy.

"You can see the situation we're in," Mekhlis said. "I am now rounding up the troops who retreated in disorder. We plan to rearm them at collection points and form new units."

I had no choice but to try to drive on toward Yukhnov, through Maloyaroslavets and Medyn, in the hope of clarifying the situation as soon as possible. As we crossed the Protva and passed through Obninskoye, I could not help remembering my childhood and youth. It was from this railroad station that my mother had sent me to Moscow as a furrier's apprentice at the age of twelve. Four years later, as a master furrier, I had often visited my parents in their village. I knew the whole area around Maloyaroslavets, having tramped through it in my early years. Just six miles from Obninskoye, which was now the headquarters of the Reserve Front, was the village of Strelkovka in Ugodsky Zavod District, where I was born and where I spent my childhood. My mother and my sister with her four children now lived there. I was concerned about what might happen to them if the Nazis came. Suppose they learned that these were Zhukov's mother, sister and nephews? And then . . . Three days later I saw to it that an adjutant moved them from the village to my Moscow apartment.

The village and the entire Ugodsky Zavod District were seized by the Germans in October, 1941. But the people of my district did not sit idly by. They organized a guerrilla group headed by a courageous fighter, Mikhail Alekseyevich Guryanov, chairman of the Ugodsky Zavod District government. The guerrillas boldly raided headquarters, rear echelons and small units of the German forces. One of these night raids destroyed the large rear headquarters of a German corps, and many Nazi officers lost their lives.

Unfortunately, Guryanov, the guerrilla commander and a member of the Party, was informed upon in November, 1941. He was seized, tortured and hanged by the Germans. To this day the people of my district tend the grave of this hero who died for his country. A monument has been erected on the grave.

When the enemy withdrew from Strelkovka, the entire village, including my mother's home, went up in flames.

When we reached Maloyaroslavets, there was not a soul in the streets. The town seemed deserted. But two light tracked vehicles were parked in front of the town hall, a driver asleep in one of them. When he was awakened, the driver told us that this was Budenny's command car. Budenny had arrived at the town hall three hours before.

I found Budenny inside, and we greeted each other warmly. It was obvious that he had lived through a great deal in those tragic days.

When I told him about my visit to Western Front headquarters, Budenny said he had been out of touch with Konev for the last two days. While he was visiting the Forty-third Army, his own headquarters had moved and he did not know where it was.

I told him that it was beyond the railroad bridge across the Protva River, seventy miles from Moscow, and that they were looking for him. I also told him that the situation was very bad and that most of the forces of the Western Front had been encircled.

"Things are no better here," he replied. "The Twenty-fourth and Thirty-second armies have been cut off, and we have no defense front any more. Yesterday I almost fell into enemy hands between Yukhnov and Vyazma. Large motorized and tank columns were moving toward Vyazma, evidently to by-pass the town on the east."

"Who is now holding Yukhnov?"

"I don't know. We have a small detachment on the Ugra River—two infantry regiments but no artillery. I think the enemy has Yukhnov."

"Then who is covering the road from Yukhnov to Maloyaroslavets?"

"When I came through there, I saw only three policemen at Medyn," Budenny said.

We agreed that he would go to his headquarters and telephone a report on the situation to Moscow. I would drive toward Yukhnov and then to Kaluga.

West of Maloyaroslavets I met the commander of the local fortified area, Colonel Smirnov, who reported on the progress of fortification work, the availability of worker battalions and the equipment of the military units capable of defending the approaches to Maloyaroslavets. After I had instructed him to organize reconnaissance and to get his fortified area into fighting shape, I drove on to Medyn. I found no one there except an old woman who was rummaging around a house that had been hit by a bomb.

"Granny, what are you doing here?" I asked.

She stood there with wide-open, wandering eyes and disheveled gray hair and said nothing.

"What's the matter, Granny?"

Without replying, the woman went back to digging.

Another woman, half-dressed and carrying a half-filled sack, appeared from the ruins.

"Don't bother asking her," she said, "she won't say anything. She has lost her mind with grief."

She told me that two days before German planes had bombed and strafed the town. Many people had been killed. The residents were getting ready to leave for Maloyaroslavets. The old woman had lived in this house with a little grandson and granddaughter. She was at the well getting water when the raid began. She saw a bomb hit her house. Somewhere under the ruins were the bodies of her grandchildren. The second woman had to hurry; her home had also been destroyed and she could not find her shoes and clothes in the rubble. Tears rolled down her cheeks. When asked whether any of our troops had passed through the town, she said that during the night several trucks had driven through toward Maloyaroslavets, followed by horse-drawn carts bearing the wounded. There had been nothing since then. I said good-bye and drove on toward Yukhnov, deeply regretting that there was nothing I could say to console this woman or any of the other Soviet people to whom the war had brought such terrible grief.

Soon after we had left Medyn, we were stopped in a forest by armed Red Army men in tank outfits. One of them told us that we could drive no farther and asked whose car it was. I identified myself and asked, in turn, where his headquarters was. It turned out to be a tank brigade headquarters a hundred yards away in the woods.

I was glad to hear this and asked him to lead me there. In the woods a tank officer of medium height and smart bearing, dressed in blue overalls, with goggles over his helmet, rose from the tree stump on which he had been sitting. He looked familiar.

"Colonel Troitsky, commander of the tank brigade of the Supreme Headquarters reserve," he said, saluting.

So that's who it was! I knew I. I. Troitsky well from Khalkhin-Gol.[4] In 1939 he served as Chief of Staff of the 11th Tank Brigade. That was the brigade, under the command of Hero of the Soviet Union Yakovlev, that defeated the 23rd Infantry Division of the Japanese Imperial Guard near the hill Bain-Tsagan.

After a hurried greeting we got down to business. Colonel

---

[4] Khalkhin-Gol was the site of the undeclared war fought in 1939 between the Russians and Japanese in which Zhukov won his first military reputation.   H.E.S.

Troitsky reported that the enemy was holding Yukhnov. German advance units had seized the bridge across the Ugra River. A reconnaissance unit sent by Troitsky toward Kaluga had found no Germans in the city, but reported heavy fighting not far from Kaluga, with the 5th Guards Rifle Division and remaining elements of the Forty-third Army engaged in the action. Although Troitsky's own brigade was part of the Supreme Headquarters reserve, it had waited at this point for two days without instructions from anyone.

I instructed Troitsky to send signal officers to Reserve Front headquarters near Obninskoye Station to inform Marshal Budenny about the situation. Part of the brigade was to occupy the terrain forward from the present position and set up defenses to cover the approaches to Medyn. I also instructed the Colonel to transmit my instructions to the General Staff through Reserve Front headquarters and to tell them that I was on my way to Kaluga, to the 5th Guards Rifle Division. We parted like two old fighting comrades.

On October 9 a staff officer of Reserve Front headquarters caught up with me and handed me a telephone message from Marshal Shaposhnikov, the Chief of General Staff. It said: "The Supreme Commander in Chief [Stalin] orders you to proceed to Western Front headquarters. You have been appointed commander of the Western Front."

Thus ended my two-day trip as a member of Supreme Headquarters investigating the situation on the orders of Stalin.

On the morning of October 10 I reached Western Front headquarters at Krasnovidovo, two or three miles northwest of Mozhaisk. There I found a special commission of the State Defense Committee, consisting of Marshal Kliment Voroshilov, General A. M. Vasilevsky, Georgi M. Malenkov and V. M. Molotov. I don't know what the commission reported to Moscow, but the simple fact that it had arrived at the Western Front at such a tense period, as well as my talks with its members, suggested that Stalin was extremely concerned about the highly dangerous situation on the approaches to Moscow.[5]

There was no doubt that the forces of the Western, Reserve and Bryansk fronts had been badly set back in the first ten days of October. It later became clear that the commands of these fronts had made serious miscalculations: although the forces of the Western and Reserve fronts had held their positions for about a month and a half and had had enough time for thorough preparations before the start of the enemy offensive, the necessary steps had not been taken; the fronts had been unable through reconnaissance to determine the strength and direction of the attack being prepared by the enemy even though Supreme Headquarters had warned about the concentration of large German forces; as a result, even though the enemy offensive had been expected, nothing had been done to provide greater defense in depth, especially antitank defenses, in the threatened sectors or to pull in the fronts' reserves; nothing had been done to organize artillery and air unit strikes at the areas from which the main enemy forces were to start their offensive; and when the enemy broke through near Vyazma, the command had done nothing to pull out the forces that were being threatened with encirclement. As a result the Sixteenth, Nineteenth, Twentieth, Twenty-fourth and Thirty-second armies were trapped.[6]

[5] Marshal Konev contends that the special commission, with his concurrence and that of Bulganin, the Military Council member of the front, asked Stalin to name Zhukov to command the Western Front. The "request" probably was inspired by Stalin. (I. S. Konev in *Bitva Za Moskvu*, Moscow, 1966, p. 52.)   H.E.S.

[6] The principal target of Zhukov's criticism, although he does not mention his name, is Marshal Konev, Zhukov's wartime rival and postwar political opponent. Konev has published a detailed defense of his conduct of the Western Front, which he directed from September 12 until he was replaced by Zhukov on October 10. Konev asserts he did everything possible to prepare for the German offensive but was hampered by the

During my talk with members of the commission, I received instructions to telephone the Supreme Commander in Chief. I went to the communications room. Stalin himself now told me of his decision to appoint me Western Front commander and asked whether I had any objections. I had no grounds for objection. It then became clear that Stalin intended to replace the entire command of the front. In my view, this was not the best way out of the existing situation. Stalin agreed to leave Konev as deputy commander and to entrust him with command of the forces guarding the approaches to Kalinin. This area was too far from front headquarters and required separate attention. I was informed that the Western Front would incorporate the remainder of the Reserve Front, the forces already on the Mozhaisk defense line and the Supreme Headquarters reserves that were being sent to reinforce that line.

"Get the Western Front into shape and act as fast as you can," Stalin said.

"I will get to work immediately," I replied, "but I must ask you to start shifting large reserves. We must expect the enemy thrust toward Moscow to increase in strength in the near future."

---

inability to get needed troops and guns from Stalin. In the critical days of late September and early October, he contends, he was being asked to give up divisions to the Supreme Headquarters reserve. He insists he warned Stalin about the critical breakthrough on the Warsaw highway toward Spas-Demensk on October 5 but admits that his telephone connections with Moscow were broken and he can find no record of the warning in the archives of the Ministry of Defense. (Konev in *Bitva Za Moskvu,* Moscow, 1966, pp. 38 ff.)   H.E.S.

2

Zhukov Takes Command

I discussed the situation with Konev and the Western Front Chief of Staff, General V. D. Sokolovsky, and we decided to move front headquarters to Alabino; Konev was to assemble a group of officers and a command staff to coordinate operations in the Kalinin sector, and Bulganin and I were to drive to Mozhaisk to confer on the spot with Colonel S. I. Bogdanov, the commander of the Mozhaisk fortified area.

The headquarters of the Mozhaisk fortified area, where we arrived in the afternoon of October 10, was located in the city Community Center. Distant artillery fire and exploding bombs could be heard clearly. Colonel Bogdanov reported fighting under way on the approaches to Borodino between the enemy's advanced mechanized and tank units and the 32nd Rifle Division, supported by artillery and a tank brigade. The division was led by Colonel V. I. Polosukhin, an experienced commander. We instructed Bogdanov to hold on at any price and returned to front headquarters at Alabino. There we found preparations in full swing to establish a strong defense zone along a line running through Volokolamsk, Mozhaisk, Maloyaroslavets and

Kaluga. It was to be developed in depth and reserves were to be assembled for the front.

The Mozhaisk line had a number of obvious tactical advantages. It was covered by the Lama, Moskva, Kolocha, Luzha and Sukhodrev rivers, whose steep banks constituted effective antitank obstacles. At the rear of the Mozhaisk line a dense net of highways and railroads offered good possibilities for troop movements. The zone was suitable for the provision of a succession of defense lines that would offer the enemy increasing opposition in depth.

The big problem was that we had very small forces along the 135-mile Mozhaisk line. On October 10 these consisted of four rifle divisions and cadets of the Moscow Artillery and Military-Political schools, the Military School named for the Supreme Soviet of the R.S.F.S.R., the Podolsk Machine-Gun and Artillery School, three reserve rifle regiments and five machine-gun battalions. The line was being held by a total of 45 battalions instead of the 150 for which it was designed. This meant a very low density of forces, on the average one battalion for every three miles of front. The road to Moscow was not fully covered.

However, the Supreme Command took emergency steps to ward off the peril to the capital. On October 9 the Mozhaisk defense zone was renamed the Moscow Reserve Front (Lieutenant General P. A. Artemyev in command; Divisional Commissar K. F. Telegin as a member of the Military Council; Major General A. I. Kudryashov as Chief of Staff). The Supreme Command reinforced it with five newly formed machine-gun battalions, ten antitank artillery regiments and five tank brigades. On October 11 all the forces on the Mozhaisk line were combined into the Fifth Army under Major General D. D. Lelyushenko. This defense zone was also reinforced with the retreating units of the Western and Reserve fronts, units of the right wing of the Western Front, from the Northwest Front and the Southwest Front as well as with reserves from the deep interior of the country. The entire country, the sons and daughters of all the Union republics, heeded the call of the Party and government for the defense of Moscow.

The command of the Western Front was expected to ensure the proper disposition of the newly arrived forces and equipment without losing a minute of precious time, to prepare a solid defense in all threatened sectors, to develop it in depth and to assemble reserves that could be shifted promptly to vulnerable spots.

Everyone worked day and night. People literally collapsed from fatigue and lack of sleep. But everyone did all he could at his post—sometimes even the impossible. Driven by a feeling of personal responsibility for the fate of Moscow, the fate of the homeland, generals and staff officers, commanders and political commissars of all ranks demonstrated unprecedented energy and dedication in seeking to organize ground and aerial reconnaissance, the firm control of forces and a steady flow of supplies, and in promoting political and Party work, to raise the morale of troops and to inculcate into every soldier a confidence in his own strength and in the inevitable defeat of the enemy on the approaches to Moscow.

A directive from Supreme Headquarters incorporated all military units and institutions of the Moscow Reserve Front into the newly formed Western Front, effective 11 P.M. on October 12.[7] In the meantime the military situation had become increasingly serious. It is reflected in the following report, made October 12 by the front's Military Council to Supreme Headquarters:

[7] General Artemyev, the commander of the Moscow Reserve Front, was made Zhukov's deputy. Major General L. A. Govorov, the deputy commander of the Moscow Reserve Front, was appointed chief of artillery of the Western Front, but a few days later he was ordered to take over command of the Fifth Army from General Lelyushenko, who had been wounded. Major General I. P. Kamera became the new artillery commander.   H.E.S.

The enemy, with two tank divisions, one motorized division and at least three infantry divisions, has seized Sychevka and Zubtsov and is continuing to advance toward Kalinin.

The advanced units of one of the tank divisions moving toward Kalinin reached a point fifteen miles southeast of Staritsa at 9:35 A.M. on October 12.

The following orders have been issued:

1. The commanders of the Twenty-second and Twenty-ninth armies are to rush one regiment each with antitank guns on trucks to the area east of Staritsa to cover the approaches to Kalinin.

2. The 174th Rifle Division, which was on the approaches to Rzhev, is being shifted to Staritsa.

3. The commander of the Twenty-second Army has been instructed to remove the 256th Rifle Division from the front and to send it by forced march to Kalinin for the defense of the city from the south.

4. The commander of the Kalinin garrison has been ordered to position detachments along the Boriskovo-Pokrovskoye line. . . .

The defense of Kalinin can be insured only by the prompt dispatch of at least one rifle division and a tank brigade, neither of which can be spared by the front.

I request your authorization for the prompt dispatch of the division to Kalinin from the reserves of the Supreme Command.

The approaches to Volokolamsk, which are completely undefended, are in the same situation, and this front can spare no forces for that sector.

At least one division should also be urgently dispatched to that area.

By the middle of October the newly formed Sixteenth, Fifth, Forty-third and Forty-ninth armies had a total strength of only ninety thousand men. These forces were far from adequate to man a continuous defense line; therefore we decided to concentrate them in the principal sectors: Volokolamsk, Istra, Mozhaisk, Maloyaroslavets and the Podolsk-Kaluga sector. Most of the artillery and antitank forces were also concentrated in these areas.

On October 13 the Volokolamsk approaches were entrusted

to the Sixteenth Army headed by General Konstantin K. Rokossovsky, A. A. Lobachev and M. S. Malinin. It included the forces of the Volokolamsk fortified zone and newly arrived units. The Fifth Army under General Govorov included the forces of the Mozhaisk fortified zone, Colonel Polosukhin's 32nd Rifle Division and newly arrived units. The Forty-third Army was commanded by Major General K. D. Golubev and included the forces of the Maloyaroslavets fortified zone. The Forty-ninth Army was commanded by Lieutenant General I. G. Zakharkin and included the Kaluga fortified zone.

All these generals were experienced commanders who knew their business and could be expected to do everything possible with the forces entrusted to them to keep the enemy away from Moscow. I also want to mention the efficient work of the staff of the front under General Sokolovsky, now a marshal, and the energy with which Major General N. D. Psurtsev, the front's chief of signal troops (and now Minister of Communications), ensured stable communications among all the parts of the front.

Extensive engineering work was under way behind the first echelon of the Western Front to ensure a defense in depth and to install antitank barriers in all sectors potentially open to tank attacks. The principal sectors were also backed up by reserves. The front headquarters was moved from Alabino to Perkhushkovo, which was linked by telephone and telegraph with all ground and air units. The headquarters was also connected by direct wire with the General Staff and Supreme Headquarters. Flows of supplies were hurriedly organized, together with medical facilities and other rear services. All this constituted the new Western Front, which was called upon to repel the attack of the German Fascist forces against Moscow.

The Communist Party began to explain the gravity of the situation, the immediacy of the threat to Moscow, to the Soviet people. The Central Committee called on all citizens to wage a determined struggle against apathy and panic and to fulfill honorably their duty to their homeland by barring the enemy from the capital.

The most important thing for us in the middle of October was to win time in order to prepare our defense. If the operations of parts of the Nineteenth, Sixteenth, Twentieth, Twenty-fourth and Thirty-second armies and the Boldin group, encircled west of Vyazma, are assessed from that point of view, these units must be given credit for their heroic struggle. Although they were cut off in the enemy's rear, they did not surrender. They continued to fight valiantly, attempting to break through to rejoin the main force of the Red Army and thus holding down large enemy formations that would otherwise have pursued the drive toward Moscow. The front command and Supreme Headquarters assisted the surrounded troops by bombing German units and with aerial drops of food and ammunition. But shortages of manpower and arms made it impossible to do more for the encircled forces at that time.

Twice, on October 10 and 12, we dispatched coded radio messages to the army commanders of the surrounded troops containing information about the enemy and ordering a breakout under the over-all command of General M. F. Lukin, commander of the Nineteenth Army. The commanders were requested to transmit a plan for the proposed breakout and to indicate the sector in which aerial support should be provided. However, there was no reply to our messages; they probably arrived too late. Over-all control of the surrounded armies was evidently lost, and troops succeeded in breaking out only in small groups.

In any case, the persistent and stubborn fight put up by the encircled forces near Vyazma held down the enemy's main units during the most critical days. We won precious time to organize our defenses along the Mozhaisk line. The sacrifice made by the surrounded forces was not in vain. A full account of their heroic struggle, representing such a great contribution to the defense of the capital, still remains to be written.

On October 13 our forces abandoned Kaluga under enemy pressure. Heavy fighting broke out on all sectors on that day as the enemy launched large mobile forces in the direction of Moscow. According to front intelligence on October 15, 50 tanks were in action in the area of Turginovo, 100 at Lotoshino, 100 at Makarovo and Karagatovo, 50 at Borovsk and 40 at Borodino.

In view of the growing threat to Moscow, the Party's Central Committee and the State Defense Committee decided to evacuate a number of agencies of the Central Committee and the government and the entire diplomatic corps to Kuibyshev, together with the most important state treasures. The evacuation began during the night of October 15–16. On the whole, Muscovites met these measures with complete understanding. But, as the saying goes, there are black sheep in every family, and, in this case, too, cowards, panicmongers and self-seekers started fleeing the capital in all directions, spreading panicky rumors about an inevitable surrender. With the aim of mobilizing the troops and civilians of Moscow to repel the enemy and of preventing a repetition of the panic stirred up by provocative elements on October 16, the State Defense Committee proclaimed a state of siege in Moscow and its surroundings on October 19.[8]

The defense line Volokolamsk–Mozhaisk–Maloyaroslavets–Serpukhov was still manned by weak forces and had been breached by the enemy in a number of places. To prevent an enemy breakthrough toward Moscow, the front's Military Council decided to establish a new defense line from Novo-Zavidov-

---

[8] The Soviet General Staff and Supreme Headquarters were divided into two on October 17, and Reserve Headquarters was set up in the east, to function in case Moscow fell. There are rumors that Stalin left Moscow briefly, but if he did, he was back by October 19, when the state of siege was proclaimed.   H.E.S.

sky through Klin, the Istra reservoir, the town of Istra, Zhavoronki, Krasnaya Pakhra and Serpukhov to Aleksin.

Because of the importance of this decision, I want to quote
in full the plan for the pull-back of the armies of the Western
Front from the Mozhaisk line. The plan, which was approved
by Stalin on October 19, contained the following provisions:

1. In case the enemy offensive cannot be halted on the Mozhaisk
line, the armies of the front, while continuing rear-guard resistance
against the enemy advance, will pull back their main forces, especially their artillery, to a newly prepared defense line running
through Novo-Zavidovsky, Klin, Istra reservoir, Istra, Zhavoronki,
Krasnaya Pakhra, Serpukhov and Aleksin. The pull-back is to be
given air support.

2. Pending the positioning of the armies on the new defense line,
strong rear guards saturated with antitank guns and provided with
mobile forces for brief counterattacks are to hold the enemy as long
as possible along an intermediate line running through Kozlovo,
Gologuzovo, Yelgozino, Novo-Petrovskoye, Kolyubakovo, Naro-
Fominsk, Tarutino, Chernaya Gryaz and the Protva River.

3. The armies will pull back within their present lateral boundaries, except for the Sixteenth and Fifth armies; the new boundary
between them will run through Zagorsk, Iksha, Povarovo and Tar-
khanovo, all these points being within Sixteenth Army territory.

4. The rear echelons of the armies are to be pulled back eastward
within their boundaries, except for the Fifth and Thirty-third
armies, whose rear echelons will have to by-pass Moscow and the
Moscow transport hub: the rear forces of the Fifth will proceed
north of Khimki and Mytishchi, and the Thirty-third south of
Peredelkino and Lyubertsy. Not a single horse-drawn cart or truck
should be permitted to move through Moscow and the Moscow
hub. This will require firm and timely traffic controls for the Fifth
and Thirty-third armies and preliminary planning of the routes of
march. Nonessential rear echelons should be pulled back early.

5. In case the Fifth Army is unable to hold the main line running
through Istra, Pavlovskaya Sloboda and Zhavoronki, it should not

be pulled back to the fortified ring around Moscow, but northeast-ward north of Khimki and, on the left flank, to the positions held by units of the Thirty-third Army south of Peredelkino and Lyubertsy so that these units may be moved into the Fifth Army reserve, by-passing the Moscow fortified area on the southeast and east to the area of Pushkino.

6. Accordingly, the Fifth Army is to be based at the railroad station of Pushkino and the Thirty-third Army at Ramenskoye. The Sixteenth, Forty-third and Forty-ninth armies should be based on the supply stations within their boundaries.

7. To insure the planned pull-back, the road junctions of Novo-Petrovskoye, Kubinka, Naro-Fominsk and Vorobyi should be previously provided with antitank defenses that would prevent a breakthrough of enemy tanks into the rear. Before the pull-back, parts of the armies should also occupy the key sectors of the new defense line with infantry units and especially artillery and signal corps detachments. In the Sixteenth Army sector, the remainder of the 126th Rifle Division is to occupy the line in the area of Klin and Troitskoye; in the Fifth Army sector, the 110th or the 113th Rifle Division the area of Davydkovo and Krasnaya Pakhra; in the Forty-third Army sector, the 53rd Rifle Division is to be stationed west of Podolsk and Lopasnya.

8. During the pull-back, the Western Front command will maintain contact with the various armies through the communications center of the People's Commissariat of Defense in Moscow while a new communications center and front headquarters will be prepared in the area of Orekhovo-Zuyevo or Likino-Dulevo.

GENERAL ZHUKOV, *Commander of the Western Front*
BULGANIN, *member, Western Front Military Council*
LIEUTENANT GENERAL SOKOLOVSKY, *Western Front Chief of Staff*

October 19, 1941

The plan was communicated on a top-secret basis to army commanders, who then worked out their own plans accordingly. Although the pull-back from the Mozhaisk line had been approved by the Supreme Command, troops of the Western Front withdrew with extremely heavy fighting in an attempt to hold up the enemy as long as possible and to gain time for the positioning of reinforcements from the Supreme Headquarters reserve and for the strengthening of the defense line in the rear. The Military Council of the Western Front addressed the following appeal to the troops:

Comrades! In this grave hour of danger for our state, the life of each soldier belongs to the Fatherland. The homeland demands from each one of you the greatest effort, courage, heroism and steadfastness. The homeland calls on us to stand like an indestructible wall and to bar the Fascist hordes from our beloved Moscow. What we require now, as never before, are vigilance, iron discipline, organization, determined action, unbending will for victory and a readiness for self-sacrifice.

I do not think it is necessary to retrace the course of military operations, which have been described in detail in many books and historical accounts. The outcome of the defensive operations of October is well known. During a month of bloody fighting the German forces advanced a total of 145 to 160 miles. But Hitler's plan to seize Moscow was disrupted, the forces of the enemy were exhausted and its shock units were overextended. Steadily losing strength, the German offensive was finally halted at the end of October along a line running through Turginovo, Volokolamsk, Dorokhovo, Naro-Fominsk, west of Serpukhov and Aleksin.

By that time troops of the Kalinin Front had stabilized the situation in the Kalinin area. [Because of the great expanse of the Western Front and because of the problem of directing the forces around Kalinin, Supreme Headquarters decided on October 17 to combine the Twenty-second, Twenty-ninth and Thirtieth armies in a new Kalinin Front, with General Konev in command, Corps Commissar D. S. Leonov as a member of the Military Council, and Major General I. I. Ivanov as Chief of

Staff.] The Bryansk Front, which by October 30 had pulled back its forces to a line running through Aleksin, Tula, Yefremov and Tim, had frustrated the enemy's plans to seize Tula and to advance toward Yelets and Voronezh.

The names of all the heroes who distinguished themselves in defense of the capital in October, 1941, could not possibly be listed. Not only individual soldiers but entire units won military glory by their feats in the name of the homeland. Such units could be found in any sector of the front. In the Volokolamsk sector, fortification troops put up a tenacious defense and particular distinction was won by the 316th Rifle Division under Major General I. V. Panfilov. It was subsequently transformed into the 8th Guards Division. It was also in this sector that a military school regiment under Colonel S. I. Mladentsev fought heroically with the support of three antitank artillery regiments.

Unparalleled bravery was displayed by M. Ye. Katukov's armored brigade, which had been incorporated into the Sixteenth Army. For its heroic fighting in October at Orel and Mtsensk, this unit, then called the 4th Tank Brigade, was awarded the great honor of being renamed the 1st Guards Tank Brigade, and its commander was awarded the Order of Lenin and the rank of major general of armored forces. In November these tank men enhanced their reputation with new exploits. During five days of defensive fighting in the Volokolamsk sector, they ambushed and destroyed more than thirty enemy tanks.

One of the best units in the Mozhaisk sector was the 32nd Rifle Division under Colonel Polosukhin. Almost 130 years after Napoleon's campaign, this division once again fought an enemy on the field of Borodino, the sacred national battlefield that has become an immortal monument to Russian military glory. The division did nothing to lessen that glory, but rather brightened it.

On the approaches to Maloyaroslavets, a heroic struggle was

put up by the 312th Rifle Division and by cadets of the Podolsk infantry and artillery schools. The area of Medyn was defended to the death by the tank men of Colonel Troitsky, whom I mentioned earlier. Around the ancient town of Borovsk, soldiers and officers of the 110th Rifle Division and the 151st Motorized Rifle Brigade added glory to their banners. Men of the 127th Tank Battalion stood shoulder to shoulder with them in repulsing the enemy.

Brilliant episodes in the chronicle of those hard days were recorded by the heroic defenders of the city of Tula. Unfortunately, this aspect of the defense has not yet been adequately covered in the Soviet histories of the war. And yet it would be difficult to exaggerate the role that the defense of Tula played in the Battle for Moscow. The city was defended by armed workers detachments and units of the Fiftieth Army that had pulled back to Tula. Particular steadfastness and courage were demonstrated by the Tula workers regiment under A. P. Gorshkov, commander, and G. A. Ageyev, political commissar. That regiment suffered heavy losses, but did not allow the enemy to enter the city. Nor did the workers of Tula lose their nerve when the enemy virtually closed the ring around the city. Together with the troops of the Fiftieth Army they continued to fight until the end, showing a high degree of organization, steadiness and courage. And they did hold out.

Until November 10, 1941, Tula had been part of the territory of the Bryansk Front. German forces were advancing on it after seizing Orel. Aside from the rear units of the Fiftieth Army, there were no forces in Tula capable of defending the city. In the second half of October three heavily mauled rifle divisions had retreated to the Tula area. These divisions ranged in strength from five hundred to fifteen hundred men, and one artillery regiment was down to four guns. These units were exhausted and required completely new equipment, none of which was available in the rear stores. The workers of Tula, under the leadership of the city's Party organizations, worked day and night sewing uniforms and repairing equipment and arms to restore these units to fighting condition.

The defense committee of Tula, headed by the regional Party secretary, Vasily Gavrilovich Zhavoronkov, was also able to assemble and arm the workers regiment of six hundred men within a short time. That regiment, together with units of the Fiftieth Army, manned the approaches to the city in the suburban area of Kosaya Gora. General V. S. Popov, commander of the Tula sector, used an antiaircraft regiment for antitank defense.

Tula repulsed an attack by Guderian's tank army on October 30. Guderian had counted on sweeping through Tula (as he had swept through Orel) and by-passing Moscow on the south. But the units of the Tula sector, including the regiment of local workers, fought the enemy with great courage and valor, setting his tanks afire with bundles of grenades and bottles of gasoline. After the Fiftieth Army had been transferred to the Western Front, it was greatly reinforced with manpower and arms available to that front.

No matter how hard the enemy tried to take Tula and thus open the road to Moscow from the south, he was unable to do so in the course of November. The city held out like an invulnerable fortress. Tula tied down the entire right flank of the German forces. When the enemy ultimately decided to by-pass Tula, Guderian's army was forced to split its forces, losing the operational effectiveness provided by tactical concentration. That is why Tula and its citizens played such an outstanding role in the defense of Moscow.

Tula, ancient city of Russian gunmakers, thus became an unconquerable outpost of the capital thanks to the solidarity and self-sacrifice of its citizens, who fought with or helped our soldiers in every possible way. I don't think I would be far wrong if I said that the glory given to Moscow as a hero city belongs also to Tula and its people.

When we speak here of heroic feats, we obviously have in mind not only our soldiers, commanders and political commissars. What was achieved at the front in October and in subsequent battles was made possible by the common and united efforts of Soviet troops and the people of Moscow and the Moscow area, unanimously supported by the entire nation.

The wide-ranging activities of the Party organization of the city of Moscow and the Moscow area in rallying the working people in defense of the capital against the enemy took on the character of a heroic epic. The fiery appeals of the Party's Central Committee and of the city and regional Party organizations awakened a deep response in the heart of every Muscovite, every soldier and the entire Soviet people. The working people of Moscow vowed to fight to the last with the soldiers rather than let the enemy through to the capital. And they kept that vow with honor.

During October and November the working people of Moscow provided five divisions of volunteers to the front. Their total contribution from the start of the war had been seventeen divisions. In addition to these divisions of the people's militia, Muscovites formed and armed hundreds of fighting teams and tank-destroyer detachments. On October 13 the Party activists in the capital decided to form workers battalions in every city borough. And within a few days Moscow mustered 25 companies and battalions with a total of 12,000 men, most of them members of the Party or the Young Communist League. An additional 100,000 workers underwent military training in their spare time and then joined military units. About 17,000 women and girls were trained as nurses and medical assistants.

Members of peacetime occupations—ordinary workers, engineers, technicians, scholars and artists—of course had few military skills. Military service was new for them, and they had a lot to learn, even as they were engaged in battle. But all of them were distinguished by common traits—a high degree of patriotism, an unshakable determination and confidence in ultimate victory. It was no accident that these voluntary units became outstanding fighting forces after they had gained some military experience. Muscovites were the core of many special reconnaissance and ski units and fought in the guerrillas.

We can never forget the contribution of residents of the capital who with their bare hands constructed fortified lines for its defense. More than half a million people of the city of Moscow and the oblast, most of them women, built fortifications on the distant and immediate approaches to the city.

Since the war a great deal has been said about the frequent references on the part of Hitler's generals and bourgeois historians to Russian mud, cold and impassable roads. These stories have already been sufficiently debunked, but I want to refer the reader once more to what Kurt Tippelskirch has said on the subject in his *History of the Second World War*: "It became impossible to move along the roads, with mud sticking to the boots, the hooves of animals, and the wheels of carts and motor vehicles. . . . The offensive ground to a halt."

Does this mean that the Nazi generals really expected to roll to Moscow and beyond on smooth, well-graded roads? In that case, too bad for them and for the German forces who, according to Tippelskirch, were halted on the approaches of Moscow by mud. In those days I saw thousands and thousands of Moscow women, who were unused to heavy labor and who had left their city apartments lightly clad, work on those impassable roads, in that mud, digging antitank ditches and trenches, setting up antitank obstacles and barricades, and hauling sandbags. Mud stuck to their boots, too, and to the wheelbarrows they used to haul earth, and added an incredible load to shovels that were unfamiliar in women's hands. I don't think there is any point in pursuing this comparison. I might merely add, for the benefit of those who look to mud to camouflage the real causes of their defeat at Moscow, that the roads were impassable for a relatively brief period in October of 1941. Early in November cold weather set in, snow began to fall, and both the terrain and the roads became passable. In the November days of the German "general offensive," the temperature ranged from 14 to 19 degrees Fahrenheit, and we know that there is no mud under such conditions.

Even in this cold, Muscovites continued to work selflessly on fortifications. Construction of the outer ring of the Moscow defense zone was completed November 25. More than 100,000 Muscovites, mainly women, had worked on it, building 1,428 artillery emplacements, 100 miles of antitank ditches, 75 miles of barbed-wire entanglements three rows deep, and a large number of other obstacles. However, their contribution to our common victory over the enemy did not end there. The self-sacrifice of the working people in defense of their capital had a tremendous moral effect on the fighting spirit of the troops, augmenting their strength and their will to fight.

Each day we received reports about the Muscovites who labored at almost all the factories of the capital and on the grounds of evacuated plants to produce arms and munitions for the front. Defense production was under way not only in large plants, but also in workshops of local craft industries and producer cooperatives.

We also must not forget that thousands of air-raid wardens were on duty day and night on the roofs of the capital. Hundreds of women and girls worked as hospital volunteers, surrounding wounded soldiers with love and care and restoring them to health. And then there was the pleasure produced at the front by letters, telegrams and packages from Muscovites and the people of the whole nation. In the entire period of the Battle for Moscow, the troops received 450,000 packages and 700,000 pieces of clothing, from as far away as the fraternal Mongolian People's Republic, which sent a delegation headed by Marshal Choibalsan to our front.

Through the efforts of the Communist Party, front and rear

were welded into a single, unbreakable unit. And that was the key factor in our victory at Moscow. Many difficult tests were still before us. Although the enemy's October offensive had failed, the situation at the front remained extremely serious. But the fighting spirit of the Soviet troops and their confidence that the enemy would be beaten and thrown back from Moscow remained unshaken.

3

The November Threat

On November 1, I was summoned to Supreme Headquarters, where Stalin said, "We want to hold the military parade as well as the ceremonial meeting marking the October Revolution [November 7]. What do you think, will the situation at the front allow us to hold these festivities in Moscow?"

I reported that the enemy was in no condition to start a major offensive in the next few days. He had suffered heavy losses in the October fighting and was now busy reinforcing and regrouping his troops. But his air force was likely to remain active even during this period.

A decision was made to strengthen the air defenses of the capital by shifting additional fighter squadrons from nearby fronts. The traditional Red Square parade took place and everything turned out all right. After their march past the Lenin Mausoleum, the military units proceeded directly to the front. That November parade was undoubtedly of tremendous political importance, both internally and abroad.

In the expectation of a renewed enemy drive against Moscow, the Soviet Supreme Command took all measures possible to break up the offensive once and for all. During the first half of November troops of the Western Front continued to regroup and to fortify their lines. As of 6 P.M. on November 10, the Fiftieth Army and the entire defense of Tula were transferred by Supreme Headquarters to the Western Front, and the Bryansk Front was disbanded. (Its Third and Thirteenth armies were transferred to the Southwest Front.) The transfer of the defense of Tula and of the Fiftieth Army to our front meant a considerable lengthening of our defense line, and the transferred army was in a weakened condition. However, we continued to receive reinforcements from the Supreme Headquarters reserve as well as tanks, arms, ammunition, signal equipment and supplies. Our quartermasters received large numbers of fur coats, felt boots, warm underwear, padded vests and fur caps. By the middle of November our soldiers had been provided with winter clothing and were a great deal more comfortable than the enemy troops, who wrapped themselves in warm clothes confiscated from local residents. Many Nazi soldiers were seen wearing bulky straw galoshes that greatly impaired movement. Nevertheless, all available reports indicated that the enemy was completing the regrouping of his forces; a continuation of his offensive could be expected soon.

The new infantry and tank units from the Supreme Headquarters reserve were concentrated in the most vulnerable sectors, mainly around Volokolamsk, Klin and Istra, where we expected the main armored attack by the enemy. The Sixteenth Army was supplemented by the 17th, 18th, 20th, 24th and 44th cavalry divisions in the Volokolamsk-Istra sector. Additional forces were also moved to Tula and Serpukhov, where the Germans' Second Tank Army and the Fourth Field Army were expected to attack. On November 9 this left flank of our front was reinforced by General P. A. Belov's cavalry corps and by the 415th Rifle Division, the 112th Tank Division and the 33rd Tank Brigade. Even though the Western Front received substantial reinforcements and deployed six armies by mid-November, it must be noted that there were few troops in depth, especially in the center, because the front line extended over 375 miles. That is why we tried to provide the best protection for the most vulnerable sectors on our flanks and to leave some forces in reserve for maneuver in case of need. However, a directive by the Supreme Commander in Chief on November 13 introduced substantial changes into our plans. Stalin called me on the telephone.

"What's the enemy up to?" he asked.

"He's completing preparations in his shock groups and will probably start an offensive soon," I replied.

"And where do you expect the main blow?"

"At Volokolamsk and Novo-Petrovskoye toward Klin and Istra. Guderian's army is likely to try to by-pass Tula toward Venev and Kashira."

"Shaposhnikov and I feel," Stalin went on, "that we must break up the enemy offensive with a preventive counterattack. One counterattack should by-pass Volokolamsk on the north, and the other should be launched from Serpukhov against the flank of the Germans' Fourth Army. Those seem to be the areas where large forces are being massed for the drive against Moscow."

"And what forces are we supposed to use for these counterattacks?" I asked. "The front has nothing available. We have just enough to hold our present positions."

"In the Volokolamsk area you could use the right-flank units of Rokossovsky's army, the 58th Tank Division, a couple of cavalry divisions and Dovator's cavalry corps. At Serpukhov use Belov's cavalry corps, Getman's tank division and parts of the Fortieth Army," Stalin suggested.

"We can't do that," I replied. "We can't throw the last reserves of our front into dubious counterattacks. We won't have any reinforcements when the enemy goes over to the offensive with his shock groups."

"But you've got six armies. Don't tell me that's too little."

I replied that the defense line of the Western Front was overextended, that it measured more than 375 miles, and that we had very few reserves in depth, especially in the center. "Consider the question of counterattacks decided and let me have your plan by tomorrow evening," said Stalin. I insisted that it would be a mistake to use our only reserves for counterattacks, and mentioned the unfavorable terrain north of Volokolamsk. But he had already hung up.

The conversation left me depressed, not, of course, because the Chief had not considered my opinion, but because Moscow, which the soldiers had vowed to defend to the last drop of blood, was in mortal danger, and we were now being ordered to throw our last reserves into extremely dubious counterattacks. With those reserves gone, we would be unable to strengthen any weak sectors in our defense lines.[9]

Fifteen minutes later Bulganin walked into my office and said, "I just had a dressing down, too."

"What do you mean?"

"Stalin said, 'You and Zhukov seem to be getting quite a high

[9] General Belov gives a sharply differing account of this episode. He says that Zhukov summoned him to his headquarters November 9, the day Belov's cavalry unit was incorporated into the Western Front, and advised him that a counterattack was being mounted in the region of Serpukhov in which the Belov group was to act in collaboration with the Forty-ninth Army. Belov was ordered to draft his plans immediately without even inspecting the lay of the land. A day later Zhukov approved his plan and took him to Moscow on November 11 to meet Stalin. Belov had not seen Stalin since 1933. He thought he had aged twenty years in nine, his eyes were shifty and his voice seemed to lack confidence. Zhukov addressed Stalin sharply in a superior tone of voice, and Belov had the impression that Zhukov, not Stalin, was in charge. Stalin seemed to take all this as though it were appropriate and occasionally a look of something like bewilderment appeared in his face. Zhukov submitted the plans for the counteroffensive and Stalin approved them with only one change—a day's delay in their start. (P. A. Belov, *Za Nami Moskva*, Moscow, 1963, pp. 40–43.)   H.E.S.

opinion of yourselves. But we'll find a way of dealing with you, too.' He ordered us to get to work immediately on the counterattacks."

"Well, in that case, you better sit down. We'll call in Sokolovsky [the Chief of Staff] and warn Rokossovsky and Zakharkin [commanders of the Sixteenth and Forty-ninth armies]."

Two hours later, front headquarters issued orders to Rokossovsky, Zakharkin and the other commanders to launch the counterattacks, and informed Supreme Headquarters of the steps taken.

These counterattacks, carried out mainly by cavalry, had, of course, no serious consequence because they were not strong enough to affect the enemy's shock forces. The counterattacking forces suffered losses and, at the crucial moment, they were not where they were most needed.

Having rebuffed our counterattacks, the enemy himself went over to the offensive two days later, on November 15, striking at the junction between the Kalinin and Western fronts.

Our counterattack in the Serpukhov sector had not achieved its objective, even though to rebuff it the Germans had to draw on part of the reserves intended for the push along the Warsaw highway. But when Guderian's army began to by-pass Tula and to drive toward Kashira, causing a serious situation in that sector, we had a great deal of trouble pulling Belov's cavalry corps and Getman's tank division out of the battle and transferring them to the Kashira area.

For the second phase of the offensive against Moscow, the German command had brought up new forces and, by November 15, faced the Western Front with 51 divisions, including 31 infantry, 13 tank and 7 motorized divisions, all up to full strength in manpower, tanks, artillery and other equipment. On the Volokolamsk-Klin and Istra sectors the enemy had concentrated the 3rd and 4th tank groups, consisting of 7 tank divisions, 3 motorized divisions and 3 infantry divisions, supported by 1,940 guns and a powerful air group. In the Tula-Kashira sector, the enemy's shock forces consisted of the Second Tank Army (4 tank divisions, 3 motorized divisions, 5 infantry divisions, an infantry brigade and the Greater Germany Motorized SS Regiment). It was also supported by a powerful air group. The Germans' Fourth Field Army, consisting of 18 infantry divisions, 2 tank divisions, a motorized and a security division, faced the Zvenigorod, Kubinka, Naro-Fominsk, Podolsk and Serpukhov sectors. That army had orders to hold down the defense forces of the Western Front, to weaken them, and then to launch an attack against the center of the front toward Moscow.

In accordance with the German operation plan, code-named "Typhoon," the second stage of the offensive against Moscow began November 15 with an attack against the right flank of the Thirtieth Army of the Kalinin Front, which was relatively weak south of the Moscow Sea [the great dam-created reservoir on the Volga River]. At the same time the enemy attacked troops of the Western Front in the sector south of the Shosha River, on the right flank of the Sixteenth Army. An auxiliary attack against the Sixteenth Army was launched near Teryayeva Sloboda.

The defenses of the Thirtieth Army gave way as the enemy threw more than 300 tanks against the Thirtieth Army's 56 light tanks. In the morning of November 16 the enemy began to pursue his attack in the direction of Klin. We had no reserves in this sector because Supreme Headquarters [Stalin] had ordered them to counterattack in the Volokolamsk sector, where they were still held down by the enemy. On the same day the Germans also attacked at Volokolamsk. Heavy fighting broke out as two tank divisions and two infantry divisions drove in the direction of Istra. Among the Soviet forces that distinguished themselves in this fighting were the 316th, 78th and 18th rifle divisions, the 1st Guards Division, the 23rd, 27th and 28th inde-

pendent tank brigades and the cavalry group of Major General
L. M. Dovator. The enemy also threw more than 400 medium
tanks against our 150 light tanks in the drive toward Istra.
On November 17, at 11 P.M., the Supreme Command ordered
the Thirtieth Army transferred from the Kalinin Front to the
Western Front. This meant that the defense line of the Western
Front was even further extended, all the way to the Moscow
Sea. Supreme Headquarters also relieved Major General V. A.
Khomenko of his command of the Thirtieth Army and replaced
him with General Lelyushenko.[10]

The fighting of November 16 to 18 was a difficult experience
for us. The enemy drove head on regardless of losses in an
effort to break through toward Moscow with his armored
wedges. But our defense in depth, with its prepared artillery and
antitank positions and its well-coordinated operations, frustrated
the enemy's plans. Thousands of enemy bodies littered the
battlefield, but at no point was the enemy able to break through.
The Sixteenth Army pulled back slowly and in complete order
to previously prepared artillery positions, where its units renewed their stand, repulsing fierce attacks and inflicting ever-
increasing losses on the enemy.[11]

[10] General Lelyushenko blamed L. Z. Mekhlis, a police general and
crony of Stalin's, for the removal and the arrest of Khomenko. Mekhlis
was responsible for many such incidents. (D. D. Lelyushenko, *Zarya
Pobedy*, Moscow, 1966, p. 88.)   H.E.S.

[11] Actually, the pull-back of the Sixteenth Army and the subsequent
German breakthrough touched off a fearsome row. Rokossovsky was concerned about the length of his lines, the exhaustion of his troops and the
increasing German pressure. He wanted to pull back to the Istra reservoir
and the Istra River. This would create a shorter line, more easily defended.
He proposed the withdrawal, but Zhukov refused to permit it. Rokossovsky appealed over Zhukov's head to the Chief of Staff, Marshal Shaposhnikov—a most unusual action. Shaposhnikov telephoned his approval
of the withdrawal a couple of hours later, making clear that Stalin had
approved the move. Rokossovsky's troops were preparing to pull out
when he got this telegram: "I am the commander of troops on this front!

Meanwhile the State Defense Committee and parts of the Party's Central Committee and the Council of People's Commissars [the government] continued to function in Moscow. The workers of the capital labored twelve to eighteen hours a day supplying the front with arms, equipment and ammunition and making repairs.

Soon after the Germans had effected their tactical breakthrough on the Thirtieth Army sector of the Kalinin Front and on the right flank of Rokossovsky's Sixteenth Army (I don't remember exactly, but I think it was on November 19) Stalin phoned me and asked: "Are you sure we are going to be able to hold Moscow? I am asking with an aching heart. Tell me honestly, as a member of the Party."

"There is no question that we will be able to hold Moscow. But we will need at least two more armies and two hundred tanks," I replied.

"I am glad that you're so sure," Stalin said. "Call Shaposhnikov and tell him where you want the two reserve armies concentrated. They will be ready by the end of November, but we have no tanks for the time being."

Within a half-hour I had arranged with Shaposhnikov to station the First Shock Army, which was in the process of being formed, in the area of Yakhroma, and the Tenth Army around Ryazan.

Meanwhile the enemy had begun his offensive November 18 in the Moscow-Tula direction. His 3rd, 4th and 17th tank divisions advanced in the Venev sector, where the 413th and 299th rifle divisions of the Fiftieth Army were dug in.

Having broken through the advanced defenses, the enemy

I revoke the order for the withdrawal of troops to the Istra reservoir and order you to defend the existing line and not retreat one step farther. General of the Army Zhukov." (K. K. Rokossovsky, *Voyenno-Istoricheskii Zhurnal*, December, 1966, p. 53.)   H.E.S.

tank group seized Bolokhovo and Dedilovo. To stem his advance, we quickly moved the 239th Rifle Division and the 41st Cavalry Division into the area of Uzlovaya. Fierce fighting, marked by the mass heroism of our troops, continued day and night. Units of the 413th Infantry Division particularly distinguished themselves.

On November 21 the main force of Guderian's tank army succeeded in occupying Uzlovaya and Stalinogorsk. The enemy's 47th Motorized Corps drove on toward Mikhailov. A serious situation was developing around Tula.

At that point the Military Council of the Western Front decided to reinforce the Kashira sector with the 112th Tank Division under Colonel A. L. Getman, the Ryazan sector with a tank brigade and other units, the Zaraisk sector with the 9th Tank Brigade and the 35th and 127th independent tank battalions, and the Laptevo sector with the 510th Rifle Regiment and a tank company.

On November 23 heavy fighting developed around Venev. Two days later, the Germans' 17th Tank Division, having by-passed Venev, approached the town of Kashira, where General Belov's reinforced 1st Guards Cavalry Corps was stationed after having been shifted from the Serpukhov area. On November 26 the enemy's 3rd Tank Division cut the Tula-Moscow railroad and highway north of Tula. On the same day the 1st Guards Cavalry Corps, the 112th Tank Division and other units concentrated in the Kashira area repulsed the enemy's attacks and threw him back southward toward Mordves. To reinforce the 1st Guards Cavalry Corps even further, the front's Military Council decided to move the 173rd Rifle Division and the 15th Guards Mortar Regiment into the Kashira sector.

On November 27 the 1st Guards Cavalry Corps, in conjunction with the 112th Tank Division, the 9th Tank Brigade, the 173rd Rifle Division and other units, launched a powerful counterattack against the enemy's 17th Tank Division, throwing it back to the south over a distance of six to ten miles. Heavy fighting continued in the Kashira-Mordves sector until November 30 as the enemy suffered heavy losses but was unable to achieve success. Guderian, the commander of the Germans' Second Tank Army, realizing that it was impossible to reach Moscow by breaking through the resistance of the Soviet forces in the Kashira-Tula area, ordered his forces to take up defensive positions.[12] The Soviet troops in the Tula area thus repulsed all attacks, causing heavy losses to the enemy and preventing his advance toward the capital.

The situation was far worse on the right flank of our front around Istra, Klin and Solnechnogorsk. Enemy tanks broke into Klin on November 23. To keep units of the Sixteenth Army from being encircled, they were pulled back to the next defense line during the following night, and Klin itself was abandoned on November 24 after heavy fighting. The loss of Klin produced a gap between the Sixteenth and Thirtieth armies that was covered by a weak, improvised group of units.

On November 25 the Sixteenth Army was forced to pull back from Solnechnogorsk, giving rise to a serious situation. The front's Military Council moved up everything available—including groups of soldiers with antitank guns, isolated groups of tanks, artillery batteries and antiaircraft divisions—in support of Rokossovsky's Sixteenth Army. The enemy had to be contained until the 7th Rifle Division from Serpukhov and two tank brigades and two antitank artillery regiments from the Supreme Headquarters reserve could be moved up into the area of Solnechnogorsk.

Our defense line began to bend inward in an arc, some sectors became greatly weakened, and it looked as if the situation were

---

[12] Guderian gave this order December 5–6. He noted in his journal: "The offensive on Moscow has ended. All the sacrifices and efforts of our brilliant troops have failed. We have suffered a serious defeat." (Heinz Guderian, *Vospominaniya Soldata (A Soldier's Memoirs)*, Moscow, 1954, p. 239.)   H.E.S.

beyond repair. But, no! The soldiers were not disheartened, and as soon as reinforcements arrived, the enemy once again faced an insurmountable defense line.

In the evening of November 29 an enemy unit took advantage of the weak defense of a bridge across the Moscow-Volga Canal near Yakhroma, seized the bridge and crossed to the east bank. There it was stopped by advance units of the newly formed First Shock Army, under the command of Lieutenant General V. I. Kuznetsov, and thrown back across the canal after fierce fighting.

On December 1 the Nazi forces launched a surprise attack at the center of the front between the Fifth and Thirty-third armies and then advanced along the Minsk-Moscow highway toward Kubinka. They were halted at the village of Akulovo by the 32nd Rifle Division, which destroyed some of the enemy tanks with its artillery fire. A number of tanks were also blown up in mine fields. The enemy's tanks, having suffered heavy losses, then turned toward Golitsyno, where they were finally stopped by the front's reserve and units of the Fifth and Thirty-third armies. By December 4 this breakthrough had been liquidated. The enemy left more than ten thousand dead, fifty destroyed tanks and a great deal of equipment on the battlefield. That was the last attempt of the German forces to break through to the Soviet capital.

The sequence of events was equally tense in other sectors under attack from the enemy's principal shock forces. The divisions on the right flank of the enemy's Volokolamsk grouping on December 2 reached a point five miles northeast of Zvenigorod, but were prevented from advancing farther on the following day. To support his other attacking forces, the enemy also opened an offensive on the quiescent Naro-Fominsk sector on December 1. He succeeded in breaking through the front of the Thirty-third Army and advanced to Aprelevka. But parts of the Fifth, Thirty-third and Forty-third armies counterattacked on December 3 and 4, throwing the enemy back to the west bank of the Nara River.

In the first few days of December it became evident from the nature of the military operations and from the strength of the attacks of the enemy forces that the offensive was grinding to a standstill and that the Germans had neither the manpower nor the arms to continue their drive.

From the interrogation of prisoners we established that all enemy forces had suffered very heavy losses, that some companies were down to twenty or thirty men, that the morale of the German troops had greatly deteriorated and that they no longer had faith in the prospect of capturing Moscow. Our troops of the Western Front also suffered great losses and were exhausted, but nowhere did they allow a major breakthrough and, reinforced by reserves and inspired by the appeals of the Party, they multiplied their strength tenfold in the struggle with the enemy before Moscow.

In the twenty days of the second phase of their offensive, the Germans lost 155,000 dead and wounded, 800 tanks, at least 300 guns and 1,500 planes. The heavy losses, the complete collapse of the plan for a blitzkrieg ending to the war, and the failure to achieve their strategic objectives depressed the spirit of the German forces and gave rise to the first doubts about a successful outcome of the war. The Nazi military-political leadership also lost its reputation of "invincibility" before world public opinion.

Former German generals and field marshals have tried to blame Hitler for the failure to take Moscow and for the failure of the war plans in general, on the grounds that, contrary to their advice, he halted the advance of Army Group Center toward Moscow in August and diverted part of the forces to the Ukraine. For example, F. W. von Mellenthin writes in his *Panzer Battles*: "The drive against Moscow, which was favored by Guderian and which we abandoned temporarily in August to seize first the Ukraine, might have been successful if we had always regarded it as the principal offensive that would decide the outcome of the war. Russia would then have been wounded at her very heart."[13]

Generals Heinz Guderian, Hermann Hoth and others attribute the defeat before Moscow to the harsh Russian climate (aside from Hitler's mistakes). Bourgeois historians and former Nazi generals have tried to convince the public that the million picked German troops were beaten at Moscow not by the iron steadfastness, courage and heroism of Soviet soldiers, but by mud, cold and deep snow. The authors of these apologetics seem to forget that Soviet forces had to operate under the same conditions. As far as the temporary halt of the drive toward Moscow in August is concerned, the Germans had no choice but to divert part of their forces to the operations in the Ukraine. Without those operations the central group of the German forces might have been in an even less favorable position: the Soviet Supreme Headquarters reserves that were thrown into operational gaps in the southwest in September would otherwise have been used against the flank and rear of Army Group Center during its drive against Moscow. Angered by the collapse of his planned blitzkrieg and looking for scapegoats, Hitler dismissed Field Marshal Walther von Brauchitsch as commander of German ground forces, Field Marshal von Bock as commander of Army Group Center, General Guderian as commander of the Second Tank Army, General Erich Höppner as commander of the 3rd Tank Group and many others whom he had generously decorated with Knight's Crosses and other high orders a month and a half or two months earlier. Hitler himself took over command of German ground forces, evidently in the belief that this would have a magical effect on his troops and inspire them to fight fanatically against the Red Army.

[13] Norman, Oklahoma, 1956.   H.E.S.

There is one more point I would like to make. Some of the
Soviet military histories, especially one titled *Razgrom nemetsko-
fashistskikh voisk pod Moskvoi* (Defeat of the German-Fascist
Forces at Moscow),[14] contend that the October fighting by the
Western, Reserve and Bryansk fronts was not part of the operations in the Battle for Moscow, that the enemy was supposedly
fully stopped on the Mozhaisk line in late October and early
November, and that the Nazi command had to prepare an entirely new "general offensive" against Moscow. I cannot agree
with any of these statements.

When the Nazi command undertook Operation Typhoon in
October, it sought to defeat the Soviet forces in the Vyazma-
Moscow and Bryansk-Moscow directions and, by-passing Moscow
on the north and south, to seize the Soviet capital as speedily
as possible. In form and method of operations, the enemy tried
to achieve that strategic plan in two pincer movements. The
first encirclement and defeat of Soviet forces was planned for
the Bryansk and Vyazma areas, and the second encirclement
and the seizure of Moscow were to be achieved by advances of
armored forces on the northwest through Klin and on the south
through Tula and Kashira and the closing of the pincers in the
area of Noginsk, east of Moscow.

In the beginning of October the enemy was able to achieve
his first objective, taking advantage of his superior manpower
and equipment and of errors made by the commands of Soviet
fronts. But his ultimate strategic objective, the seizure of Moscow, failed because the main forces of the enemy were held down
by the Soviet troops surrounded in the Vyazma area (parts of
the Sixteenth, Nineteenth, Twentieth, Twenty-fourth and

---

[14] This volume was prepared under the editorship of Marshal V. D.
Sokolovsky and mentions Zhukov by name only four times. Marshal Konev
gets six notices, Sokolovsky four, Timoshenko three, Belov thirty-four and
Cavalry General L. M. Dovator seven. (*Razgrom nemetsko-fashistskikh
voisk pod Moskvoi*, Moscow, 1964.)   H.E.S.

Thirty-second armies and the Boldin group). The limited forces thrown by the enemy against the Mozhaisk line with the aim of breaking through to Moscow succeeded in pushing the Soviet troops back to a line running through Volokolamsk, Dorokhovo, the Protva River, the Nara River, Aleksin and Tula. They were not able to break through.

The fact that the Germans substantially reinforced their troops and equipment in November and regrouped their tank forces on the left flank is, in my view, not sufficient ground for the conclusion offered in the book under discussion. Reinforcements and regroupings are common in all strategic offensive operations and do not determine the beginning and end of such operations.

Since the end of the war I have often been asked how we were really able to stop the strong German drive against Moscow. A great deal has already been written about the battle, and, on the whole, it is correct. Nevertheless, as the former commander of the Western Front, I would like to add my opinion.

In planning Operation Typhoon, the Nazi Supreme Command seriously underestimated the strength, the condition and the potentialities of the Red Army in the Battle for Moscow. Similarly, it grossly overestimated the capabilities of its own forces to break through our defense lines and seize the Soviet capital.

The Germans also made mistakes in organizing their armored shock groups for the second stage of the offensive. Their flank groups, especially those operating around Tula, were weak and were inadequately supplied with infantry. Experience should have shown that exclusive reliance on armored forces was insufficient under those conditions. The tank units were worn down, had suffered heavy losses and had lost their striking power.

Nor was the German command able to launch the associated attack in the center of our front in time even though its forces were adequate for the purpose. In the absence of attacks at the center we were able to shift all our reserves, down to divisional reserves, from the center of the front to parry the enemy's strike forces on the flanks. Heavy losses, a lack of preparation for winter conditions and the stubborn resistance of Soviet forces, all affected the enemy's fighting capacity.

By November 15 our intelligence was able to establish that the enemy was massing strike forces on the flanks of our defense line and to determine the exact direction of the main enemy attacks. We opposed these armored blows with a defense in depth that was relatively well provided with antitank obstacles and other engineering devices, and that was where we concentrated our basic tank forces. Our soldiers were fully conscious of their personal responsibility for the fate of Moscow, for the fate of their homeland, and were determined to die rather than let the enemy through to Moscow.

A major role was also played by the decree of the State Defense Committee of October 19, proclaiming a state of siege in Moscow and adjoining areas, and by the determined effort to ensure strict discipline and order among the forces defending Moscow. Every violation was promptly stopped by decisive measures. We were able to improve the control of forces at all command and staff levels, especially in the heat of battle, thus ensuring precise fulfillment of orders.

A major contribution to the organization of our defenses was made by the Operational Administration of the General Staff and personally by Lieutenant General A. M. Vasilevsky, the Deputy Chief of the General Staff. His assessment of the situation on the Western approaches during the period of October 2–9 and his recommendations furnished the basis for the steps taken by Supreme Headquarters. The untiring officers of the General Staff followed every step of the enemy forces day and night and made constructive suggestions during dangerous moments.

4

Zhukov's Counteroffensive

The enemy had been unable to break through our defense lines. He could not surround a single division nor fire a single artillery salvo at Moscow. By the beginning of December he was exhausted and out of reserves, while our Western Front was reinforced with two newly formed armies, the First Shock Army and the Tenth Army, and a number of other units that had been combined into a third army, the Twentieth.

These enabled the Soviet command to organize a counteroffensive.

The counteroffensive was being prepared while the defensive operations around Moscow were still going on, and the final plans took shape when the German forces—having suffered tremendous losses—became too exhausted to withstand our attacks. The Moscow counteroffensive was thus a continuation and a logical culmination of the successful counterattacks begun by our troops on the flanks of our front in the last few days of November.

In an effort to take advantage of the favorable conditions developing for us around Moscow, Supreme Headquarters ordered the troops of the Kalinin Front (Konev) and the right flank of the Southwest Front (Timoshenko) to begin a counter-offensive along with the Western Front. At the end of November and the beginning of December the Supreme Command, by agreement with the Military Council of the Western Front, had concentrated the First Shock Army northwest of Moscow and east of the Moscow-Volga Canal. At the same time the Tenth Army had massed its forces around Ryazan.

The Soviet people and its armed forces were going through a difficult period. Soviet troops had broken up the German plan to capture Leningrad and form a junction between German and Finnish forces. At Tikhvin the Red Army went over to the counteroffensive, defeated the enemy and recaptured the town. In the south, forces of the Southern Front had also gone over to the counteroffensive and freed Rostov-on-Don.

On November 29 I telephoned the Supreme Commander in Chief and, after having reported on the situation, asked that the First Shock Army and the Tenth Army be placed under my jurisdiction so that I could strike stronger blows against the enemy and throw him back farther from Moscow.

Stalin listened attentively to what I had to say and then asked: "Are you sure that the enemy has reached a state of crisis and is incapable of introducing new groups into his forces?"

"The enemy is exhausted," I said. "But without the help of the First Shock Army and the Tenth Army the troops of my front will be unable to eliminate any dangerous salients. If we don't eliminate these salients now, the enemy may be able to reinforce his groups in the Moscow area by bringing up large reserves from the north and south later. Then our situation would be much more serious."

Stalin said he would discuss the matter with the General Staff.

I did not want to telephone the General Staff, and instead

asked my Chief of Staff, General Sokolovsky (who agreed that
the time had come to move the First Shock Army and the Tenth
Army into battle), to call the General Staff and persuade it to
deploy the two reserve armies immediately. Late in the evening
of November 29 we were informed that Supreme Headquarters
had decided to transfer the First Shock Army and the Tenth
Army to the Western Front. At the same time Supreme Headquarters [Stalin] asked to see our plan for the use of these
armies. This plan, of which the essential elements follow, was
submitted the following day.[15]

The First Shock Army, after it had eliminated the German
bridgehead on the east bank of the Moscow-Volga Canal, was
to concentrate its forces in the Dmitrov-Yakhroma sector and,
in conjunction with the Thirtieth and Twentieth armies, strike
toward Klin and beyond in the general direction of Teryayeva
Sloboda.

The Thirtieth Army was to be charged with the task of defeating the enemy around Rogachevo and Borshchevo and, with
the First Shock Army, of seizing Reshetnikovo and Klin, and
continuing its advance toward Kostlyakovo and Lotoshino.

The Twentieth Army, together with the First Shock Army
and the Sixteenth Army, was instructed to strike from the areas
of Krasnaya Polyana and Bely Rast toward Solnechnogorsk,
seizing it from the south, and driving on toward Volokolamsk.
In addition, the right wing of the Sixteenth Army was to strike
against Kryukovo and Istra.

The Fiftieth Army at Tula would strike toward Bolokhovo
and Shchekino. Belov's operational group at Mordves was to

---

[15] Zhukov's unwillingness to telephone the General Staff reflected a
continuing disagreement between himself and Marshal Shaposhnikov,
Chief of Staff, concerning strategy and tactics. The disagreement deep-
ened as the winter went on. Zhukov's plan for the Moscow counteroffensive
was approved by Stalin November 30. (A. M. Samsonov, *Velikaya Bitva
pod Moskvoi*, Moscow, 1958.)   H.E.S.

advance toward Venev and then Stalinogorsk and Dedilovo in conjunction with the right wing of the Tenth Army. The Tenth Army, to be deployed between Serebryanye Prudy and Mikhailov, would strike toward Uzlovaya and Bogoroditsk and beyond, south of the Upa River.

The additional strength of three new armies (the First Shock, Tenth and Twentieth) would thus be thrown against the enemy's northern and southern groupings.

The immediate aim of the counteroffensive was to eliminate the two wedges on the northern and southern flanks of our front. Subsequent operations were to be determined in the course of the counteroffensive, depending on the existing situation, with the over-all objective of inflicting maximum losses on the enemy and pushing him as far back from Moscow as possible, thus eliminating the immediate threat to the Soviet capital.

The Western Front did not have the resources for achieving more ambitious objectives than this. Despite the transfer of the three reserve armies, the front still lacked numerical superiority over the enemy (except in the air), and the enemy still remained superior in tanks and artillery. Because of these circumstances, our forces in the center of the Western Front were given the task, in the first stage of the counteroffensive, of tying enemy forces down by active operations in preparation for an ensuing offensive.

I don't remember exactly, but I think it was on the morning of December 2 that Stalin, speaking with me on the telephone, asked, "How do you evaluate the enemy and his possibilities?"

I replied that the enemy was completely exhausted. He seemed to have no reserves to strengthen his shock groups, and without them the Nazis could not continue their offensive. The Chief replied, "Good. I will call you again."

From this I understood that Headquarters would consider the further action of our troops.

Stalin called about an hour later and asked what I thought the front should do in the next few days. I proposed that the troops be prepared for the counteroffensive according to the approved plan.

Headquarters was considering what assistance the other fronts —the Kalinin Front and the right wing of the Southwest Front— could give in order to provide the most effective support of the Western Front. Deputy Chief of Staff Vasilevsky discussed the question by high-security phone with Colonel General Konev, the Kalinin Front commander, on December 1: "Smashing the German offensive on Moscow not only to save Moscow but to begin the serious defeat of the enemy requires active fighting for definite objectives. If we do not begin in the very near future, it may be too late. The Kalinin Front, which occupies a very effective position, cannot stand idle."

In conversation by telephone on December 2 Stalin said that the Kalinin Front and the right wing of the Southwest Front had been given orders to support us. Our drive was to be timed to coincide with theirs.

Late in the evening of December 4 the Chief telephoned me and asked, "Is there anything else you need beyond what we gave you?"

I said I still needed air support from the Supreme Headquarters reserve and the air defense forces and at least two hundred tanks with crews. The front had too few tanks and needed more for the rapid development of the counteroffensive.

"We can't give you any tanks; we don't have any," Stalin said. "But you'll get your air support. Arrange it with the General Staff. I am going to call them now. Just remember that the Kalinin Front offensive begins on December 5 and the operational group on the right wing of the Southwest Front around Yelets on the sixth."

It was bitter cold at this season. Deep snow slowed troop movements to the take-off points for the counteroffensive. But despite these difficulties all forces were in position on the morning of December 6.

On that day the troops of the Western Front, after concentrated bombing and artillery bombardment, went over to the offensive north and south of Moscow. The adjoining fronts, meanwhile, had begun their offensives around Kalinin and Yelets. The great battle had begun. The initiative had passed to our side.

On December 5 the Kalinin Front drove a wedge into the enemy line south of Kalinin but could not break through. It was not until the sixteenth, after the right wing of the Western Front (the Thirtieth, First Shock, Twentieth and Sixteenth armies) had defeated the enemy around Rogachevo and Solnechnogorsk and seized Klin, that the Kalinin Front could advance against the enemy's rear guard, which was covering the retreat of the main forces.

The First Shock Army reached the outskirts of Klin on December 13 and, together with the Thirtieth Army, began the battle for the town. Having surrounded Klin, the Soviet forces broke into the town and, after fierce fighting during the night of December 14–15, cleared it of the enemy.

The Twentieth[16] and Sixteenth armies also advanced successfully. The Twentieth, after overcoming fierce enemy resistance, approached Solnechnogorsk late on December 9, while the Sixteenth Army, having seized Kryukovo on the eighth, advanced toward the Istra reservoir. The enemy was forced to

---

[16] The Twentieth Army was commanded by General A. A. Vlasov, then one of the brightest young stars in the Red Army. In July, 1942, having lost most of his Second Shock Army in the Nazi encirclement south of Leningrad, he surrendered to the Germans. Later he put himself at the head of an anti-Soviet military organization and at the end of the war was seized by the Russians, tried and executed as a traitor. This is why Zhukov never mentions the name of the Twentieth Army commander. H.E.S.

abandon Solnechnogorsk on December 12. The right wing of the Fifth Army also advanced, thanks to a large extent to the progress of the Sixteenth Army.

The advance of the right wing of the Western Front was steadily supported by the front's own air units, the air defense forces and the bombers of our long-range air force, which was then commanded by General A. Ye. Golovanov. Our planes attacked artillery emplacements, tank units and command centers, and when the enemy began his retreat, the planes strafed and bombed infantry, armored and truck columns, littering all the roads to the west with the remains of motor vehicles and other equipment.

The Western Front command dispatched ski units, cavalry and parachutists to the rear of the enemy to harass his retreating forces. Guerrilla units went into action, greatly complicating the situation for the German command.

I must say here that the experience of war revealed to me the absolute necessity of a front commander's working with his military units up until the very beginning of an operation or battle. This is essential in order to help the troops to understand the situation and to organize their action. With the beginning of an operation and during its course commanders should be with their staffs or at command points from which they can direct the troops.

In directing the troops in the Battle of Moscow I was guided by these principles. In the period of defensive action the great length of the front (more than 375 miles) and the complex and crucial situation did not permit the front commander to be separated from his staff. All information about the actions of the enemy, of our own troops and of the neighboring fronts, rapidly accumulated at the command post, and we were in constant communication with Supreme Headquarters and the General Staff.

However, on one occasion during the defensive operations I

was compelled to leave my staff and visit one of the divisions of the Sixteenth Army. Here is how it happened:

Somehow Stalin had got word that our troops had abandoned the city of Dedovsk, northwest of Nakhabino. This was very close to Moscow (within ten miles), and he was naturally very disturbed at such unexpected intelligence, especially since on November 28 and 29 the 9th Guards Rifle Division, commanded by Major General A. P. Beloborodov, had successfully held off repeated attacks of the enemy in the nearby region of Istra. Yet, here twenty-four hours later, it seemed that Dedovsk was in the hands of the Germans.

Stalin called me on the telephone: "Do you know that they've occupied Dedovsk?"

"No, Comrade Stalin, I didn't know that."

The Chief didn't wait to find out why I was uninformed. He snapped angrily: "A commander should know what's going on at the front!" He ordered me to proceed immediately to the spot and "personally organize a counterattack and retake Dedovsk." I argued that it was not wise to leave front headquarters at such a tense moment.

"Never mind," Stalin said. "We'll get along somehow. Leave Sokolovsky [the Chief of Staff] in charge."

Hanging up the phone, I quickly got hold of General Konstantin K. Rokossovsky of the Sixteenth Army and asked why headquarters knew nothing about the loss of Dedovsk. He explained that the Germans didn't have Dedovsk and that the place in question must be the village of Dedovo. He said that the 9th Guards Rifle Division was engaged in heavy battle in the region of Khovanskoye, Dedovo and Snigiri, in an attempt to prevent a breakthrough of the Germans along the Volokolamsk highway toward Dedovsk and Nakhabino. It was plain that the report Stalin had received was all a mistake. I decided to call Headquarters and explain the misunderstanding. But it was like trying to drive a nail into a stone. Stalin was in a towering rage and demanded that I go immediately to Rokossovsky and do everything necessary to see that this miserable village was recovered from the enemy. Moreover, he demanded that I take along the Fifth Army commander, General Leonid A. Govorov, because "he is an artilleryman and he can help Rokossovsky organize artillery fire to help the Sixteenth Army."

There was no sense in arguing. When I called General Govorov, he protested vigorously that there was no point in such a trip. The Sixteenth Army had its own chief of artillery, Major General V. I. Kazakov; moreover, Rokossovsky himself knew what to do, and why should he, Govorov, leave his army at such a critical time? In order to end the debate I told Govorov that it was an order from Stalin.

We went to see General Rokossovsky and then with him to Beloborodov's division. Beloborodov was not exactly happy to see us. He was already up to his neck in problems, and now he was being asked to explain why the Germans had occupied a few houses in the village of Dedovo on the far side of a deep gully. He outlined the situation and made it plain that there was no tactical reason for trying to recapture the houses since they were on the far side of a deep ravine.

Unfortunately, I couldn't tell him that tactical principles had nothing to do with our presence there. So I ordered Beloborodov to send a rifle company and two tanks to drive the Germans out of the houses. It was done at dawn, December 1.

Meanwhile, it turned out that I was wanted on the telephone. The line to Sixteenth Army headquarters had been cut, but a communications officer appeared at Beloborodov's division with word for me to call my command post. When I managed to get through to my Chief of Staff, Sokolovsky reported that Stalin had called three times asking, "Where is Zhukov? Why has he gone away?" It appeared that on the morning of December 1 the enemy had launched an attack on the Thirty-third Army at a point that had been relatively quiet.

Sokolovsky and I agreed on steps to liquidate this new threat, and then I got through to Headquarters. Vasilevsky gave me Stalin's orders: return immediately to front headquarters; in the meantime the Supreme Command would decide how to provide additional reserves to wipe out the enemy's breakthrough toward Aprelevka.

Returning to my GHQ, I telephoned Moscow and spoke with Stalin. I reported that I was acquainted with the situation and advised him of the measures I was taking to liquidate the German breakthrough on the center of the front. Stalin mentioned neither my trip to the Sixteenth Army with Govorov nor the reasons he had ordered us there. But at the very end of the talk he asked, "Well, and what about Dedovsk?" I replied that I had sent a rifle company, supported by two tanks, to oust the Germans from the village of Dedovo. So ended one of my absences from front headquarters during the defensive Battle of Moscow.

Then, in the course of the Moscow counteroffensive I found a trip to the troops essential. I visited the Sixteenth Army of Rokossovsky, the Fifth Army of Govorov, the Forty-third Army of Golubev and the Forty-ninth Army of Zakharkin. This was necessary, principally, to assist the commanders in better coordinating their actions with those of their neighboring units, to warn them against frontal attacks, and to persuade their troops to by-pass strongpoints of the enemy and pursue him relentlessly.

A week after the beginning of the counteroffensive I issued a directive cautioning against head-on assaults. This was based on the experience of the first days of the offensive. The fact was that in a number of instances especially created shock groups had been drawn into heavy and bloody frontal attacks. In the region of Klin, for example, the advance of the Thirtieth and First Shock armies had been held up in this way.

In the course of an attack on December 19 on the village of

Palashkino, fourteen miles northwest of Ruza, Major General L. M. Dovator, commander of the 2nd Guards Cavalry Corps, lost his life. His body was sent to Moscow for burial. Upon my request, the Presidium of the Supreme Soviet of the U.S.S.R. on December 21 posthumously awarded him for courage and valor the title of Hero of the Soviet Union. Dovator was succeeded in his cavalry command by Major General I. A. Pliyev, who had commanded the 3rd Guards Cavalry Division.

On the left wing of the Western Front, units of the Fiftieth Army and General Belov's cavalry corps had opened their offensive December 3 in an effort to defeat Guderian's tank army around Tula. The Germans' 3rd and 17th tank divisions and the 29th Motorized Division pulled back from Venev, leaving seventy tanks on the battlefield.

Guderian's Second Tank Army had greatly overextended itself in its effort to by-pass Tula and had no reserves left. On December 6 our new Tenth Army joined the battle at Mikhailov, where the enemy put up a stubborn defense in an effort to cover the flank of the retreating Second Tank Army. On December 8 the Fiftieth Army launched its attack from Tula and threatened to cut off the enemy forces retreating from Venev and Mikhailov. Both the Western Front command and Supreme Headquarters provided constant air support for the advance of the Belov cavalry corps and the Fiftieth and Tenth armies. Guderian's army, threatened by deep inroads on its flanks and lacking the forces to parry the attacks of the Western Front and of the operational group provided by the Southwest Front, began to pull back rapidly through Uzlovaya and Bogoroditsk toward Sukhinichi, leaving behind heavy weapons, trucks, tractors and even tanks.

In the course of ten days, troops on the left wing of the Western Front inflicted a serious defeat on the Second Tank Army under Guderian and advanced eighty-five miles.

To the left of the Western Front, troops of the Bryansk

Front, which had been reconstituted on December 18, also pursued their advance. The first phase of our counteroffensive ended with Soviet forces holding a line running through Oreshki, Staritsa, the Lama and Ruza rivers, Maloyaroslavets, Tikhonova Pustyn, Kaluga, Mosalsk, Sukhinichi, Belev, Mtsensk and Novosil.

The German armies, weakened and worn down by fighting, suffered heavy losses and retreated westward under the pressure of our forces.

In my capacity as member of Supreme Headquarters, I was summoned to the Supreme Command on the evening of January 5 to discuss plans for a general offensive. Marshal Shaposhnikov, the Chief of General Staff, gave a brief report on the situation at the front and presented his draft plan for future operations. Then Stalin said, "The Germans seem bewildered by their setback at Moscow and are poorly prepared for the winter. Now is the time to go over to a general offensive."

Shaposhnikov's plan was essentially as follows:

In view of the success of the counteroffensive along the fronts to the west, forces on all other fronts were also to begin offensives. The objective of such a general offensive was to defeat the enemy at Leningrad, west of Moscow and in the south. The main attack was to be directed against Army Group Center. The combined forces of the Northwest, Kalinin, Western and Bryansk fronts would form a pincers that would trap the main forces of the enemy around Rzhev, Vyazma and Smolensk.

Troops of the Leningrad Front, the right wing of the Northwest Front and the Baltic Fleet were to defeat Army Group North and lift the blockade of Leningrad. Troops of the Southwest and Southern fronts were supposed to defeat Army Group South and liberate the Donets Basin. The Caucasus Front and the Black Sea Fleet were expected to free the Crimea. The general offensive was to start within an extremely short time.

Those present at the conference were asked for their opinions.

"We should continue the offensive on the Western Front," I said. "There conditions are most favorable and the enemy has not had time to restore the fighting capacity of his forces. But a successful continuation of the offensive will require reinforcements in manpower and equipment, especially tanks, without which we cannot expect to make much progress. As for offensives near Leningrad and in the southwest, forces there face formidable enemy defenses. Without powerful artillery support our troops would be unable to break through, they would be worn down and suffer heavy and completely unjustified losses. I would favor reinforcing our troops on the Western Front and waging a stronger offensive there."

From Stalin's reaction to my speech I understood that the decision had already been taken and that there would be no reconsideration. However, speaking after me, N. A. Voznesensky [Chairman of the State Planning Commission][17] also spoke against the general offensive. He argued that we did not have material means sufficient to support simultaneous offensives on all fronts.

As soon as he had finished Stalin said, "I've talked with Timoshenko, and he favors the attack. We must quickly smash the Germans so that they cannot attack when spring comes."

Stalin was supported by Malenkov and Beria, who said that Voznesensky was always finding unforeseen difficulties, which could be overcome. No one else wanted to speak. The Chief concluded by saying, "So this, it seems, ends the discussion."

I had the impression that Stalin had called his generals to Supreme Headquarters not for a discussion of the expediency of the general offensive but to "nudge the military," as he sometimes loved to put it.

When we left the office, Boris M. Shaposhnikov said, "It was foolish to argue. The Chief had already decided. The directives

[17] Voznesensky was arrested in 1949 and executed by Stalin in the so-called "Leningrad Affair." H.E.S.

have already gone out to almost all the fronts, and they will launch the offensives very shortly."

"Then why did Stalin ask for my opinion?"

"I just don't know, old fellow, I just don't know," Shaposhnikov said with a heavy sigh.[18]

My front headquarters received the directive for the offensive on January 7. Accordingly, additional assignments were issued to the troops by the Military Council.

The forces of the right wing (First Shock Army and Twentieth and Sixteenth armies) were to continue their offensive toward Sychevka and, together with the Kalinin Front, were to smash the enemy in the Rzhev-Sychevka sector.

The center of the front (Fifth and Thirty-third armies) was ordered to strike toward Mozhaisk and Gzhatsk; the Forty-third, Forty-ninth and Fiftieth armies were to drive toward Yukhnov, defeat the enemy in the Yukhnov-Kondrovo sector and drive on toward Vyazma.

General Belov's reinforced cavalry corps was supposed to drive toward Vyazma and join up with the 11th Cavalry Corps under Major General S. V. Sokolov, operating within the Kalinin Front, for a joint strike into the rear of the enemy's Vyazma grouping. (At that time large guerrilla forces were also active in the Vyazma area.)

The Tenth Army was ordered to advance toward Kirov, covering the left flank of the Western Front.

Our neighbor on the right, the Kalinin Front, was expected to drive in the direction of Sychevka and Vyazma, by-passing Rzhev, while its Twenty-second Army struck toward Bely.

The Northwest Front was supposed to launch its offensive

---

[18] Stalin's (and Shaposhnikov's) plans for a general winter offensive turned into a disaster on almost all the fronts. The attack that was opened January 13 on the Leningrad front led to a dreadful winter of fighting in frozen bogs and marshes, no material successes and extremely heavy Russian losses.   H.E.S.

in two diverging directions. Its Third Shock Army, under Lieutenant General M. A. Purkayev, was to drive toward Velikiye Luki, and the Fourth Shock Army, under Colonel General A. I. Yeremenko, toward Andreapol, Toropets and Velizh. Our neighbor on the left, the Bryansk Front, was charged with the seizure of Orel and Kursk. Troops of the Southwest Front were to capture Kharkov and establish bridgeheads across the Dnieper near Dnepropetrovsk and Zaporozhye.

This broad plan for an offensive on all fronts turned out to be supported with neither the required manpower nor the necessary arms, and most of the fronts had no success. The only exception was the Northwest Front, which was able to advance because the Germans had no continuous defense line in that sector. At the beginning of February the Third and Fourth shock armies of the Northwest Front reached the approaches to Velikiye Luki, Demidov and Velizh after an advance of 150 miles. The Twenty-second Army of the Kalinin Front was fighting on the outskirts of the town of Bely, and the 11th Cavalry Corps had reached the area northwest of Vyazma. The Thirty-ninth and Twenty-ninth armies of the Kalinin Front were advancing slowly west of Rzhev. Troops on the left wing of the Kalinin Front were up against strong enemy defenses and made no progress.

The Western Front (the Twentieth Army, parts of the First Shock Army, Pliyev's 2nd Guards Cavalry Corps, the 22nd Tank Brigade and five ski battalions) opened its offensive on January 10 after a ninety-minute artillery preparation and sought to break through the enemy lines near Volokolamsk. The enemy gave way after two days of fierce fighting, and the cavalry corps, the five ski battalions and the 22nd Tank Brigade poured through a breach in the enemy lines toward Shakhovskaya.

As a result of this decisive operation, the right wing of our front, with the help of guerrillas, seized Lotoshino and Shakhovskaya on January 16 and 17, cutting the Moscow-Rzhev railroad. But instead of adding forces to allow us to exploit this success, Supreme Headquarters on January 19 ordered the First Shock Army to rejoin the reserves. The transfer of the Thirtieth Army to the Kalinin Front on December 16 and now the pull-out of the First Shock Army seriously weakened the right flank of the Western Front. Since I felt that the pressure on the enemy should not be relaxed in that sector, no matter what, Sokolovsky and I telephoned the General Staff for permission to keep the First Shock Army. The answer was simple: it was the Chief's order. I phoned Stalin. I got his answer: "Don't argue. Send it along." To my declaration that the removal of this army would weaken our shock group, he replied, "You have plenty of troops—just count them." I said that our front was very wide and that in all sectors hard fighting made it impossible to regroup. I begged to keep the First Shock Army on the right wing of the Western Front until we had completed the current offensive. We did not want to lessen our pressure on the enemy.

Instead of answering, Stalin hung up. That meant the conversation was finished.

My talks with Shaposhnikov on this subject were also fruitless.

"My dear fellow," Shaposhnikov said, "there is nothing I can do; it is the Chief's personal decision."

When the weakened forces on the right wing approached Gzhatsk, they were stopped by the enemy's organized defense and could not proceed further.

The Fifth and Thirty-third armies, which were advancing in the center, had seized Ruza, Dorokhovo, Mozhaisk and Vereya by January 20. The Forty-third and Forty-ninth armies had reached Domanovo and engaged the enemy's Yukhnov group in battle.

Two battalions of the 201st Airborne Brigade and the 250th Airborne Regiment were dropped near Zhelanye, twenty-five miles south of Vyazma, between January 18 and 22, to cut the enemy's escape routes.

The Thirty-third Army received orders to expand the salient it had driven in the direction of Vyazma and, with Belov's 1st Cavalry Corps, the airborne units, guerrillas and the 11th Cavalry Corps of the Kalinin Front, to win control of Vyazma. On January 27 Belov's corps drove across the Warsaw highway twenty miles southwest of Yukhnov and three days later joined up with the airborne units and guerrillas south of Vyazma. On February 1 they were also joined by three rifle divisions of the Thirty-third Army (the 113th, 338th and 160th) under the personal command of Lieutenant General M. G. Yefremov and began the battle for Vyazma. To reinforce Belov's 1st Cavalry Corps and coordinate operations with the 11th Cavalry Corps of the Kalinin Front, Supreme Headquarters ordered the 4th Airborne Corps to be dropped in the area of Ozerechnya, west of Vyazma, but because of the lack of transport planes only the 8th Airborne Brigade of two thousand men could be delivered to the target area.

At this point I would like to go into greater detail concerning the operations of Belov's cavalry corps, the two reinforced divisions of the Thirty-third Army and the units of the 4th Airborne Corps in the rear of the enemy lines. In the course of its drive from Naro-Fominsk toward Vyazma, the Thirty-third Army had advanced rapidly by January 31 to the area of Shansky Zavod and Domanovo, where it found a broad gap in the enemy defenses. The absence of a continuous front line suggested that the Germans did not have enough forces for a strong defense of Vyazma. We decided therefore to drive on toward Vyazma before the enemy had time to move up reserves, and, by capturing the town, to place his entire Vyazma grouping in an extremely serious situation. General Yefremov decided to lead the strike group of his army himself.

When General Yefremov's group reached the outskirts of Vyazma, the enemy pinched off the base of the gap in his front, cutting off the Yefremov group and restoring the front line along the Ugra River. The right flank of the Thirty-third Army was then at Shansky Zavod, while its neighbor to the left, the Forty-third Army, was held up at Medyn and was thus unable to go to the relief of the Yefremov group as ordered.

When Belov's cavalry corps reached the Vyazma area and joined Yefremov, it also found itself cut off in the rear. By the time the 8th Airborne Brigade could be dropped to reinforce our troops around Vyazma, the Germans had been able to bring up large reserves from France and other areas, greatly strengthening their defenses. We were forced to abandon the entire group in the rear of the enemy lines in a forested area southwest of Vyazma, where several guerrilla units were based. For the next two months the Belov corps, the Yefremov group, the airborne units and the guerrillas operated in the rear of the enemy, inflicting serious blows on enemy manpower and equipment.

On February 10, for instance, the 8th Airborne Brigade and guerrillas occupied the area of Morshanovo and Dyaglevo, destroying the headquarters of the 5th German Tank Division and seizing many trophies.

After establishing radio contact with Belov and Yefremov, the front command did all it could to supply their forces by air with munitions, medicine and food. A large number of wounded were also evacuated by air. Major General V. S. Golushkevich, operations chief at front headquarters, and a number of signal officers repeatedly visited the isolated group. But by the beginning of April its position had deteriorated seriously. The enemy massed large forces in an attempt to eliminate this "thorn" in his side before spring. A thaw that set in at the end of April hampered the group in its maneuverability and in its links with the guerrillas, who had provided food and fodder.

On request from Generals Belov and Yefremov, the front command gave its approval to a plan under which the isolated troops were to attempt to rejoin the main forces. They were to proceed through guerrilla territory toward Kirov, where the Tenth Army was planning to break through the enemy's defenses to meet them.

Belov's cavalry corps and the airborne units executed these orders precisely and, after traveling over a long horseshoe-shaped course, reached the Tenth Army sector at the end of May and the beginning of June.

General Yefremov, on the other hand, considered the escape route too long for his exhausted troops and appealed directly to Supreme Headquarters by radio to permit a direct breakout across the Ugra River. Stalin telephoned me and asked whether I agreed. I replied with a categorical no. But the Chief maintained that Yefremov was an experienced commander and should have his way. Stalin ordered an attack in the direction of the proposed breakout. The attack was prepared by the Forty-third Army and carried out, I think on May 17 or 18, but there was no movement from the other side.

We learned later that the Germans had detected Yefremov's movement toward the Ugra River and intercepted the breakout attempt. Yefremov, who fought like a hero, was killed in the unequal battle that followed, and with him died a substantial number of the heroic soldiers in his detachment. General Yefremov had taken command of the Thirty-third Army on October 25, when the Germans were driving toward Moscow. His forces fought courageously and did not let the enemy break through their lines. Yefremov was awarded the Order of the Red Banner for valor in the Battle of Moscow. Among those who died with him was his army's artillery chief, Major General P. N. Ofrosimov, who was a classmate of mine in 1929–30 in the Red Army courses for higher commanders. General Ofrosimov was a fine, able artillery officer, a man with a soul.

Belov's group traveled a long and difficult road, skillfully avoiding large enemy forces and destroying small enemy units along the way until it rejoined the main Soviet forces through the gap driven by the Tenth Army. The group lost the bulk of its heavy weapons and equipment during its operations in the enemy's rear and in the breakout. But most of the men made it back to the main front. They were exhausted when they finally linked up in a joyous meeting with the troops who had launched the attack to meet them. Soldiers and commanders shed tears without embarrassment—tears of happiness and the fraternal friendship of our fighting men.

In making a critical review of the events of 1942, I find that we made a mistake in our assessment of the situation around Vyazma. We overestimated the capabilities of our forces and underestimated the enemy's, and the nut proved to be harder to crack than we had expected.

In February and March, Supreme Headquarters demanded that we increase our offensive operations, but the manpower and equipment available to the front were exhausted, and we were especially short on ammunition. Thus, in comparison with planned deliveries during the first ten days of January the front received: 82-mm mortar shells, 1 percent; artillery shells, 20 to 30 percent. For all of January: 50-mm mortar shells, 2.7 percent; 120-mm mortar shells, 36 percent; 82-mm mortar shells, 55 percent; artillery shells, 44 percent. The planned deliveries for February were also not fulfilled. Of 316 carloads of munitions planned for the first ten days, we received not one. Because ammunition for our rocket artillery was exhausted, we had to send these units to the rear. It may be hard to believe, but we had to ration the expenditure of shells to one or two per gun per day. And this during an offensive!

A report I wrote to Stalin in this connection on February 14, 1942, stated: "Experience has shown that a shortage of shells makes it impossible for us to carry out artillery barrages. The enemy's firing system remains unharmed; and our forces, attacking without artillery support, suffer heavy losses and do not achieve the expected progress."

Supreme Headquarters decided to reinforce the sectors making up the Western Front, but it was too late. The enemy, alerted by the course of events, had greatly strengthened his Vyazma grouping and, basing himself on previously prepared positions, resumed his own attacks on both the Western and Kalinin fronts.

Our overstrained and extremely weakened troops found it more and more difficult to overcome the opposition of the enemy. Repeated reports and recommendations by the commander and the Military Council on the urgency of halting and fortifying our lines were rejected. Stalin demanded that we attack. "If you don't achieve results today," he said, "you will tomorrow. If you attack, you may at least tie down the enemy, and the results will be felt on other parts of the front."

In a directive dated March 20, the Chief again demanded a more energetic pursuit of our objectives.

In late March and early April, the Western fronts attempted to implement the directive which called for defeat of the enemy's Rzhev-Vyazma grouping, but our efforts failed. Supreme Headquarters was finally obliged to accept our recommendation that the Soviet forces take up defensive positions along a line running through Velikiye Luki, Velizh, Demidov, Bely, Dukhovshchina, Nelidovo, Rzhev, Pogoreloye Gorodishche, Gzhatsk, Ugra River, Spas-Demensk, Kirov, Lyudinovo, Kholmishchi and the Oka River. Troops of the Western Front had thus advanced forty-five to sixty-five miles during the winter offensive and had somewhat improved the operational strategic situation in the west.

At the same time the operations of the Leningrad, Volkhov, Southern and Southwest fronts failed to achieve their objectives because the Soviet forces lacked superiority in manpower and arms and were met by fierce enemy resistance.

Events demonstrated the error of Stalin's decision calling for a general offensive in January. It would have been wiser to have concentrated more strength on the Western sector (Northwest, Kalinin, Western and Bryansk fronts) and to have struck a devastating blow at Army Group Center, forcing it back to a line running through Staraya Russa, Velikiye Luki, Vitebsk, Smolensk and Bryansk before we took up defensive positions to prepare for the summer campaign of 1942.

If the nine armies in the Supreme Headquarters reserve had not been scattered over the entire front but had been concentrated in the west, the enemy's central group would have been smashed and the entire course of the war might have been affected.

The final results of the great Battle of Moscow proved to be inspiring for the Soviet side and depressing for the enemy.

A German general, Westphal, in describing the battle, has acknowledged that the "German army, once considered invincible, was on the brink of destruction."[19] Similar acknowledgments have been made by other German generals, including Tippelskirch, Günther Blumentritt, Fritz Bayerlein and F. von Manteuffel. You can't argue against facts. The Germans lost a total of more than half a million soldiers, 1,300 tanks, 2,500 guns, 15,000 trucks and a great deal of other equipment. They were thrown back toward the west over a distance of one hundred to two hundred miles from Moscow.

The Soviet counteroffensive of the winter of 1941–42 was conducted under the difficult conditions of a snowy, cold winter and, what is most important, without numerical superiority over the enemy. Moreover, our mechanized and tank divisions were below strength, and we know from experience that under such conditions offensive operations cannot be carried out on a large scale. The enemy's maneuvers can be anticipated, his forces outflanked and his escape routes cut only with powerful mechanized and tank units.

[19] *The Fatal Decisions*, Seymour Freidin and William Richardson, eds., New York, 1956.   H.E.S.

For the first time in six months of war, in the Battle of Moscow the Red Army inflicted a major defeat on the main forces of the enemy. It was the first strategic victory over the Wehrmacht since the beginning of World War II. Even before the Battle of Moscow, the Soviet armed forces had conducted a number of important operations that slowed the advance of the Wehrmacht in the three principal sectors of the Soviet front. But none of those operations was equal in scale or results to the great battle before the walls of the Soviet capital. The skilled conduct of defensive operations, the successful launching of counterattacks and the swift transition to a counteroffensive greatly enriched Soviet military art and demonstrated the growing strategic and operational-tactical maturity of Soviet military commanders and the improved military mastery of Soviet soldiers in all services.

The defeat of the Germans at Moscow was also of great international significance. The people in all the countries of the anti-Nazi coalition received the news of the outstanding victory of Soviet arms with great enthusiasm. All progressive mankind linked that victory to its hopes for an approaching liberation from Fascist slavery.

The failures of German forces at Leningrad, at Rostov, near Tikhvin and in the Battle of Moscow had a sobering effect on the reactionary circles of Japan and Turkey and forced them to assume a more cautious policy toward the Soviet Union.

After the defeat of the Germans before Moscow, the strategic initiative on all sectors of the Soviet-German front passed to the Soviet command. In an effort to restore the fighting capacity of its forces, the Nazi military-political leadership had to undertake a number of far-reaching measures and move large numbers of troops out of France and other occupied countries to the Soviet-German front. The Nazis had to bring pressure on the governments of their satellites to induce them to send additional forces and supplies to the Soviet front, thus aggravating the domestic political situations in those countries.

After the defeat of the Nazis at Moscow, not only ordinary Germans but many German officers and generals were convinced of the might of the Soviet state and recognized that the Soviet armed forces represented an insurmountable obstacle to the achievement of Hitler's objectives.

Despite their careful preparations, the Germans encountered a number of important and unforeseen circumstances in the war against the Soviet Union. They never expected, for example, that they would have to fight on two fronts: against the Red Army and against powerful guerrilla forces, who waged active operations under the guidance of underground Party organizations. Nor did the Nazis expect their forces to be worn down without having achieved a single strategic objective in 1941 so that they had to take up defensive positions along the entire Soviet-German front, thus losing their strategic initiative.

The strategic defeat of German forces at Moscow made it plain to the whole world that Hitler's plans for a blitzkrieg against the Soviet Union had collapsed, that the defeat of the German Fascist forces had begun and that the Soviet state was invincible.

All Soviet military units fought with extraordinary courage and valor in the fierce Battle for Moscow. Everyone, from private to general, displayed great heroism in fulfilling his sacred duty to the homeland, sparing neither his strength nor his very life in the defense of the city.

In voicing my profound gratitude to all survivors of the battle, I bow my head before the serene memory of those who stood unto death but did not let the enemy penetrate to the heart of our homeland, our capital, the hero city of Moscow.

I am often asked the question: "Where was Stalin at the time of the Moscow battle?"

Stalin was in Moscow, organizing the forces and means for the defeat of the enemy. He must be given his due. As head of the

State Defense Committee, and with the members of Supreme Headquarters and the leaders of the People's Commissariats, he carried on major work in the organizing of strategic reserves and the material-technical means essential for the military struggle. With his harsh demands, he achieved, one might say, almost the impossible. In the period of the Battle for Moscow he was very attentive to advice but, regrettably, sometimes took decisions not in accordance with the situation. So it was with the transfer of the First Shock Army to the reserves and with the scattered offensives on all fronts.

When I am asked what I remember most of all of the past war, I always answer: the Battle for Moscow. A quarter of a century has passed, but these historic events and battles still remain in memory. Under hectic, almost catastrophically complicated and difficult conditions our troops were tempered, matured, accumulated experience and, once the absolutely essential minimum of arms were in their hands, moved from retreat and defensive maneuver to a powerful offensive. Our grateful descendants will never forget the difficult and heroic sacrifices of the Soviet people and the military achievements of the Soviet armed forces during that period. The Battle for Moscow laid the firm foundations for the ensuing defeat of Nazi Germany.

The Battle of

STALINGRAD

AUGUST, 1942–FEBRUARY, 1943

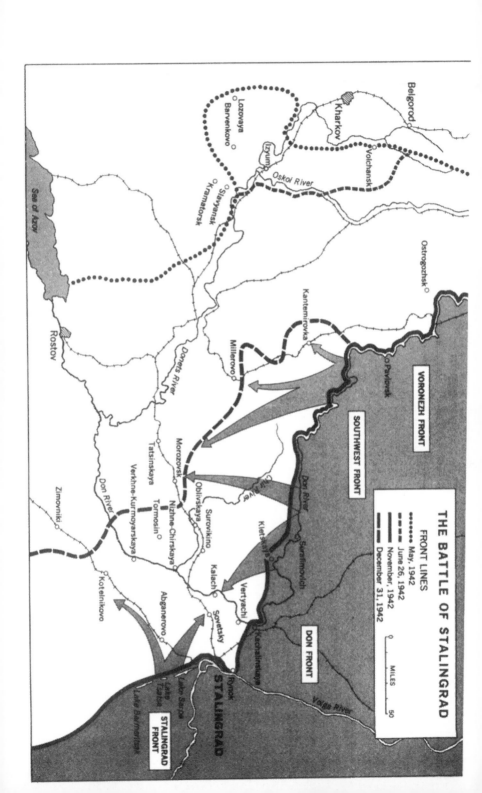

THE BATTLE OF STALINGRAD

FRONT LINES

• • • • • May, 1942
▬ ▬ ▬ June 26, 1942
━━━━━ November, 1942
▬▬▬▬ December 31, 1942

MILES
0   50

VORONEZH FRONT

SOUTHWEST FRONT

DON FRONT

STALINGRAD FRONT

STALINGRAD

Belgorod

Kharkov

Lozovaya
Barvenkovo

Izyum

Oskol River

Volchansk

Ostrogozhsk

Kantemirovka

Pavlovsk

Slavyansk

Kramatorsk

Sea of Azov

Rostov

Millerovo

Donets River

Morozovsk

Tatsinskaya

Verkhne-Kurmoyarskaya

Tormosin

Nizhne-Chirskaya

Oblivskaya

Surovikino

Zimovniki

Don River

Koteinikovo

Abganerovo

Kalach

Sovetsky

Vertyachi

Kletskaya

Serafimovich

Don River

Chir River

Kremenskaya

Don River

Rynok

Lake Sarpa

Lake Tsatsa

Lake Barmantsak

Volga River

Editor's Note

Disaster once again overtook Russian arms with the end of the winter of 1941-42 and the coming of spring. Stalin had overestimated the ability of his armies to carry the war to the Germans during the winter months. His enforced offensives left the Soviet troops tired, dispirited and short of arms, supplies and transport. Several major forces were encircled or virtually so (Vlasov's Second Shock Army near Chudovo, south of Leningrad; and two forces subordinate to Zhukov —Belov's cavalry group and General Yefremov's Thirty-third Army, both trapped near Vyazma).

Soviet troops in the south found themselves in equally difficult situations. The Germans were bringing new pressures to bear on the isolated Soviet units in the Crimea, and a disaster at Kerch, the eastern strait separating the Crimea from the Caucasus, was in the making. Stalin's grandiose plans for a victory in the Crimea were collapsing, at least partly because of the ineptitude and stupidity of two of his police generals, Kulik and Mekhlis.

In fact, it was hard to find any sector where the situation was genuinely favorable to the Russians. They had been unable in a winter's desperate fighting to lift the siege of Leningrad. A dangerous salient around Rzhev and Vyazma still threatened Moscow. At this moment Stalin launched one of his most disastrous offensives—an effort to retake Kharkov.

Zhukov was still in command of the Western Front, worrying about his encircled units near Vyazma and trying to persuade Stalin and Marshal Shaposhnikov, Chief of Staff, not to carry out the Kharkov attack but, instead, to let him strike at the dangerous Nazi spearheads on his front.

Stalin brushed aside Zhukov's representations. He ordered the

Kharkov operation carried out. The attack, led by Marshal Timoshenko with Nikita S. Khrushchev as his Military Council member, got under way May 12. Utter disaster followed. The Germans had also been preparing an attack. A powerful German group under Field Marshal von Kleist struck Timoshenko's forces almost as soon as they began to move. Within ten days three Soviet armies, the Sixth, Fifty-seventh and part of the Ninth, as well as General L. V. Bobkin's operations group, were surrounded. Thousands of Soviet troops were captured, killed or wounded. The Germans claimed 239,000 prisoners were taken. Command losses were great. The killed included Generals F. Ya. Kostenko, deputy commander of the Southwest Front, K. P. Podlas of the Fifty-seventh Army, A. M. Gorodnyansky of the Sixth Army and L. V. Bobkin of the operations group.

Typically, Stalin sought to shift the blame. Lieutenant General F. M. Kharitonov of the Ninth Army was removed from his command and ordered to summary court-martial. He was saved from the firing squad by the personal intervention of General A. M. Vasilevsky.[1] Major General I. Kh. Bagramyan, one of the most brilliant of Russia's World War II commanders, was relieved as Chief of Staff of the Southwest Front and severely censured, and soon Timoshenko also was removed from his post.

Controversy over the catastrophe was still lively more than twenty-five years after the event. Khrushchev, in his famous "secret speech" of February, 1956, sought to absolve himself of blame. He contended that he tried to persuade Stalin to call off the offensive because the Soviet forces were threatened with encirclement by the sudden blow of von Kleist's group. According to Khrushchev, he presented his argument first to the Acting Chief of Staff, General Vasilevsky, who unsuccessfully argued the case with Stalin. When Vasilevsky reported failure, Khrushchev described how he telephoned Stalin directly. But Stalin refused to speak to him. Malenkov took the telephone. Khrushchev

[1] A. M. Vasilevsky, *Voyenno-Istoricheskii Zhurnal*, January, 1966, p. 18.

had to put his case to Malenkov, who, in turn, passed on the arguments to Stalin. Stalin again declined to call off the attack, saying, "Let everything remain as it is." The result, said Khrushchev, was that hundreds of thousands of Soviet troops were lost. Histories written in the Khrushchev era put blame for these losses on Stalin. Zhukov, who loses no opportunity to indict Khrushchev, blames him and Timoshenko, the Southwest commander. Other Soviet authorities believe Rodion Ya. Malinovsky, commander of the Southern Front, shared culpability.

The disaster set the stage for much worse to follow. Stalin remained convinced that the greatest danger lay in a new Nazi thrust toward Moscow. He concentrated large numbers of reserves to meet a Nazi thrust toward the city from the Bryansk area.

"Actually," observes Marshal Vasilevsky in his memoirs, "the chief blow of the Germans was mistakenly expected not in the South but on the Central Front. Supreme Headquarters weakened the South in order to strengthen the Center, especially along the flanks."

This put the Russians completely off balance. The Germans struck hard across south Russia and soon had the Red Army reeling. The Nazis liquidated the Soviet bridgehead at Kerch. They smashed the Soviet siege lines and captured the naval base of Sevastopol on the tip of the Crimea, completing their conquest of that peninsula and freeing a whole army for use elsewhere. They launched a major offensive in the Kursk-Voronezh sector, south of Moscow, and almost broke through once again to the near approaches of the Soviet capital.

Most importantly, they began to drive with rapidly increasing momentum toward the Don River bend and Stalingrad.

The unfolding of the summer warfare was taking a far more dangerous shape than that envisaged by Stalin, who had looked to fresh attacks by almost all his front commanders to start the Germans back toward their homeland. Instead, there was every sign that a new and critical battle would be fought in which the stakes were no less than the cutting of Russia in two, the severing of north-south communications, especially along the Volga, the pinching off of the Caucasus and the Maikop and Baku oil fields, and the breach of the new Anglo-American supply line across Iran which was just beginning to deliver materials in quantity. There was even the direct possibility that the Germans would break through the Near East land bridge and threaten India.

During the curtain-raising of the Stalingrad crisis Zhukov remained commander of the Western Front, where little was happening. He was not always to be found at Western Front headquarters, however, since, as his account makes clear, he was often at Supreme Headquarters in Moscow, advising Stalin or arguing with him about the major decisions of the war.

As the tension over the south and over Stalingrad rose, Stalin began to reorganize his forces. He created new commands at the front and he began to send in his most battle-tested commanders. First, General Vasilevsky was sent to the scene. Then major political associates were directed there—Georgi M. Malenkov, Nikita S. Khrushchev and Vyacheslav Malyshev, the commissar of the armament industry.

But none of these moves halted the Nazis in their pell-mell rush for the Volga and Stalin's name city. Finally, on August 27, 1942, Zhukov was summoned from the Western Front and named Deputy Supreme Commander in Chief. Stalin was Supreme Commander in Chief. There never before had been a deputy supreme commander, and after Zhukov there would never be one again.

Once again, in an hour of deadly danger Stalin turned to Zhukov. Stalingrad hung in the balance. Its fate and quite probably the fate of Russia were placed in Zhukov's hands.

The Battle of Moscow had made Zhukov a national hero. Stalingrad demonstrated his towering domination of the Soviet military apparatus. Every Russian commander of consequence participated in some way in the Stalingrad fighting. Men like General Chuikov made their reputation in the titanic struggle that raged in the ruins of the Stalingrad tractor factory and the building-by-building and room-by-room defense of the city on the Volga. But it was Zhukov who bore responsibility for all the armies, all the generals, for the defense of the city and, most important of all, for the concept, organization and carrying out of the grandiose counteroffensive which finally shattered the myth of Nazi military invincibility beyond repair. Many men, naturally, worked together in this endeavor. Zhukov's closest and most important collaborator was his brilliant General Staff colleague, General Vasilevsky.

After Stalingrad no one really challenged Zhukov's primacy. His fellow marshals still competed with him for top honors. But he was No. 1.

And after Stalingrad no one really doubted that Russia with Zhukov at the head of her armies would finally defeat Germany.

H.E.S

5

The Dangerous Spring

The international and domestic situation of the Soviet Union improved somewhat toward the end of the spring of 1942. The anti-Fascist front continued to expand and to strengthen. In January twenty-six nations signed a declaration in which they agreed to use all the means at their disposal in the fight against the aggressors and not to conclude a separate cease-fire or a separate peace. The Soviet Union reached complete agreement with the United States and Britain that a second front would be opened in Europe in 1942. All these and other factors, especially the defeat of German forces before Moscow and the disruption of German plans for a blitzkrieg, greatly invigorated anti-Fascist forces in all countries.

A quiet period had set in on the Soviet-German front. Both sides had taken up defensive positions. Troops dug trenches, built dugouts, mined the approaches to forward positions, placed barbed-wire entanglements and carried out other defensive chores. Commanders and headquarters staffs worked out firing systems, coordination between the various services and other problems.

Both Supreme Headquarters and individual military units summed up the first phase of the war, reviewed and discussed both successful and unsuccessful operations, and devoted more time to the study of tactics and the operational and strategic skill of the enemy, its strong and its weak aspects.

The Soviet people, inspired by the Red Army's great victory around Moscow, which laid the basis for a fundamental turning point in the war, completed the wartime reorientation of the Soviet economy. Increasing numbers of new tanks, planes, artillery pieces, rockets and munitions began to reach the armed forces.

New strategic reserves of all services were being formed in the interior of the country. The increasing production capacity of the Soviet tank and artillery industries enabled the Supreme Command to start the formation of separate tank corps and tank armies supplied with the most modern equipment of the period.

The armed services began to be provided with modernized 45-mm antitank guns and new 76-mm guns. New antitank brigades and divisions intended for combat against large enemy tank units were formed.

Steps were taken to improve the air defenses of the armed services and of the country as a whole. The Soviet armed forces began to form separate air armies. By June the country had eight such armies. The long-range bomber force and the air reserve of the Supreme Command began to receive reinforcements. The total strength of the Soviet forces rose to 5,534,500 men, 4,959 tanks, 40,798 guns and mortars and 2,480 planes. The armed services expanded military training and mastered both the latest war experience and the new weapons.

The Party's Central Committee, after a review of political agitation work in the armed services, took a number of steps to improve the structure of the Party apparatus and of propaganda in the armed forces. L. Z. Mekhlis was replaced by A. S.

Shcherbakov, a national Party secretary and Moscow Party chief, as the head of the Main Political Administration of the armed services. The Central Committee asked the military councils of individual fronts and armies to improve their political work among soldiers and officers so as to tighten discipline and strengthen the staying power and fighting capacity of the troops.

The German command was also getting ready for the summer campaign, still viewing the Soviet front as its main theater of operations. The Nazi leadership continued to send satellite forces to the Eastern Front. Along the entire front from the Barents Sea to the Black Sea, Nazi Germany and its allies had arrayed 217 divisions and 20 brigades, of which 178 divisions, 8 brigades and 4 air fleets were German. Because of the absence of a second front, Germany was able to keep as little as 20 percent of its armed forces on other fronts and in occupied countries.

By May, 1942, the enemy's strength on the Soviet-German front included an army of 6,198,000 men (including 810,000 allied troops), 3,230 tanks and self-propelled guns, 56,940 guns and mortars and 3,395 planes. The Germans continued to be superior in manpower, artillery and mortars. We had a slight numerical superiority in tanks, but in quality most of ours lagged behind the Germans'.

In its general outlines, Hitler's political and military strategy for 1942 called for the defeat of Soviet forces in the south, the conquest of the Caucasus, an advance to the Volga River and the seizure of Stalingrad and Astrakhan, thus setting the stage for the destruction of the U.S.S.R. as a state.

Although the German command still retained superiority over the Soviet armed forces in manpower and matériel, its plans for the 1942 offensive had to take account of the fact that it was no longer capable of launching offensives simultaneously on all strategic sectors as it had done in 1941 in Operation Barbarossa.

The spreading of the German forces from the Barents Sea to the Black Sea resulted in a corresponding decline in operational density along the front.

By means of a series of "total" measures, the German command was able to reconstitute Army Group South, concentrating in it forces far superior to Soviet strength in the southwest sector of the front.

Hitler's Directive No. 41, dated April 5, 1942, called on the German armed forces to gain control of the Soviet Union's richest industrial and agricultural regions, thus obtaining additional economic resources (especially the oil of the Caucasus) and winning a dominant strategic position for the achievement of his military and political goals.

Hitler and his associates hoped that as soon as the German forces had gained victory in the south of the Soviet Union they would be able to again attack Leningrad and Moscow.

In planning their push into the Caucasus and toward the Volga, the Germans also sought to deprive the Soviet Union of its communications with its allies through the Caucasus.

I spent a great deal of time at Supreme Headquarters in the spring of 1942, and I knew how Stalin assessed the situation and the prospects for 1942.

It was quite obvious that he did not believe assurances by Churchill and Roosevelt that a second front would be opened in Europe, but he had not lost hope that they would somehow try to open a second front elsewhere. Stalin trusted Roosevelt more than Churchill, whom he considered insincere and anti-Soviet to the core.

Stalin assumed that the Germans would be capable of waging major offensives in two strategic sectors in the summer of 1942, most likely in the Moscow sector and in the south. As for the north and northwest, there Stalin expected no significant German activity. At most he thought that in those areas the enemy would seek to straighten the front and improve the disposition of his forces.

Of the two sectors in which Stalin expected major enemy offensives, he was most concerned about the Moscow sector, where the Germans had massed seventy divisions.

As for our own plans for the spring and summer of 1942, he believed that we had neither the manpower nor the matériel for major offensive operations. He thought that for the immediate future the Soviet armed forces should restrict themselves to an active strategic defense in addition to some limited offensives in the Crimea, around Kharkov and in the Lgov-Kursk and Smolensk sectors as well as around Leningrad and Demyansk.

I knew that Marshal Shaposhnikov, the Chief of General Staff, generally agreed with Stalin except that he felt the Soviet operations plan should provide for an active strategic defense to wear the enemy down at the beginning of the summer and then, as soon as reserves became available, undertake broad counteroffensive operations. I supported Shaposhnikov with one qualification. I considered it essential that we take steps at the beginning of summer to eliminate the enemy's Rzhev-Vyazma grouping, where the Germans held a large salient with strong forces. Supreme Headquarters and the General Staff were more concerned with the Orel-Tula and Kursk-Voronezh sectors in view of a possible enemy strike by-passing Moscow from the southwest. Accordingly, a decision was taken to concentrate a large part of the Supreme Command reserves on the Bryansk Front by the end of spring. By the middle of May the Bryansk Front received 4 tank corps, 7 rifle divisions, 11 independent rifle brigades, 4 independent tank brigades and a large quantity of artillery. In addition, the Fifth Tank Army of the Supreme Headquarters reserve took up positions behind the Bryansk Front for a strong counterstrike in case the enemy attacked the Bryansk Front.

I was basically in agreement with Stalin's operational and strategic predictions, but I could not agree with him on the number of proposed separate offensive operations on the grounds that they would absorb our reserves and make it more difficult to prepare for a general offensive.

I proposed, instead, that we launch a strong offensive against the enemy's Rzhev-Vyazma salient with troops of the Western and Kalinin fronts, air support from units of the Supreme Command and the Moscow air defense forces, and with some of the troops of the Northwest Front.

In my view, such a thrust against the Germans west of Moscow would greatly weaken the enemy and force him to abandon major offensive operations, at least in the immediate future. By hindsight, this may seem open to dispute, but at the time, in the absence of complete information about enemy intentions, I was convinced that I was right.

Because of the complexity of the problem, Stalin called a conference to discuss the general situation and the various alternatives for the summer campaign. The conference, held in the State Defense Committee at the end of March, was attended by Voroshilov, Timoshenko, Shaposhnikov, Vasilevsky, Bagramyan and myself.

Shaposhnikov gave a detailed report that generally reflected Stalin's own forecasts. But in view of the enemy's numerical superiority and the absence of a second front in Europe, Shaposhnikov proposed that we restrict ourselves to active defense for the immediate future. He favored concentrating the main strategic reserves in the central section of the front, including the Voronezh area, where the General Staff expected the major action to unfold in the summer of 1942.

Shaposhnikov was discussing some organizational problems in a plan for an offensive drafted by Timoshenko's Southwest command (involving forces of the Bryansk, Southwest and Southern fronts), when Stalin interrupted him: "We cannot remain on the defensive and sit on our hands until the Germans strike first! We must launch preventive strikes on a broad front and probe enemy intentions."

Then he added, "Zhukov proposes that we launch an offensive in the western sectors and remain on the defensive elsewhere. I think that is a half-measure."

Timoshenko spoke next. He said that troops of the Southwest command were ready and should launch a preventive strike against the Germans to disrupt their offensive plans against the Southern and Southwest fronts. Otherwise the enemy would repeat what he had achieved at the beginning of the war. As for an offensive in the western sectors, he said, he supported me in my view that this would tie down the forces of the enemy.

I spoke up once again in opposition to the plan for several offensives. Although Shaposhnikov, as far as I know, also opposed a large number of separate operations, he remained silent on that occasion. The conference ended with an order by Stalin that offensive operations be launched in the near future in the Crimea, at Kharkov and elsewhere. We all returned to our regular posts.

The events of May and June bore out the miscalculations of Supreme Headquarters. Our armed forces were once again put to a severe test in the south. The offensive launched at the end of April in the Crimea failed. Troops of the Crimean Front, headed by Lieutenant General D. T. Kozlov, did not gain their objectives and suffered heavy losses. Supreme Headquarters ordered the front command to take up firm defensive positions.

But on May 8 the enemy, having massed his shock forces and extensive air support against the Crimean Front, broke through the defenses. Our troops found themselves in a serious situation and were forced to abandon Kerch.

That defeat greatly complicated the situation at Sevastopol, which had resisted stubbornly since October. Having seized Kerch, the German command was now able to concentrate its forces against Sevastopol.

On July 4, after a nine-month siege and fierce fighting in which Soviet sailors and soldiers gained immortal glory, Sevastopol was abandoned by our forces. This meant the complete loss of the Crimea, greatly complicating the over-all picture and naturally improving the position of the enemy, who now had an additional army available for reinforcement.

On May 3 the Northwest Front began an offensive against the Sixteenth German Army at Demyansk. The battle, which lasted an entire month, did not bring success even though heavy losses were inflicted on the enemy.

At about that time, I spoke to Stalin by telephone about the Crimean Front and the situation in the Southwestern command.

He said, "Now you see where defense is getting us." And he added, "We should severely punish Kozlov, Mekhlis and Kulik for their carelessness so that others will stop dillydallying. Timoshenko will start his offensive soon. What about you? You still haven't changed your mind about our tactics in the south?"

I said, no, I still felt that we should harass the enemy in the south with air strikes and artillery fire, wear him down with defensive actions and only then go over to the offensive.

However, troops of the Southwest command began an offensive on May 12 in the direction of Kharkov by making two thrusts, one out of the Volchansk area and the other from the Barvenkovo salient. The Southern Front was charged with the operation in the Barvenkovo salient. However, the Southwestern command had neglected to consider the threat posed by a large concentration of German forces in the area of Kramatorsk at the base of the salient.

After launching their offensive from the Barvenkovo salient, troops of the Southwest command broke through enemy defenses and advanced fifteen to thirty miles in three days. But that was as far as the operation got.

In the morning of May 17 eleven divisions of German Army Group Kleist went over to the offensive in the Slavyansk-Kramatorsk sector, at the base of the Barvenkovo salient, against the

Ninth and Fifty-seventh armies of our Southern Front. The enemy broke through the Soviet defenses, advanced thirty miles in two days and drove a wedge into the flank of the left wing of the Southwest Front at Petrovskoye.

I was present during a conversation between Stalin and Timoshenko in mid-May and clearly remember that Stalin expressed serious concern about the threat posed by the enemy's Kramatorsk grouping.

Timoshenko reported that his Military Council felt the threat had been exaggerated and that it was not sufficient ground for halting the Kharkov operation. That same evening Stalin discussed the matter with N. S. Khrushchev, a member of the Military Council of the Southwestern command, who expressed the same views as Timoshenko. The Southwestern command maintained these views until May 18. On the evening of that day the deteriorating situation began to give serious concern to General Vasilevsky, the Acting Chief of General Staff, who urged Stalin to halt the Kharkov operation and to use our forces in the Barvenkovo salient to parry the attack by the enemy's Kramatorsk grouping.

But Stalin rebuffed Vasilevsky by citing the recommendations of the Southwestern command. The existing version [Khrushchev's] that the Military Council of the Southwestern command warned Stalin against continuing the Kharkov operation does not correspond to the facts. I can make this statement because I was present during Stalin's conversations.[2]

On May 19 the Military Council of the Southwestern command finally understood the situation and began to take steps to rebuff the German attack, but it was too late. By May 22 the Sixth and Fifty-seventh armies, parts of the Ninth Army and General L. V. Bobkin's operations group were completely encircled. Many units succeeded in breaking out, but others could

[2] This constitutes a direct denial by Zhukov of Khrushchev's version, which sought to put the blame on Stalin.   H.E.S.

not, and fought till the end rather than surrender.

Among those who lost their lives in this battle was General F. Ya. Kostenko, deputy commander of the Southwest Front, a Civil War hero and former commander of the 19th Manych Regiment of the 4th Cavalry Division, which I commanded from 1932 to 1936. Others who died were General K. P. Podlas, Fifty-seventh Army commander; General A. M. Gorodnyansky, Sixth Army commander, and General Bobkin. The latter had been a classmate of mine in refresher courses for senior commanders. All of them were remarkable men, excellent commanders and loyal sons of our Party and our country.

When we analyze the failure of the Kharkov operation, it is easy to see that the basic reason for it was an underestimation of the serious threat posed to the Southwest command and our failure to position Supreme Headquarters reserves in the area. If several reserve armies had been available in the rear of the front, we could have avoided the catastrophe of the Kharkov operation in the summer of 1942.

Heavy fighting continued in June along the entire Southwestern sector. Under heavy enemy pressure our forces pulled back with great losses to the Oskol River, where they attempted to set up defense lines.

On June 28 the enemy opened a broader offensive, striking out of the Kursk area in the direction of Voronezh against the Thirteenth and Fortieth armies of the Bryansk Front. On June 30 the German Sixth Army in the Volchansk sector went on the offensive in the direction of Ostrogozhsk, breaking through the defenses of the Twenty-first and Twenty-eighth armies. The situation of our forces in the Voronezh area steadily deteriorated, with some of them caught in a trap.

Here is how Marshal Vasilevsky assessed the situation in his memoirs:

The situation in the Voronezh area greatly deteriorated by the end of July 2. The enemy had broken through our defenses at the junction of the Bryansk and Southwest fronts to a depth of fifty miles. The front reserves available in this sector were thrown into battle. There was evident danger that the enemy's strike forces would break through to the Don River and seize Voronezh. To prevent the enemy from forcing the Don River and to stem his advance, Supreme Headquarters assigned two of its reserve field armies [the Sixth and the Sixtieth—G. Zh.] to the Bryansk Front command and ordered them stationed along the right bank of the Don River between Zadonsk and Pavlovsk. At the same time the Fifth Tank Army was transferred to the Bryansk Front with the objective of joining the front's own tank units in counterattacks against the flank and the rear of the German forces driving toward Voronezh. . . . Prompt decisive action by the Fifth Tank Army could have changed the situation in our favor. . . . However, the tank army received no instructions from the front command on July 3. Having first instructed the commanders of the army and of the Bryansk Front to prepare promptly for a counterattack, I myself went to Yelets on orders from Supreme Headquarters, to speed the movement of the Fifth Tank Army. Despite the assistance provided by Supreme Headquarters and the General Staff, the situation on the Bryansk Front continued to deteriorate, largely because of command failures at the front and army levels. Supreme Headquarters therefore ordered the Bryansk Front broken up into two fronts, with a new Voronezh Front under N. F. Vatutin, and K. K. Rokossovsky replacing F. I. Golikov in command of the Bryansk Front.[3]

The participation of the Sixth and Sixtieth field armies and the Fifth Tank Army somewhat strengthened our defenses in the Voronezh area, but did not entirely eliminate the danger of an enemy breakthrough across the Don and a thrust along the Don toward Stalingrad.

As a result of our loss of the Crimea and the defeat of the Soviet forces in the Barvenkovo salient, in the Donets Basin and near Voronezh, the enemy had once again seized the strategic initiative and, with the help of fresh reserves, began

[3] *Voyenno-Istoricheskii Zhurnal,* August, 1965, pp. 7–8.

his rapid advance toward the Volga River and into the Caucasus. By the middle of July the Germans had thrown our troops back to the Don River from Voronezh to Kletskaya and from Surovikino to Rostov and had launched a battle in the bend of the Don River in an effort to break through to Stalingrad.

6

The Stalingrad Crisis

Due to our forced retreat, the enemy gained control of the rich regions of the Don and the Donets Basin. We were faced with the direct threat of an enemy breakthrough to the Volga and into the Northern Caucasus, and the loss of the Kuban Plain and of all communications with the Caucasus, a key economic region that was supplying oil to both the army and industry. At that point the Supreme Commander in Chief issued his Order No. 227, which set in motion severe measures to combat panicmongers and violators of discipline and condemned "defeatist" tendencies. Order No. 227 was backed up by intensive political agitation and other measures on the part of the Party's Central Committee.

Troops of the Southwest Front suffered heavy losses in their retreat from the Kharkov area and were unable to halt the enemy's advance. The Southern Front, which was also suffering substantial losses, was unable to stem the Germans' advance into the Caucasus.

In an effort to prevent the Germans from reaching the Volga River, Supreme Headquarters set up a new Stalingrad Front on July 12, including in it: the Sixty-second Army under Major General V. Ya. Kolpakchi, the Sixty-third Army of Lieutenant General V. I. Kuznetsov, the Sixty-fourth Army and the Twenty-first Army of the abolished Southwest Front. The over-all Southwestern command, which had lost its purpose, had been liquidated on June 23.

The entire Military Council of the former Southwest Front went over to the new Stalingrad Front, which was further reinforced with the First and Fourth tank armies, in process of formation, and remaining elements of the Twenty-eighth, Thirty-eighth and Fifty-seventh armies. The Volga Flotilla was also placed under the front command.[4]

The construction of defense lines and fortifications got under way on the approaches to Stalingrad. As in the defense of Moscow, thousands of citizens took part in this effort and selflessly prepared the city for defense.

Both the regional and city Party committees of Stalingrad organized the formation and training of people's militia and worker defense detachments, reorganized production for the needs of the front, and evacuated children, old people and valuables from the city.

On July 17 the Stalingrad Front held a defense line running from Pavlovsk along the left bank of the Don River to Serafimovich and Kletskaya, then south to Surovikino and Verkhne-Kurmoyarskaya.

Meanwhile the Southern Front had suffered irreplaceable losses in its retreat. Its four armies numbered little more than 100,000 men. In an effort to strengthen the command of forces in the Northern Caucasus, Supreme Headquarters abolished the Southern Front and transferred all its remaining troops to the North Caucasus Front under Marshal S. M. Budenny.

[4] This means that Timoshenko was placed in charge of the Stalingrad Front, with Khrushchev as his deputy. Zhukov rarely mentions either by name. H.E.S.

The Thirty-seventh and Twelfth armies of the North Caucasus Front were given the assignment of covering the Stavropol sector, and the Eighteenth, Fifty-sixth and Forty-seventh armies the Krasnodar sector.

By the end of July the Stalingrad Front was made up of 38 divisions, of which half had 6,000 to 8,000 men, and the others from 1,000 to 3,000 men, or a total of 16 divisions of normal strength. These small forces had to cover a front 330 miles in length. The total strength of the front during that period included 187,000 men, 360 tanks, 337 planes and 7,900 guns and mortars.

Against this front the enemy had massed 250,000 men, 740 tanks, 1,200 planes and 7,500 guns and mortars, which meant a ratio of 1.3:1 in manpower, 1:1 in guns and mortars, 2:1 in tanks and 3.6:1 in planes. Because of the Soviet resistance on the approaches to Stalingrad, the enemy later shifted the Fourth Tank Army from the Caucasus for a thrust from Kotelnikovo and threw additional satellite troops into the battle.

Directive No. 45 of the German High Command, dated July 23, ordered Army Group B to cover its northern flank along the middle course of the Don River (where Hungarian, Italian and Rumanian forces took up positions), to seize Stalingrad and Astrakhan and gain a stronghold on the Volga River, thus cutting off the Caucasus from the rest of the Soviet Union. To achieve this objective, the army group had the support of the Fourth Air Fleet, with 1,200 planes.

On July 26 German armored and mechanized forces broke through the defenses of the Sixty-second Army in the Don River bend and reached the Don in the area of Kamensky, north of Kalach. Supreme Headquarters ordered the front reinforced with the First and Fourth tank armies, which were still in process of formation and had a total of only 240 tanks, and with two rifle divisions. These additional forces were unable to stop the enemy's advance but helped to slow it to some extent.

It is, of course, not desirable to resort to units that are still in the process of being formed, but the road to Stalingrad was greatly undermanned and Supreme Headquarters had no other choice. Heavy fighting also broke out in the Sixty-fourth Army sector, south of Kalach, but there, too, the enemy was prevented from driving straight through to Stalingrad.

With the troops of the Stalingrad Front now stretched over a front of more than four hundred miles, Supreme Headquarters decided on August 5 to break the front into two: a Stalingrad Front and a Southeast Front.

Lieutenant General V. N. Gordov, who had succeeded Marshal Timoshenko July 23, remained in command of the Stalingrad Front, with Major General D. N. Nikishev as Chief of Staff. The front included the Sixty-third, Twenty-first, Sixty-second field armies, the Fourth Tank Army, and the Sixteenth Air Army, which was in process of being formed under Major General S. I. Rudenko.

The Southeast Front included the Fifty-seventh, Fifty-first and Sixty-fourth armies, the First Guards Army and the Eighth Air Army. The front was under the command of Colonel General A. I. Yeremenko, with Major General G. F. Zakharov as Chief of Staff.[5]

Colonel General A. M. Vasilevsky, now Chief of General Staff, was assigned by the State Defense Committee on August 12 to coordinate operations at Stalingrad. Operationally the Stalingrad Front was placed under the jurisdiction of the commander of the Southeast Front.

After fierce fighting the enemy's 14th Tank Corps broke through Soviet Don River defenses at Vertyachi on August 23

---

[5] Khrushchev continued as Military Council member of both the Stalingrad and Southeast fronts, but Zhukov, as usual, omits Khrushchev's name. The two fronts were put under the united command of General Yeremenko after a very short interval. General Vasilevsky called the splitting of the front a major error and noted that it was quickly corrected.   H.E.S.

and, cutting the Stalingrad sector into two, reached the Volga River in the area of Latoshinka and Rynok, just north of Stalingrad. The Sixty-second Army was thus cut off from the rest of the Stalingrad Front, and was therefore transferred to the jurisdiction of the Southeast Front.

German bombers carried out barbarous air strikes against the city, turning it into a pile of rubble. Peaceful residents were killed and industrial enterprises and cultural institutions were destroyed.

On the morning of August 24, elements of the enemy's 14th Tank Corps opened an attack against the Stalingrad tractor plant, in the northern part of the city, but without success. Armed workers of Stalingrad factories joined the battle.

At the same time, troops of the Stalingrad Front who had pulled back toward the northeast attacked the enemy's Volga River wedge from the north, forcing him to divert substantial troops intended for the seizure of Stalingrad. This Soviet maneuver greatly weakened the enemy's strike against the city, and his 14th Tank Corps was, in fact, cut off from its support units for a few days and had to be supplied by air.

But after crossing the Don River with his main forces, the enemy developed a more energetic offensive against the city with the support of powerful air strikes.

By August 30 the troops of the Southeast Front, under enemy pressure, had been forced back first to the outer defense ring and then to the inner defense ring. The Sixty-second and Sixty-fourth armies were attempting to hold a line on the western outskirts of Stalingrad, running through Rynok, Orlovka, Gumrak, Peschanka and Ivanovka. The Sixty-second Army was then under the command of Lieutenant General A. I. Lopatin. He did all that was expected of him, and more, since it was perfectly clear that the enemy was operating with superior forces against his army. But Lopatin chose to preserve the Sixty-second Army for a stand within the city, where the enemy forces were ultimately to be depleted and destroyed.[6]

In those crucial days at Stalingrad, Supreme Headquarters ordered diversionary offensive operations west of Moscow in an effort to tie down enemy reserves and prevent them from being shifted to Stalingrad.

On the Western Front, where I was in command at the time, events unfolded as follows: On the left wing the Sixteenth and Sixty-first armies opened an attack on July 10 in the Kirov-Bolkhov sector in the direction of Bryansk. On the right wing, at Pogoreloye Gorodishche, the reinforced Twentieth Army, in coordination with the left wing of the Kalinin Front, made a successful offensive in August with the objective of defeating the enemy in the Sychevka-Rzhev area.

The offensive was halted after it had broken through the German defenses and reached the Rzhev-Vyazma railroad, but the town of Rzhev remained in enemy hands. The Germans suffered heavy losses in the fighting, and, in an effort to halt the advance of the troops of the Western Front, the German command was forced to make use of a substantial number of divisions that had been intended for the campaign at Stalingrad and in the Caucasus.

A German general, Kurt Tippelskirch, has the following to

---

[6] These seemingly innocent words of praise for General Lopatin are the iceberg tip of the raging feud between Marshal Zhukov and Marshal V. I. Chuikov, one of the great heroes of Stalingrad. Chuikov succeeded Lopatin as commander of the famous Sixty-second Army, the army which fought the Stalingrad battle from inside the city, building by building. Chuikov in his memoirs singled out Lopatin for savage criticism, calling him "plump and fair and outwardly very calm." He contended Lopatin lacked self-confidence, was unable to stand up to the harsh conditions of Stalingrad and, in Khrushchev's words, thought Stalingrad could not be held. (V. I. Chuikov, *V Nachale Puti*, Moscow, 1959, p. 57.) Zhukov is saying in effect that had it not been for Lopatin there would have been no Sixty-second Army for Chuikov to command. In his account of Stalingrad Zhukov manages to mention Chuikov only once by name.   H.E.S.

say in that connection: "A breakthrough was prevented when three tank divisions and several infantry divisions that were already getting ready to move to the Southern Front were held back and thrown into the battle first to localize the breakthrough and then to counterattack."[7]

If we had had one or two more armies at our disposal, we could have defeated the enemy, in conjunction with the Kalinin Front, not only in the Rzhev area but in the entire Rzhev-Vyazma salient, and could thus have improved our operational situation on the entire front west of Moscow, but our forces were extremely limited at the time.

On August 27, as I was conducting the offensive operation in the area of Pogoreloye Gorodishche, I had a call from A. N. Poskrebyshev.[8] He told me that in view of the situation in the south the State Defense Committee had decided the previous day, August 26, to appoint me Deputy Supreme Commander in Chief. Poskrebyshev told me to be at my command center at 2 P.M. and wait for a telephone call from Stalin. Poskrebyshev seemed very reluctant to talk and answered all my questions by saying, "I don't know. I assume he will tell you himself." I gathered, however, that the State Defense Committee was extremely concerned over developments around Stalingrad.[9]

Soon Stalin was on the high-security line. After asking about the situation at the Western Front, he said, "You better come to

---

[7] Kurt Tippelskirch, *History of the Second World War.*

[8] Chief of Stalin's secretariat and an incredibly sinister figure, associated with all the purges of the late Stalin years.   H.E.S.

[9] Actually, at this moment the Stalingrad Front was tottering. The Nazis had broken through to the Volga on August 23, which Vasilevsky called "an unforgettably tragic day." They had cut off the Sixty-second Army inside Stalingrad from the rest of the Soviet forces. Telephone communications had been severed and Vasilevsky had to communicate with Stalingrad by open radio. Whether the Russians could hold even the small remaining foothold inside Stalingrad on the west bank of the Volga was dubious.   H.E.S.

Supreme Headquarters as soon as you can. Put the Chief of Staff in charge." Then he added, "Give some thought to who should be appointed commander in your place."

That ended the conversation. Stalin said nothing about my having been appointed Deputy Supreme Commander. He was evidently saving that for our personal meeting. In general Stalin used to limit his telephone conversations to whatever was absolutely essential at the moment. He also expected us to be extremely careful in the use of the telephone, especially in zones of operations, where we had no scrambling devices.

I left for Moscow without returning to front headquarters. I arrived at the Kremlin late that evening. Stalin was at work in his office. Several members of the State Defense Committee were with him. Poskrebyshev announced my arrival, and I was admitted at once.

Stalin said that the situation in the south was very bad and that the Germans might seize Stalingrad. It was no better in the Northern Caucasus. The State Defense Committee had decided to appoint me Deputy Supreme Commander and to send me to Stalingrad. Vasilevsky, Malenkov [Politburo member] and Malyshev [arms commissar] were there already. Malenkov was supposed to remain there with me and Vasilevsky was to return to Moscow.

"How soon can you take off?" Stalin asked me.

I said I needed a day to study the situation and would fly to Stalingrad on the twenty-ninth.

"Well, that's fine," Stalin said, adding, "Aren't you hungry? It wouldn't hurt to have a little refreshment."

Over tea Stalin briefed me on the situation as of 8 P.M. on August 27. Having told me quickly about developments at Stalingrad, where German troops had crossed the Don in force, Stalin said he had decided to transfer the Twenty-fourth Army, the First Guards Army and the Sixty-sixth Army to the Stalingrad Front. The Twenty-fourth Army was commanded by

General Kozlov, the First Guards by Major General K. S. Moskalenko, and the Sixty-sixth by Malinovsky.

The First Guards Army was to be shifted to Loznoye, north of Stalingrad, and open an attack on September 2 against the Germans' Volga River wedge in an effort to link up with the Sixty-second Army.

Stalin then said, "Under the cover of Moskalenko's army you must then promptly move the Twenty-fourth and Sixty-sixth armies into battle. Otherwise we may lose Stalingrad."

It was clear to me that the Battle for Stalingrad was of the utmost military and political importance. The fall of the city would enable the German command to cut off the south of the Soviet Union from the rest of the country. We might lose the great waterway of the Volga River, on which a heavy flow of goods was moving from the Caucasus.

The Supreme Command had moved everything it had, except for the newly formed strategic reserves intended for subsequent operations, into the Stalingrad area. Urgent measures were being taken to speed the production of planes, tanks, guns, munitions and other supplies in order to have them ready in time for the defeat of the enemy forces that had broken through to Stalingrad.

7

The Battle Grows

I took off from Moscow's Central Airport on August 29 and landed four hours later on an airstrip near Kamyshin (on the Volga, north of Stalingrad). I was met by Vasilevsky, who filled me in on the latest developments. After a short talk we drove to the headquarters of the Stalingrad Front at Malaya Ivanovka.[10]

We reached the headquarters about noon. General Gordov was somewhere near the front lines. Nikishev, the Chief of Staff, and Rukhle, the operations chief, gave us a report on the situation. As I listened to them, I had the impression that they were not entirely clear about the situation and were not sure

[10] The Stalingrad Front, so called, was at this time the designation of the group of armies just north of the city. Malaya Ivanovka is about fifty miles due north of Stalingrad. The so-called Southeast Front at that time incorporated the region of Stalingrad proper. Its headquarters was on the east bank of the river, across the Volga from Stalingrad, which is a west-bank city. It was located in the little town of Krasny Sad (Red Gardens). Georgi Malenkov was the Politburo member attached to the "Stalingrad Front" at this time; Khrushchev was attached to the "Southeast Front," which was commanded by Yeremenko. Malenkov was on the scene most of the time, but his presence is ignored by Zhukov.   H.E.S.

that the enemy could be stopped at Stalingrad.

I reached General Gordov by telephone at the headquarters of General Moskalenko's First Guards Army, and told him to wait there for Vasilevsky and myself. When we arrived, we found Generals Gordov and Moskalenko and their reports very encouraging. I felt that they were thoroughly familiar with the enemy's strength and with the capabilities of their own forces.

After a discussion of the situation and of the state of our troops, we agreed that the combined forces of the three armies could not be ready for a counterattack before September 6. I immediately called Stalin over the high-security line and informed him of our decision. He said he had no objection.

Since Vasilevsky had been ordered to return to Moscow, he took off shortly thereafter, I believe on September 1.

The First Guards Army was unable to open the offensive ordered for September 2 by Supreme Headquarters. Because of a shortage of fuel and delays en route its elements had not yet reached their jumping-off areas. At General Moskalenko's request, I postponed the attack to the next day. In my report to Supreme Headquarters, I said:

The First Guards Army could not launch its offensive on September 2 because its units had been unable to reach their jumping-off points, to bring up munitions and fuel, and to organize for battle. Rather than send unorganized troops into battle and risk unwarranted losses, after having inspected the situation on the spot, I postponed the attack to 5 A.M. on September 3. The attack by the Twenty-fourth and Sixty-sixth armies has been set for September 5–6. The operations plan is now being worked out in detail by commanders, and steps are being taken to insure a steady flow of supplies.

On the morning of September 3, after artillery bombardment, troops of the First Guards Army attacked, but they advanced only a couple of miles toward Stalingrad, inflicting a slight setback on the foe. Continuous enemy air strikes and counterattacks by tanks and infantry, supported by artillery, prevented further advance.

On that day I received the following telegram over Stalin's signature:

The situation at Stalingrad has deteriorated further. The enemy stands two miles from the city. Stalingrad may fall today or tomorrow if the northern group of forces does not give immediate assistance. See to it that the commanders of forces north and northwest of Stalingrad strike the enemy at once and come to the aid of the Stalingraders. No delay can be tolerated. To delay now is tantamount to a crime. Throw all your air power to the aid of Stalingrad. The city has few planes.

I telephoned Stalin immediately and told him I could order the offensive to begin the next morning, but that the troops of the three armies would have to start battle almost without ammunition, which would not reach artillery positions before the evening. Furthermore, it would also take until evening for infantry operations to be coordinated with artillery, tanks and air support, and nothing would come of the offensive without such coordination.

"And you think the enemy is going to wait while you're getting organized?" Stalin said. "Yeremenko insists the enemy is going to take Stalingrad on his first try unless you strike from the north."

I replied that I did not share that view and asked permission to start the offensive on the fifth as planned. As for air support, I would issue orders immediately to bomb the enemy with all the strength we had.

"Well, all right," Stalin said. "But if the enemy begins a general offensive against the city, attack immediately. Do not wait for the troops to be completely ready. Your main job is to keep the Germans from taking Stalingrad and, if possible, to eliminate the German corridor separating the Stalingrad and Southeast fronts."

At dawn on September 5, advance artillery, mortar and air action was begun on the entire front of the Twenty-fourth, First Guards and Sixty-sixth armies. But the density of artillery fire was insufficient, even in the sectors of the principal thrusts, and failed to yield the required result. The ground attack followed salvos of Katyusha rockets. I watched the attack from the observation post of the First Guards Army. We could tell from the strength of the enemy's counterfire that our artillery bombardment had not been effective and that no deep penetration by our forces was to be expected.

And that is precisely what happened. Within one and a half to two hours it became clear from the reports of commanders that the foe had halted our advance in a number of sectors with his fire and was counterattacking with infantry and tanks. Aerial reconnaissance showed that large groups of tanks, artillery and motorized infantry were moving northward from Gumrak, Orlovka and Bolshaya Rossoshka, on the western outskirts of Stalingrad. Enemy bombers also began to attack our positions.

The enemy reinforcements joined the battle in the second half of the day and pushed our forces back to their original positions in some sectors.

The battle died down by evening, and we summed up its results. Our forces had advanced little more than one to two miles, and the Twenty-fourth Army remained practically in its original positions.

By evening additional shells, mines and other ammunition reached our forces. Using fresh intelligence about the enemy gathered during the day, we decided to prepare a new attack for the morning, regrouping our forces as best we could during the night.

Late in the evening I had a call from Stalin.

"How are things at Stalingrad?" he wanted to know.

I reported on the heavy daylong battle and said that the

enemy had shifted some of his forces from Gumrak to the front north of Stalingrad.

"That is very good," Stalin said. "It is of great help to the city."

But I continued: "Our forces did not advance very far, and in some sectors they remained in their original positions."

"Why was that?"

"Because we did not have enough time to prepare the offensive and reconnoiter the enemy's artillery positions and therefore could not aim our preparatory fire effectively. When our ground forces attacked, the enemy was able to stop them with his fire and counterattacks. In addition, enemy planes had superiority in the air and bombed our positions all day."

"Just continue the attacks," Stalin ordered. "Your job is to divert as many of the enemy forces as possible from Stalingrad."

The following day the battle was renewed with even greater ferocity. During the night our planes had bombed the enemy's positions. In addition to our front-line air force, these strikes were joined by the long-range bombing force under the command of Lieutenant General A. Ye. Golovanov, who was with me at the command center of the First Guards Army.

On September 6, the enemy brought up new forces and dug in tanks and self-propelled guns on dominant elevations as strongpoints. These could be rendered harmless only by powerful artillery fire, and we had very few big guns at our disposal at the time. On the third and fourth days the battle was limited largely to artillery exchanges and aerial dogfights.

On a tour of front-line units on September 10 I reached the conclusion that we would be unable to break through the German lines and eliminate the enemy's corridor with our available forces. Generals Gordov, Moskalenko, Malinovsky and Kozlov concurred in that view.

In reporting to Stalin that day, I said, "We will not be able to break through the enemy corridor and join up with the Southeast Front with the forces at the disposal of the Stalingrad

Front. The Germans have greatly strengthened the northern front with units brought up from Stalingrad. Further attacks with the present forces would be useless and would result in heavy casualties. We need reinforcements and time to regroup for a more concentrated frontal assault. Thrusts by individual armies are not sufficient to dislodge the enemy."

Stalin said in reply that it might be well for me to fly to Moscow and report on the situation in person.

I flew to Moscow on September 12 and was at the Kremlin within four hours. Vasilevsky, who had also been summoned, reported on the movement of new German forces toward Stalingrad from the direction of Kotelnikovo, on fighting near Novorossisk, and on the German drive toward Grozny.

Stalin listened closely and then summed up: "They want to get at the oil of Grozny at any price. Well, now let's see what Zhukov has to say about Stalingrad."

I repeated what I had told him by telephone, adding that the Twenty-fourth, First Guards and Sixty-sixth armies, which had taken part in the battle of September 5 to 11, were basically good fighting units. Their main weakness was the absence of reinforcements and the shortage of howitzers and tanks needed for infantry support. The terrain on the Stalingrad Front was extremely unfavorable to us—it was open terrain dissected by deep gullies that provided excellent cover for the enemy. Having occupied a number of commanding heights, the Germans could now maneuver their artillery fire in all directions. In addition, they could also direct long-range artillery at our forces from the area of Kuzmichi, Akatovka and the experimental state farm. Under those conditions, I concluded, the Twenty-fourth, First Guards and Sixty-sixth armies of the Stalingrad Front were unable to break through the enemy defenses.

"What would the Stalingrad Front need to eliminate the enemy corridor and link up with the Southeast Front?" Stalin asked.

"At least one full-strength field army, a tank corps, three tank brigades and four hundred howitzers. In addition, the support of at least one air army during the time of the operation."

Vasilevsky expressed agreement with my estimate.

Stalin reached for his map showing the disposition of Supreme Headquarters reserves and studied it for a long time. Vasilevsky and I stepped away from the table and, in a low voice, talked about the need for finding another way out.

"What other way out?" Stalin suddenly interjected, looking up from the map.

I had never realized he had such good hearing. We stepped back to the map table.

"Look," he continued, "you better get back to the General Staff and give some thought to what can be done at Stalingrad and how many reserves, and from where, we will need to reinforce the Stalingrad group. And don't forget about the Caucasus Front. We will meet again tomorrow evening at nine."

Vasilevsky and I spent the entire following day studying possible alternatives. We concentrated on the possibility of a single major operation which would avoid using up our reserves in a large number of isolated operations. By October we were to have completed the formation of strategic reserves that would include well-equipped new tank forces. By that time Soviet industry would also have increased the production of newly designed planes and of ammunition for our artillery.

After discussing the various alternatives, Vasilevsky and I decided to submit the following plan to Stalin: first, to continue to wear down the enemy by an active defense; second, to prepare a counteroffensive of such magnitude against the enemy at Stalingrad as to shift the strategic situation in the south decidedly in our favor.

As for a detailed plan for such a counteroffensive, we were, of course, unable in one day to prepare all the necessary calculations, but it seemed clear to us that the main thrusts would have to be directed against the Rumanian-held flanks of the

Stalingrad grouping. Rough estimates showed that such a counteroffensive could not be prepared before the middle of November. Our assessment was based on the assumption that the Germans were in no condition to fulfill their strategic plans for 1942 and that the forces at their disposal in the autumn of 1942 would not suffice to achieve their objectives either in the Northern Caucasus or on the Don and the Volga.

All the forces that the German command could send into the Caucasus and toward Stalingrad had been greatly worn down and weakened. The enemy was evidently incapable of moving additional troops into the south and would ultimately have to go over to the defensive on all sectors just as had happened after the Battle for Moscow.

We knew that Paulus' Sixth Field Army and Hoth's Fourth Tank Army, two of the Wehrmacht's most effective striking forces, had been so weakened in the grueling fighting for Stalingrad that they would be unable to complete the capture of the city.

As for the Soviet troops, they had suffered such heavy casualties in the fierce fighting on the approaches to Stalingrad, and were to suffer more within the city itself, that they were unable to defeat the enemy with existing forces. The large strategic reserves equipped with new arms were not yet ready. But by November Supreme Headquarters would have at its disposal strong new mechanized and tank forces equipped with the world-famous T-34 tanks, which would enable us to undertake more far-reaching tasks. In addition, our senior commanders had learned a great deal in the first period of the war and, through hard experience with a strong enemy, had become masters of the military art. Commanders, political commissars and ordinary fighting men of the Red Army had also learned through bitter experience how to meet the enemy in any situation.

On the basis of front-line reports, the General Staff had

studied the strong and weak sides of the German, Hungarian, Italian and Rumanian troops. The satellite forces were found to be less well armed, less experienced and less capable, even in defense, than the German units. And, most important, their soldiers and even many of their officers had no desire to die for others on the distant fields of Russia, where they had been sent by Hitler, Mussolini, Antonescu, Horthy and the other Fascist leaders.

The situation of the enemy was further complicated by the fact that he had few troops in his operational reserve in the Volga-Don sector. They amounted to no more than six divisions and were scattered over a broad front. We were also favored by the operational configuration of the front. Soviet forces held enveloping positions with respect to the enemy and might relatively easily improve their bridgeheads south of the Don River at Serafimovich and Kletskaya.

In the evening of September 13, Vasilevsky called Stalin and said we were ready to report. Stalin said he would be busy until ten o'clock and that we should come at that time. We were in his office at the appointed hour.

He greeted us by shaking hands (which he seldom did) and said with an air of annoyance, "Tens and hundreds of thousands of Soviet people are giving their lives in the fight against Fascism, and Churchill is haggling over twenty Hurricanes. And those Hurricanes aren't even that good. Our pilots don't like them."

Then, in a quiet tone without any transition, he continued: "Well, what did you come up with? Who's making the report?"

"Either of us," Vasilevsky said. "We are of the same opinion."

Stalin stepped up to our map.

"What have you got here?" he asked.

"These are our preliminary notes for a counteroffensive at Stalingrad," Vasilevsky replied.

"What are these troops at Serafimovich?"

"That would be a new front. We will have to set it up to launch a powerful thrust into the rear of the German forces at Stalingrad."

"We don't have the forces now for such a big operation."

I said that according to our calculations we would have the necessary forces and could thoroughly prepare the operation in forty-five days.

"Wouldn't it be better to limit ourselves to a thrust from north to south and from south to north along the Don?" Stalin said.

I explained that the Germans would then be able to shift their armored forces from Stalingrad and parry our thrusts. An attack west of the Don, on the other hand, would prevent the enemy from quickly maneuvering his forces and bringing up his reserves because of the river obstacle.

"Aren't you out too far with your striking forces?" Stalin said.

Vasilevsky and I explained that the operation would proceed in two stages: after a breakthrough of the German defenses, the enemy's forces at Stalingrad would be surrounded and a strong outer front would be created, isolating his forces from the outside; then we would proceed to destroy the trapped Germans and stop any attempts to come to their aid.

"We will have to think about this some more and see what our resources are," Stalin said. "Our main task now is to hold Stalingrad and to keep the enemy from advancing toward Kamyshin."

At that point Poskrebyshev walked in and said Yeremenko was on the phone.

After his talk with Yeremenko, Stalin said, "Yeremenko says the enemy is bringing up tank forces near the city. He expects an attack tomorrow."

Turning to Vasilevsky, Stalin added, "Issue orders immediately to have Rodimtsev's 13th Guards Division cross the Volga and see what else you can send across the river tomorrow."

Then Stalin told me: "Call Gordov and Golovanov and tell them to start air attacks immediately. Gordov will have to attack first thing in the morning to tie down the enemy. You better get back to the Stalingrad Front and size up the situation around Kletskaya and Serafimovich. In a few days Vasilevsky will have to visit the Southeast Front and study the situation on its left wing. We will talk about our plan later. No one, beyond the three of us, is to know about it for the time being."[11]

I boarded my plane an hour later and flew back to the headquarters of the Stalingrad Front.

[11] Vasilevsky supports Zhukov's reference to Stalin's insistence on extreme secrecy. Stalin warned both generals that they were not to discuss the intentions of Supreme Headquarters with anyone. (Vasilevsky, in *Stalingradskaya Epopeya*, Moscow, 1968, p. 83.)   H.E.S.

8

The Balance Tips Toward Russia

September 13, 14 and 15 were difficult days, very difficult days, for Stalingrad. Regardless of cost, the enemy kept pressing step by step through the ruins of the city toward the Volga bank. It almost seemed as if we could not stop him. But the men of the Sixty-second and Sixty-fourth armies stood their ground and turned the ruins of the city into a fortress.

The turning point in those days, and in what seemed to be the last few hours, was the introduction of Rodimtsev's 13th Guards Division into the battle (after its transfer from the Supreme Headquarters reserve). It crossed the Volga and immediately counterattacked the enemy in what was evidently an unexpected blow. On September 16 we recaptured the hill of Mamayev Kurgan. The Stalingrad defenders were also aided by air strikes from Golovanov's long-range bombers and Rudenko's Sixteenth Air Army as well as by attacks and artillery fire from troops of the Stalingrad Front in the north against elements of the Germans' 8th Army Corps.

A great deal of credit must be given to the soldiers of the Twenty-fourth, First Guards and Sixty-sixth armies of the Stalingrad Front and to the airmen of the Sixteenth Air Army and the long-range bombing force, who, at no matter what sacrifice, gave invaluable help to the Sixty-second and Sixty-fourth armies of the Southeast Front in holding Stalingrad.

Here is what a German officer with Paulus' army has written: "At the same time our corps suffered heavy casualties in September in repulsing fierce attacks by the enemy, who was trying to break through our lines in the north. The divisions on that sector were greatly weakened, with company strengths down to 30 or 40 men."[12]

At about this time General Yeremenko, with Stalin's approval, visited the command center of the First Guards Army to discuss the situation. General Golovanov and I were also there, and Gordov and Moskalenko briefed Yeremenko on all details.

Since Stalin had told me not to talk about our plan for a counteroffensive, the discussion ranged mainly over reinforcements for the Southeast and Stalingrad fronts. When Yeremenko asked whether a more powerful counterattack was in the offing, I said that Supreme Headquarters hoped to launch stronger counterattacks at a later date but did not have the forces for such a plan for the time being.[13]

Toward the end of September I was again summoned to Moscow by Stalin to discuss the plan for a counteroffensive. By that time Vasilevsky had also returned to Moscow from his visit to the Southeast Front. He and I met for a discussion before going to Supreme Headquarters.

There Stalin asked me what I thought of General Gordov, the commander of the Stalingrad Front. I said he was a skilled operations man, but seemed to be unable to get along with his staff and his commanders.

Stalin said in that case we'd better get another commander for

[12] Joachim Wieder, *Stalingrad*, Munich, 1962.
[13] This is a dig at Yeremenko, who has tried to claim some credit for the plan of the Stalingrad counteroffensive.   H.E.S.

that front. I suggested Rokossovsky. Vasilevsky agreed. We also decided [as of September 28] to change the name of the Stalingrad Front to Don Front, and the Southeast Front to Stalingrad Front (to reflect their geographical locations more accurately). Rokossovsky was appointed commander of the Don Front, with M. S. Malinin as his Chief of Staff. Lieutenant General N. F. Vatutin was suggested as candidate for the command of a newly created Southwest Front. The headquarters of the First Guards Army was to serve as the nucleus of a headquarters for the new Southwest Front. The First Guards Army commander, General Moskalenko, was transferred to the Fortieth Army.

After a detailed discussion of our counteroffensive plan, Stalin said to me, "You better fly back to the front and take all the steps necessary to wear down the enemy. Have another look at the proposed concentration areas for reserves and the jumping-off areas for the Southwest Front and the right wing of the Stalingrad Front, especially around Serafimovich and Kletskaya. Comrade Vasilevsky will have to have another look at the left wing of the Southeast Front."

After another on-the-spot examination of all conditions for the counteroffensive, Vasilevsky and I returned to Supreme Headquarters for another round of discussions. At that time the plan was officially approved. Vasilevsky and I signed the map showing the counteroffensive plan, and Stalin added the word "Approved" and his signature.[14]

Stalin then told Vasilevsky, "Without divulging our plan, we should now ask for the views of the front commanders concerning future operations."

The Stalingrad Front became the Don Front as of September 28. I had been instructed to inform the Military Council of the Don Front personally about future operations. I still remember that conversation of September 29 in a dugout in the

---

[14] The code name of the plan was "Uran"—Uranus.   H.E.S.

ravine north of Stalingrad where General Moskalenko had his command center.

In reply to my instructions to keep up active operations to prevent the enemy from shifting forces from the Don Front to the storming of Stalingrad, Rokossovsky said our strength had been depleted and there was not much that we could accomplish. He was right, of course. I held the same view, but without our help the Southeast (now the Stalingrad) Front would not be able to hold the city.

On October 1 I returned to Moscow for more work on the plan for the counteroffensive. I flew with General Golovanov, the commander of the long-range bomber force, who was at the controls of the plane. It was a pleasure to fly with such an excellent pilot.

We were still some distance from Moscow when the plane suddenly made a turn and began to descend. I figured that we were changing course. But a few minutes later Golovanov landed the plane on an unfamiliar airfield. I asked him, "Why did we land here?"

"We were lucky that we were so close to this field, otherwise we might have crashed."

"What happened?"

"Icing."

While we were talking, my own plane, which had been following, also touched down, and I flew on to Moscow's Central Airport.

All those hurried flights under difficult conditions could, of course, not always end happily. I remember another plane incident that almost cost me my life. It was on a flight from Stalingrad to Moscow a few days later. It was raining and Moscow reported fog and limited visibility. But we had to fly; Stalin had summoned me.

The flight to the Moscow area was not bad, but at Moscow visibility was down to three hundred feet. My pilot was ordered by the flight command of the air force to land at another airfield. In that case I would have arrived late at the Kremlin, where Stalin was waiting.

Taking all responsibility upon myself, I ordered the pilot to land at Central Airport and remained with him in the cockpit. As we passed over Moscow, we suddenly saw the top of a factory chimney thirty to fifty feet from the left wing of the plane. I looked at the pilot. "Without batting an eye," he lifted the plane just a bit, and two or three minutes later we were safe on the ground.

"That was a close shave," I told the pilot.

He smiled, and said, "Anything is possible if you disobey the flying rules."

"It was my fault," I replied, firmly shaking his hand.

In the intervening years I unfortunately have forgotten the pilot's name, though I think it was Belyayev, a wonderful man and a highly experienced pilot. I must have flown a total of 130 hours with Comrade Belyayev. He was later killed in an air accident, I am sorry to say.

In October Supreme Headquarters ordered six reconstituted divisions across the Volga into Stalingrad to reinforce the Sixty-second Army, of which little remained beyond headquarters and support units. The Don Front was also reinforced to some extent with manpower and equipment.

Supreme Headquarters and the General Staff gave particular attention to the formation of the newly constituted Southwest Front.

Heavy fighting continued throughout October in Stalingrad itself and in adjoining areas. Hitler issued orders to the command of Army Group B and to Paulus, the Sixth Army commander, to seize Stalingrad in the immediate future.

For its decisive thrust the German command shifted German forces from the flanks and replaced them by Rumanian troops, thus greatly weakening its defensive positions near Serafimovich and south of Stalingrad.

In the middle of October the enemy launched one more

offensive in the hope of finishing off Stalingrad once and for all. But again the Soviet forces stood fast. The units that distinguished themselves particularly were A. I. Rodimtsev's 13th Guards Division, V. A. Gorishny's 95th Division, V. D. Zholudev's 37th Division, I. Ye. Yermolkin's 112th Division, S. F. Gorokhov's group, I. I. Lyudnikov's 138th Division, and D. N. Bely's 84th Tank Brigade.

The battle raged without stopping for several days and nights, in the streets of the city, in buildings, in factories, on the Volga River bank, everywhere. But our forces, though suffering heavy casualties, held on to a few small "islands" in the city.

To provide some relief for Stalingrad, troops of the Don Front began an offensive on October 19. The Germans were again compelled to divert a substantial amount of air power, artillery and tanks from the battle for the city to deal with the new offensive. At the same time the Sixty-fourth Army made a counterattack against the enemy flank in the sector of Kuporosnoye and Zelenaya Polyana, just south of the center of Stalingrad.

Both the Don Front offensive and the counterattack by the Sixty-fourth Army to some extent eased the situation of the Sixty-second Army in the city and frustrated the enemy's plans. Without this relief the Sixty-second Army might not have been able to hold on to the city and the Germans might possibly have taken it.

At the beginning of November the Germans tried several times to eliminate a number of nests of resistance in the city, and, on November 11, when our forces were completing the vast preparations for their counteroffensive, the enemy attempted one more attack, again without result.

By that time the Germans were at the end of their strength. Prisoner interrogations revealed that the enemy's forces had been greatly reduced, that the morale and political conviction of both soldiers and officers were low, and that few expected to emerge alive from the inferno of Stalingrad.

During the entire period of June through November the enemy had lost 600,000 men, 1,000 tanks, 2,000 guns and mortars, and 1,400 planes in the region of the Don, the Volga and at Stalingrad. The operational situation of German forces on the Volga had deteriorated. Divisional and corps reserves had been used up, and the flanks of Army Group B were held by unreliable Rumanian, Italian and Hungarian troops that were beginning to understand their hopeless situation.

The Soviet forces on the Don River were in a favorable position for a counteroffensive by the Southwest and Don fronts. South of Stalingrad the Fifty-first Army, in a local counterattack, had expelled the enemy from the lake defiles and was in complete control of the favorable defense line along lakes Sarpa, Tsatsa and Barmantsak. On Vasilevsky's recommendation, this line had been selected as the jumping-off point for the November counteroffensive by the left wing of the Stalingrad Front.

The fierce battle for Stalingrad was in its fourth month. The entire world followed developments with bated breath. The success of the Soviet forces and their courageous struggle against the enemy inspired all mankind and instilled confidence in ultimate victory over Fascism.

The Battle of Stalingrad was also a tremendous education for victory for our troops. Unit headquarters and staffs received practice in coordinating infantry, tanks, artillery and air power. Our troops learned how to put up stubborn resistance in city streets, combining it with maneuvers on the enemy's flanks. The morale of our forces rose substantially. All this provided favorable conditions for our counteroffensive.

The defensive fighting around Stalingrad and in the Northern Caucasus in the middle of November of 1942 marked the end of the first period of the Great Patriotic War, which played such a special role in the life of the Soviet people. This was an extremely difficult period for the nation and its armed forces, for the German troops, sowing death and destruction, had driven to the very outskirts of Leningrad and Moscow and occupied most of the Ukraine.

By November, 1942, enemy troops occupied a huge part of the Soviet Union, with an area of 700,000 square miles and a prewar population of eighty million. Millions of Soviet people who had been caught by the war were compelled to abandon their cities, villages, factories and plants and move eastward to avoid the enemy occupation. Soviet troops were forced by the military situation to retreat into the interior, suffering substantial losses in manpower and matériel.

But even during that difficult period neither the Soviet nation nor its armed forces lost faith in the prospect of the ultimate defeat of the enemy hordes. The mortal danger helped to rally our people even more closely around the Communist Party, and, despite every hardship, the enemy was finally stopped in all sectors.

The first period of the war provided a serious education in armed struggle with a strong and experienced enemy. The Soviet Supreme Command, the General Staff and the unit commanders and staffs received invaluable experience in organizing and conducting defensive battles and counteroffensives.

The mass heroism of Soviet soldiers and the courage of their commanders, reared by our Party, were demonstrated with particular force during the fierce fighting of that period. A positive role was played by the personal example of Party members and Young Communists who, when necessary, sacrificed themselves for the sake of victory. Bright pages in the chronicle were also contributed by the heroic resistance of the frontier fortress of Brest and of Leningrad, Moscow, Odessa, Sevastopol, Stalingrad, Liepaja, Kiev and the Caucasus.

The first period of the war also saw the emergence of the

Soviet Guards. The honorary title of Guards, for mass heroism and valor, was given to four cavalry corps, 36 rifle divisions, 27 tank brigades, 32 air regiments and other units. In the Navy the Guards title was awarded to two cruisers, four submarines, one destroyer and one mine sweeper. Among the first units to receive the title were: the 1st Moscow Motorized Rifle Division of Colonel A. I. Lizyukov, the 2nd Cavalry Corps of General P. A. Belov, the 3rd Cavalry Corps of General L. M. Dovator, the 4th Tank Brigade of General M. Ye. Katukov, the 26th Fighter Plane Regiment of Major A. P. Yudakov, the 31st Dive Bomber Regiment of Lieutenant Colonel F. I. Dobysh, the 215th Assault Air Regiment of Lieutenant Colonel L. D. Reino, the 440th Artillery Regiment of Major A. I. Bryukhanov, and the 289th Antitank Artillery Regiment of Major M. K. Yeremenko.

The tense armed struggle against the German forces required great expenditure of arms, munitions and supplies. But despite the loss of key economic regions, factories and plants, the Soviet people strove with self-sacrificing labor to provide the armed forces with the equipment of war. By the end of the first phase of the war the country had been converted into a military camp. The Soviet people considered it their duty to do everything in their power for victory over the enemy.

Heroic work was also accomplished by members of the Red Army's support services. As many as 6.4 million carloads of military supplies moved over the railroads in the first year and a half of the war. The army was provided with 113,000 carloads of munitions, 60,000 carloads of arms and equipment, and 210,-400 carloads of fuel and lubricants. In 1942 truck transport units alone carried 2.7 million men, 12.3 million tons of supplies, 1,923 tanks and 3,674 guns. Transport planes carried 532,000 men, including 158,000 wounded.

The reorganization of the support services undertaken at the beginning of the war was a complete success. The new organizational structure and skillful selection of commanders, political commissars and Party unit leaders ensured proper use of the tremendous resources that were being made available to the armed forces.

And what were the capabilities of the enemy whom the Soviet forces confronted during this first period?

That question demands an answer, if only to make clear to our young generation the gravity of the struggle waged by the Soviet people in defense of their homeland. Some of the memoirs and works of fiction do not always show the preparation, experience and strength of the enemy with whom Soviet soldiers had to deal.

First of all, let us consider the basic mass of German troops— soldiers and officers.

The German forces invaded the Soviet Union intoxicated by their easy victories over the armies of Western Europe; they were poisoned with Goebbels' propaganda, and firmly convinced both of the possibility of an easy victory over the Red Army and of their own superiority over all other nations. The younger soldiers and officers of the armored forces and air units were in a particularly arrogant mood. I had occasion to interrogate prisoners in the first few months of the war, and I must say they really believed in Hitler's adventurist promises.

Their fighting capacity, their special training and military indoctrination were without question on a high level, particularly in armored units and the air force. The German soldier knew his business in battle and in service in the field; he was steadfast, self-assured and disciplined.

In short, the Soviet soldier faced an experienced, strong enemy who was not to be easily defeated.

German headquarters forces and smaller military units were trained in all the techniques of modern warfare. Communications with fighting units in battle were assured mainly by radio, for which equipment was available in abundance at all command levels. Ground forces did their utmost to fulfill their assignments, benefiting from skillful air support that would often clear the way for them.

In this initial period of the war I also had a rather high opinion of the upper German command levels. It was obvious that they had carefully planned and organized their initial thrusts in all strategic sectors; they had picked experienced commanders for armies and other major units, and had correctly evaluated the direction, manpower and troop composition needed for strikes against weak sectors in our defense lines. Despite all this, the military and political strategy of German Fascism turned out to be deeply erroneous and shortsighted. Gross miscalculations and mistakes were made in political and strategic estimates. The forces at Germany's disposal, even including satellite reserves, were clearly inadequate for waging simultaneous operations in the three major sectors of the Soviet-German front.

Because of this the enemy was compelled to halt his drive toward Moscow and to assume defensive positions on that front in order to divert part of the forces of Army Group Center to the support of Army Group South, facing our troops on the Central and Southwest fronts.

Similarly, before the Germans were able to carry through their offensive at Leningrad, they were compelled to divert air power and armor from that city and regroup them west of Moscow for the support of Army Group Center. In October and November, 1941, the German forces were in a position to concentrate their offensive in only one sector, the Moscow sector, but even there the growing Soviet resistance demonstrated that the enemy lacked sufficient forces to achieve the objectives of Operation Typhoon. The same gross strategic miscalculation was made in planning the summer campaign of 1942.

At the basis of all these miscalculations were an obvious underestimation of the strength of our Socialist land and its people under the guidance of the Party of Lenin and an over-estimation of the Germans' own forces and capabilities.

In planning the invasion of the Soviet Union, Hitler and his associates intended to throw all their available forces against us. This was the miscalculation of a reckless gambler. Despite the treason of the Pétain Government, the working people of France did not bow their heads before the German occupation. Nor did the freedom-loving peoples of Yugoslavia, Poland, Czechoslovakia and other countries. All of them kept up an armed struggle against the occupying forces. The enemy was thus confronted with a massive resistance movement. Britain also continued to fight, even though she did not use her capabilities to the fullest.

Despite their initial successes up to the Battle of Moscow, the German forces were confronted with a number of unforeseen circumstances as soon as they invaded the Soviet Union. They never expected that they would have to fight both the Red Army at the front and a powerful guerrilla movement led by underground Party units at the rear.

Nor did the Germans anticipate the failure to achieve a single strategic objective that compelled them to take up defensive positions along the entire Soviet front in 1941. They lost their strategic initiative, and their troops were exhausted and demoralized. The same thing happened at Stalingrad at the end of 1942.

Enemy troops suffered tremendous losses in the first sixteen months of fighting on the Soviet-German front. By November, 1942, their losses exceeded two million dead, wounded and missing in action. The best elements of the German forces were among the casualties, and the Nazi command had no replacements for them at the end of this first phase of the war.

Nor did the enemy expect that the Soviet people, rallying around the Party, would so swiftly effect the nation's changeover to a wartime economy and launch the mass production of tanks, planes, artillery, munitions and everything else needed by the Red Army to achieve superiority over the German forces and ultimate victory.

Despite the setbacks in the first phase of the war, the Red Army did not collapse under the German onslaught the way the Western armies had. On the contrary, the rugged conditions of war served to toughen and mature our troops so that when they were supplied with the necessary arms, they were able to transform a defensive, retreating army into an offensive force.

The organization and inspiration of our entire Party yielded brilliant results both in the field and at home. The Soviet people quickly mobilized to provide the materials and supplies for the Red Army's struggle against the German forces.

And so the first period of the Great Patriotic War ended with the imminent collapse of all the strategic plans of the Nazi command and with substantial depletion of the forces and capabilities at Germany's disposal. This basic result of the struggle thus far predetermined to a large extent the subsequent course of the entire Second World War.

9

Operation Uranus Takes Shape

After the heavy fighting in the south, around Stalingrad and in the Northern Caucasus, the Nazi military leadership believed that Soviet troops were in no condition to carry out a major winter offensive in the region.

To confuse the enemy, we conducted operations against Army Group Center west of Moscow in the summer and autumn of 1942. Supreme Headquarters intended to give the impression that it was there, and nowhere else, that we were preparing a winter offensive.

In October, therefore, the Nazi command began to concentrate large forces opposite our western sectors. A tank division, a motorized division and an infantry division were shifted from Leningrad to Velikiye Luki. Seven divisions from France and Germany showed up in the area of Vitebsk and Smolensk. Two tank divisions previously identified at Voronezh and Zhizdra were moved to the area of Yartsevo and Roslavl. By the beginning of November a total of twelve divisions plus other reinforcements had been shifted to strengthen Army Group Center.

These operational miscalculations by the Germans were

further aggravated by poor intelligence. They were unable to detect preparations for our Stalingrad counteroffensive, which involved 11 armies, several separate mechanized, cavalry and tank corps, brigades and other units, 13,500 guns and mortars, 1,100 antiaircraft guns, 115 detachments of rocket artillery, 900 tanks and 1,115 planes.

By the start of our counteroffensive the enemy's operational-strategic dispositions in the south of the Soviet Union were as follows:

The main forces of Army Group B operated in the area of the middle Don, at Stalingrad and farther south along the Sarpa Lakes, and included the Italian Eighth Army, the Rumanian Third and Fourth armies, and the Germans' Sixth and Fourth tank armies. The average sector per division was ten to fifteen miles.

This army group contained more than a million men, 675 tanks and self-propelled guns, and 10,000 guns and mortars. Numerically the two sides were almost equal, except for a slight Soviet superiority in tanks.

Army Group B was supported by the Fourth Air Fleet and the 8th Air Corps.

In working out its plan for a counteroffensive, the Soviet Supreme Command assumed that a defeat inflicted on the enemy at Stalingrad would also seriously endanger enemy forces in the Northern Caucasus and compel them to pull back in a hurry or face entrapment.

Since Stalin's death there has been some confusion as to the real author of the counteroffensive plan, whose scale and results would be so far-reaching. Even though the question of authorship is not so important under Socialism and I have already described the various steps in the formulation of the plan, I would like to make some additional comments.

It has been assumed that the first outlines were worked out at Supreme Headquarters as early as August, 1942, and that the

first version called for a rather limited counteroffensive.
Actually, that was not the plan for the great counteroffensive, but one for a counterattack intended to stop the enemy on the approaches to Stalingrad. At that time no one at Supreme Headquarters even dreamed of a major counteroffensive since we lacked both the manpower and the matériel for such a massive operation.[15]

It has also been said that the Military Council of the Stalingrad Front [the former Southeast Front] on its own initiative recommended the organization and execution of a counteroffensive to Supreme Headquarters on October 6. To this Vasilevsky has given the following reply:

> At dawn on October 6 N. N. Voronov, V. D. Ivanov and I visited the observation post of the Fifty-first Army [near Lake Tsatsa]. There we heard a report by the army commander N. I. Trufanov. That same evening, at a meeting with the front commander [Yeremenko] and his Military Council [Khrushchev] at front headquarters, we again discussed Supreme Headquarters' counteroffensive plan. Since the front command had no basic objections to the plan, we drafted a report accordingly to the Supreme Commander in Chief during the night. The following day I asked the commander of the Don Front to prepare a similar report on his own front for Supreme Headquarters.[16]

I do not think there is anything to add to this. Vasilevsky convincingly shows that it was Supreme Headquarters and the General Staff that played the main role in the planning of the counteroffensive.

Some of the historical accounts say that General Vatutin, the

[15] Zhukov emphasized earlier that the first discussion of the great counteroffensive was on September 13. Here he is seeking to rebut a version that was incorporated in histories written in the Khrushchev period which sought to blur the authorship of the great design by confusing the early minor counterattack discussion with the plans for the major operation. H.E.S.

[16] *Voyenno-Istoricheskii Zhurnal*, October, 1965, p. 20.

commander of the Southwest Front, later offered a plan for a counteroffensive. This raises the following questions: how much later, what plan, and was it a plan for his own front or a general plan for a counteroffensive?

We know that the Southwest Front was not formed until the end of October, when manpower and matériel for the new front were already being massed according to the plan for the general counteroffensive, which Supreme Headquarters had already approved.

Perhaps we need only point out that, according to existing practice and regulations, every front commander was expected to work out an operations plan for his front and to submit it either to Supreme Headquarters or to its representative on the scene for approval. In that process the front commander could of course express his views about coordination with neighboring fronts and make other recommendations.

The magnitude of the Stalingrad counteroffensive required a plan based not only on operational considerations but also on concrete calculations of supplies and matériel.

Who was able to make the necessary calculations for an operation on such a scale? Naturally only the agencies that controlled the manpower and matériel. And that could only be Supreme Headquarters and the General Staff. It must be remembered that the General Staff was the creative and working apparatus of the Supreme Command throughout the war and that not a single strategic operation could be carried out unless the General Staff had initiated and organized it.

Supreme Headquarters and the General Staff thoroughly analyzed as a matter of course all the intelligence about the enemy received from individual fronts and armies in order to determine enemy intentions and the character of his military operations. They also considered suggestions advanced by the various staffs, front commanders and services before arriving at a particular decision.

Consequently, a plan for any strategic operation of magnitude could evolve only as a result of the combined effort of all services, staffs and commanders.

But the final and decisive responsibility for the planning and organization of such a major strategic operation belongs without question to Supreme Headquarters and the General Staff. It is equally evident that the actual defeat of the enemy was the work of those who risked their lives smashing the enemy with their bold thrusts, accurate fire, courage and military skill. I am referring to our glorious soldiers, sergeants and generals who, after the test of the first phase of the war, were now ready to take the initiative and to inflict a catastrophic defeat on the Germans.

Supreme Headquarters and the General Staff should be given credit for having analyzed all the factors of this great operation with scientific precision and for having anticipated the progress and conclusion of the battle. But the total plan for the counteroffensive cannot be attributed to any particular person.[17]

[17] Vasilevsky supports Zhukov's view that plans for the counteroffensive were worked out by the General Staff, and that the coordination of the Stalingrad fronts was handled by himself and Zhukov. Zhukov had responsibility for the Southwest and Don fronts (north of Stalingrad) and Vasilevsky for the Stalingrad Front (the city and the region just to the south). The local commanders worked out details, but the General Staff handled the over-all outline and concept. Secrecy was intense. No official order on the formation of the new Southwest Front or the naming of General N. F. Vatutin to head it and of General S. P. Ivanov as his Chief of Staff was issued until October 25. Vatutin and Ivanov worked out their plans on a single map. At a large command meeting near Filonovo in late October, presided over by Zhukov, Colonel General A. A. Novikov, chief of the Red Air Force, Colonel General N. N. Voronov, chief of artillery, and Lieutenant General Ya. N. Fedyunenko, chief of tanks, were present. It was apparent from Novikov's comments that he had no notion of the scale of the counteroffensive being planned. Zhukov worked out even tiny details—supply questions and recognition signals to be used when the Southwest Front and Stalingrad Front troops met after encircling the Nazis. He refused to permit any written orders to be drafted lest the secrecy break down. As troops were brought up for the counteroffensive, they were

The main role in the first phase of the counteroffensive was to be played by the Southwest Front under General Vatutin. This front was to strike powerful, deep-ranging blows out of its bridgeheads on the south bank of the Don near Serafimovich and Kletskaya. The Stalingrad Front was to attack from the area of the Sarpa Lakes south of Stalingrad. Shock forces of the two fronts were to meet near Kalach and Sovetsky, trapping the main forces of the enemy at Stalingrad.

The Southwest Front, with a main striking force consisting of the Twenty-first Field Army, the Fifth Tank Army and elements of the First Guards Army, was to break out of its bridgeheads, smash through the defenses of the Rumanian Third Army, and drive with its mobile units toward the southeast to reach the Don between Bolshe-Nabatovsky and Kalach. This would place the troops of the Southwest Front in the rear of the enemy forces at Stalingrad, cutting off their communications with the west.

This advance was to be protected on the southwest and west by an outer front formed by the First Guards Army under General Lelyushenko and later by the Fifth Tank Army under Lieutenant General P. L. Romanenko. These forces, driving toward the west, southwest and south, by the third day of the operation were supposed to reach a line running through Veshenskaya, Bokovskaya and along the Chir River to Oblivskaya.

The ground forces of the Southwest Front were to be supported by the Second and Seventeenth air armies, commanded by Major Generals K. N. Smirnov and S. A. Krasovsky.

The Don Front was expected to launch two auxiliary attacks. One, coordinated with the Southwest Front, involved a thrust by the Sixty-fifth Army from the bridgehead east of Kletskaya,

---

permitted to move only at night and were dispersed into villages. No reference to the upcoming attack was permitted in either letters or telephone conversations. (S. P. Ivanov, *Novaya i Noveishaya Istoriya,* January, 1969, pp. 20–21.)   H.E.S.

with the objective of rolling back enemy defenses along the south bank of the Don River. The other called for a thrust by the Twenty-fourth Army from the area of Kachalinskaya southward along the east bank of the Don in the general direction of Vertyachi, with the objective of cutting off enemy forces in the small Don bend from the troops at Stalingrad.

The Sixty-sixth Army north of Stalingrad was to engage the enemy so as to prevent him from maneuvering his reserves. The ground operations of the Don Front were to be supported by the Sixteenth Air Army under General Rudenko.

The Stalingrad Front was expected to launch an offensive with its main forces, consisting of the Fifty-first, Fifty-seventh and Sixty-fourth armies, on a sector running from Ivanovka, south of Stalingrad, to the northern end of Lake Barmantsak. Their objective was to break through enemy defenses and drive northwestward for a link-up with forces of the Southwest Front near Kalach and Sovetsky, thus completing the entrapment of the German forces at Stalingrad.

The Fifty-first Army under Major General N. I. Trufanov had the task of breaking through enemy defenses from bridge-heads in the strips of land between Lakes Sarpa, Tsatsa and Barmantsak and driving toward the southwest in the general direction of Abganerovo.

The Fifty-seventh Army of General F. I. Tolbukhin and the Sixty-fourth Army of General M. S. Shumilov were to attack from the area of Ivanovka to the west and northwest, with the aim of enveloping the enemy forces at Stalingrad on the south.

Troops of the Sixty-second Army of General Chuikov were to tie down enemy forces in the city and be ready to go over to the offensive.

The advance of the Stalingrad Front was to be protected on the southwest by the creation of an outer front by the Fifty-first Army, including General T. T. Shapkin's 4th Cavalry Corps, which was to advance southwestward in the general direction of Abganerovo and Kotelnikovo. All these operations were to be supported by the Eighth Air Army under T. T. Khryukin. Preparations for the counteroffensive involved the transportation of vast numbers of troops and quantities of supplies for all fronts, especially the newly formed Southwest Front. Credit for this must be given to the General Staff and to the staff of the Red Army's support services. They did a brilliant job in massing men and matériel for the operation. A total of 27,000 trucks were used to transport men and goods. The railroads delivered 1,300 carloads a day. Men and matériel for the Stalingrad Front had to be ferried across the Volga River under difficult autumn-ice conditions. From November 1 to 19 the Volga ferries handled 160,000 soldiers, 10,000 horses, 430 tanks, 600 guns, 14,000 trucks and 7,000 tons of ammunition.

Vasilevsky and I, along with other representatives of Supreme Headquarters, spent the end of October and the beginning of November at the front, going over the operations plan with commanders and staffs. Review conferences held at the headquarters of fronts, armies and lesser units demonstrated that commanders and political commissars had carried out the complex planning work with a high degree of responsibility and initiative.

Operation plans for the Southwest Front were reviewed and revised between November 1 and 4, followed by a similar review of those for the Twenty-first Field Army, the Fifth Tank Army and the First Guards Army. I and other representatives of Supreme Headquarters took part in these preparations, closely coordinating the operational plans of the air force, artillery, armored forces and army engineers.

On November 4 we reviewed the plans of the Twenty-first and Sixty-fifth armies at a conference held at Twenty-first Army headquarters. The commands of the Don Front and of the Sixty-fifth Army were present. At the same time Vasilevsky was reviewing plans with the Fifty-first, Fifty-seventh and Sixty-fourth armies. I was to join him later.

In preparation, we concentrated first on the enemy, learning all we could about him, the nature of his defenses, the disposition of his main forces and general firing systems, and the location of antitank defenses and antitank strongpoints.

We were also concerned with our artillery preparations—the barrage density that would be needed, the likelihood of destroying enemy targets, and coordination between artillery and ground forces during the offensive. We also worked on coordinating air support and artillery, assigning them targets, and coordinating them, in turn, with tank forces both during and after the breakthrough. Operations between neighboring armies also had to be coordinated, especially in the case of mobile forces advancing deep into the enemy's defenses. In the course of this review, we made practical recommendations, suggesting what more had to be learned about the enemy, what further plans should be drawn up and what work remained to be done.

The commanders and political commissars focused on the need for a rapid breakthrough in the enemy's tactical defenses, first stunning them with a powerful blow and then quickly bringing up the second echelons so as to turn the tactical breakthrough into an operational offensive.

This was painstaking work for commanders and political commissars, but it paid off well during the actual counteroffensive.

As Vasilevsky and I had agreed, I arrived at the command center of the Fifty-seventh Army at Tatyanovka in the morning of November 10 to go over the final preparations. In addition to members of the front's Military Council, among those present were M. M. Popov, M. S. Shumilov, F. I. Tolbukhin, N. I. Trufanov, corps commanders V. T. Volsky and T. T. Shapkin and other generals of the front. Before the conference, we took a last look at the terrain over which the forces of the Stalingrad Front were to attack.

After this reconnaissance we discussed problems of coordination with the Southwest Front, the details of the proposed link-up near Kalach and other aspects of the impending operation. After discussing problems at the top-command level, we reviewed the operations plans of individual armies as reported by the various army and corps commanders.

In the evening of November 11 I sent the following telegraphic message to Stalin:

I have just spent two days with Yeremenko. I personally examined enemy positions facing the Fifty-first and Fifty-seventh armies and went over in detail with divisional, corps and army commanders their assignments under Operation Uranus. I noted that Tolbukhin's preparations for Uranus are the most advanced. . . . I gave instructions for further reconnaissance and work on the operations plan on the basis of information obtained. Comrade Popov seems to be doing his job well.

Two rifle divisions (the 87th and the 315th) assigned to Yeremenko by Supreme Headquarters have not yet arrived because of a shortage of transport and horses. Only one of the mechanized brigades has arrived so far. The operation will therefore not be completely prepared by the stated deadline. I gave orders to be ready by November 15.

We must make 100 tons of antifreeze available to Yeremenko immediately or he will not be able to move his mechanized units. Transportation should be provided quickly for the 8th and 315th rifle divisions, and it is urgent that the Fifty-first and Fifty-seventh armies be provided with warm outfits and ammunition no later than November 14.

KONSTANTINOV [my code name]

No. 4657
November 11, 1942

It should be noted that Stalin gave a great deal of attention to the problem of air support. In reply to a message of mine complaining of unsatisfactory preparations for the counteroffensive in this area, Stalin sent me the following telegram:

COMRADE KONSTANTINOV:

If air support for Yeremenko and Vatutin proves unsatisfactory, the entire operation will fail. Experience shows that we can defeat the Germans only with superiority in the air. Our air force must do the following:

First, concentrate its attacks in the area of operation of our shock forces, harass the German air units and cover our own troops.

Second, open the way for our advancing forces by systematic bombing of German positions.

Third, pursue the retreating enemy with systematic bombing and harassment to disorganize him and prevent his making a stand on another defense line.

If Novikov [the air force commander] thinks our air force is not yet ready to carry out these functions, we had better delay the operation until we have massed more air power.

Talk this over with Novikov and Vorozheikin [deputy commander of the air force] and let me have your general opinion.

VASILYEV [one of Stalin's code names]

No. 170686
November 12, 1942. 0400 hours

After our review of operations plans at the Stalingrad Front, Vasilevsky and I telephoned Stalin on November 12 and told him that we wanted to discuss a number of aspects of the forthcoming operation in person.

We were at the Kremlin the next morning. Stalin was in a good mood as he inquired about the situation at Stalingrad and the progress of the preparations.

The substance of our report was as follows:

Concerning the relationship of forces, both in quality and in numbers, we pointed out that the lines facing our main thrusts on the Southwest and Stalingrad fronts were still held mainly by Rumanians. If we could trust prisoner interrogations, they were not of high fighting caliber. We would have numerical superiority in those sectors unless the German command decided to regroup its reserves. So far our intelligence had detected no such moves. Paulus' Sixth Army and the main force of the Fourth Tank Army remained in the neighborhood of Stalingrad, where they continued to be tied down by troops of the Stalingrad and Don fronts.

Our forces continued to mass in the designated areas and, so far as we could tell, the enemy had not detected the troop concentrations. We had taken even more precautionary measures than usual to conceal movements of troops and matériel.

The operations plans of fronts, individual armies and lesser units had been reviewed meticulously. Coordination between services had been worked out on the spot. The proposed link-up of the shock forces of the Southwest and Stalingrad fronts had been reviewed with the commanders and staffs of the two fronts, and with their armies and the units that were actually expected to link up near Sovetsky and Kalach. The air armies would evidently not be ready before November 15.

The formation of both the outer and inner fronts that were to encircle and liquidate the German forces trapped in Stalingrad had been reviewed in detail.

The flow of ammunition, fuel and winter uniforms had been slightly slowed down, but all supplies could be expected to be at the front by November 16 or 17.

The counteroffensive could be launched by the Southwest and Don fronts on November 19, and by the Stalingrad Front one day later. The difference in jumping-off times was due to the fact that the Southwest Front faced a greater task. It was farther from the proposed link-up area of Kalach and Sovetsky and, in addition, would have to force the Don River.

Stalin gave us all his attention. We could tell he was pleased because he puffed unhurriedly on his pipe, smoothed his mustache and listened to us without interrupting. The Stalingrad operation meant the assumption of the initiative by the Soviet forces. We all had confidence in its success, which could have such far-reaching consequences for our country.

While we were making our report, Stalin was joined by members of the State Defense Committee and the Politburo; and we had to repeat some of the basic points we had covered in their absence. After a brief discussion the plan for the counteroffensive was fully approved.[18]

Vasilevsky and I drew Stalin's attention to the fact that as soon as the enemy was in trouble at Stalingrad and in the Northern Caucasus, the German command would be compelled to move relief forces from other sectors, especially from the Vyazma area, west of Moscow. To prevent this, we proposed an offensive north of Vyazma against the German salient around

---

[18] Vasilevsky gives the following account of their report:

"After these meetings Zhukov and I checked the work of the front commanders and agreed on the tenor of the report we would make to Supreme Headquarters on the state of preparedness of the troops of the Stalingrad fronts. The concrete details of the operation were based on the preparatory work of the fronts, and transferred to the map for our report to Supreme Headquarters.

"In our oral report we said:

" '1. Data from the fronts, which have been verified by the General Staff, indicate equal strength on both sides in the Stalingrad sectors.

" 'Because of the creation of powerful groupings from Headquarters reserves and the temporary slackening of operations in the secondary areas of the fronts, we have achieved a significant superiority over our opponent in the area of the chief thrusts of the front. This will unquestionably contribute toward the success of the operation.

" 'No significant shift of enemy reserves from distant points to the Stalingrad sectors has been noted. Nor has any essential regrouping of the enemy forces active on the over-all front been observed. The German groupings remain essentially unchanged; their main forces (the Sixth and Fourth tank armies, as before) are engaged in protracted battle in the region of the city. The flanks of these groups—that is, in the areas of our future strikes—are defended by Rumanian units. On the whole, the relative balance of forces in the Stalingrad sectors is favorable for carrying out the tasks assigned by Supreme Headquarters.

" 'In the course of the operation it is essential to devote special attention

Rzhev. Such an operation could be launched by troops of the Kalinin and Western fronts.

"That would be a good idea," Stalin said. "But which of you would handle it?"

Vasilevsky and I had agreed on that point beforehand, and therefore I said, "The Stalingrad operation is essentially all prepared. Vasilevsky could take over the coordination of operations around Stalingrad, and I could handle preparations for the counteroffensive on the Kalinin and Western fronts."

Stalin agreed, saying, "Return to Stalingrad tomorrow morn-

---

to the constant strengthening of the fronts with air support, rapid replacement of losses in troops, especially in tank and mechanized forces, and the accumulation of new Headquarters reserves in the area to ensure the successful conclusion of the operation and ensuing developments.

" '2. The concentration of troops and essential matériel as ordered by Headquarters, as well as all supplemental measures ordered by the State Defense Committee, especially the development of rail facilities in the front areas, have been carried out with only slight deviation from schedule thanks to enormous efforts on the part of rail and river authorities.

" '3. The operational tasks of all front commands down to company commands are correctly understood and have been worked out in practical terms in the terrain. Cooperation of infantry and artillery, and tanks and aviation, has also been worked out down to the company level. Special attention has been given to the preparation of tank, mechanized and cavalry corps.

" 'With the completion of the area plans of operation no supplemental corrections in the operational orders given the front commanders and armies, and already approved by Headquarters, are needed.

" 'From the plan it is apparent that the basic role in the opening stage of the operation will be carried out by the Southwest Front, which, in our opinion and in the opinion of the front commander, has sufficient forces and matériel for the task.

" 'The link-up of the tank and mechanized troops of the Southwest and Stalingrad fronts should occur on the east bank of the Don in the region of Sovetsky and Kalach in the course of the third or fourth day of the operation.

" 'Measures to establish the outer ring of encirclement provided for in the

ing and make a final check that troops and commands are ready to start the operation."

On November 14 I was back with Vatutin's forces, and Vasilevsky was with Yeremenko's. The following day I received a telegram from Stalin:

COMRADE KONSTANTINOV: *Personal*
You can set the moving date for Fedorov and Ivanov [the offensives by Vatutin and Yeremenko] as you see fit, and let me know when you come back to Moscow. If you think it necessary that either one or the other move one or two days earlier or later, I empower you to decide that question according to your best judgment.

VASILYEV
1310 hours
November 15, 1942

After some discussion Vasilevsky and I set November 19 as the date for the offensive of the Southwest Front and the Sixty-fifth Army of the Don Front, and November 20 for that of the Stalingrad Front. Stalin approved that decision.

---

plan have been worked out with the front commanders and armies and with the commanders of the appropriate military units under their leadership.

" 'As a result of the enormous political work carried out among the troops, the morale of the forces is good and their fighting spirit is high.

" 'Everything is set for the offensive by the troops of the Southwest and Don fronts to begin on November 19 and that by the Stalingrad Front on November 20.

" 'The commanders of the fronts and armies have been instructed to announce the order to their troops on the night before the offensive.

" 'In conclusion, we wish to report that all commanders of the units which are to participate in this Soviet operation of unprecedented scale and significance share our confidence in its success.'

"After the discussion of questions about the plan and the date for putting it into operation, it was finally approved by Headquarters. The coordination of action on all three fronts for the duration of the operation was placed in my hands." (Vasilevsky, in *Stalingradskaya Epopeya*, Moscow, 1968, pp. 87–98.)   H.E.S.

On November 17 I was summoned back to Supreme Head-quarters to work out the operations plan for the Kalinin and Western fronts.[19]

[19] There apparently was a bit more to Zhukov's return to Moscow on November 17 than the question of the Kalinin and Western fronts offensive. Vasilevsky was called back the same day by Stalin—a remarkable thing with the Stalingrad counteroffensive almost at zero hour. An urgent meeting of the State Defense Committee was convened to consider a letter sent to Stalin by General V. T. Volsky, whose 4th Mechanized Corps was to be the southern arm of the pincers that would trap the Germans at Stalingrad. Volsky warned Stalin "as an honest Communist" that the forthcoming Stalingrad operation was doomed to disaster because of lack of manpower and matériel. Vasilevsky (and presumably Zhukov) had to defend their plans. After Vasilevsky spoke Stalin telephoned Volsky from the Kremlin council room. Volsky agreed to withdraw his objections and carry out his orders. To everyone's surprise Stalin spoke calmly, without losing his temper. Apparently satisfied, he permitted Vasilevsky to fly back to Stalingrad, where he arrived on the morning of the nineteenth, just too late for the jump-off of the troops. What this curious episode implied is not clear unless it was to establish grounds for charges against Vasilevsky and/or Zhukov in the event that the counteroffensive fizzled. Meanwhile, Zhukov, supposedly planning the Kalinin and Western fronts offensives, apparently stayed on at Supreme Headquarters in constant touch with Stalin and Stalingrad. Even after going to the Kalinin Front he continued to advise Stalin on the Stalingrad operation.   H.E.S.

10

Stalingrad Strikes Back

At 7:30 in the morning of November 19 troops of the Southwest Front thrust powerfully through the defenses of the Rumanian Third Army on two sectors: General Romanenko's Fifth Tank Army advanced from the bridgehead southwest of Serafimovich and Major General I. M. Chistyakov's Twenty-first Army from the Kletskaya bridgehead.

Enemy troops were unable to resist and either retreated in panic or surrendered. German forces behind the Rumanians attempted to halt our advance with a strong counterattack, but were smashed by our 1st and 26th tank corps. A tactical breakthrough in the Southwest Front sector had been achieved.

General Romanenko was in his element. He was a gallant officer and a highly capable commander. His character was singularly suited to this type of mobile operation.

The enemy first expected the main thrust to develop in the Twenty-first Army sector and threw his reserves, consisting of the Rumanian 1st Tank Division and the Germans' 14th and 22nd tank divisions and 7th Cavalry Division, against General Chistyakov's forces. But later the German 22nd Tank Division and the Rumanian 1st Tank Division were moved against the 1st Tank Corps of the Fifth Tank Army under the command of Major General V. V. Budkov.

The 26th Tank Corps under Major General A. G. Rodin inflicted a heavy defeat on the 1st Tank Division and captured the headquarters of the Rumanian Fifth Army Corps. Some of the Rumanians fled in panic, but most of them surrendered.

As soon as our forces had emerged into operational terrain, the main force of the Rumanian Third Army and the German reserves that had been rushed to its relief were completely smashed and virtually ceased to exist. The 26th Tank Corps of General Rodin and the 4th Tank Corps of A. G. Kravchenko pressed their advance toward Kalach for the planned link-up with the 4th Mechanized Corps of the Stalingrad Front.

During the night of November 22–23 an advanced detachment of the 26th Tank Corps led by Lieutenant Colonel G. N. Filippov seized a bridge across the Don River in a bold thrust, thus ensuring a rapid crossing for the entire tank corps and the capture of the town of Kalach. The Colonel was awarded the title of Hero of the Soviet Union for his heroic feat, and his men were decorated with orders and medals.

On November 24 the Twenty-first Field Army and the Fifth Tank Army took more than thirty thousand prisoners in mopping up a trapped enemy force.

To the left of the Twenty-first Army, the Sixty-fifth Army of the Don Front went over to the offensive under the command of Lieutenant General P. I. Batov.

Stalin, who was seriously worried over the operations on the right flank of the Don Front, sent the following message to General Rokossovsky on the evening of November 23:

COMRADE ROKOSSOVSKY:
Copy for Comrade Vasilevsky

Vasilevsky reports that the Germans have shifted part or all of their 3rd Motorized Division and 16th Tank Division from your front and are throwing these forces against the Twenty-first Army. This opens up a situation favorable to greater activity by all the armies of your front. Galanin [Twenty-fourth Army commander] is too slow; tell him he has to take Vertyachi no later than November 24.

Also tell Zhadov [Sixty-sixth Army commander] to start more active operations and try to tie down the enemy.

You also have to give Batov a push; he could be much more forceful in the present situation.

STALIN

November 23, 1942
1940 hours

As a result of the successful offensive of the Twenty-first Army and a number of steps taken by the command of the Don Front, the situation with the Sixty-fifth Army was soon straightened out. The Twenty-fourth Army of the Don Front opened its offensive three days later, driving along the east bank of the Don River. But it was generally weak and did not achieve very much.

The Fifty-first, Fifty-seventh and Sixty-fourth armies of the Stalingrad Front opened their offensive on November 20, as planned. The Fifty-first attacked in the direction of Plodovitoye and Abganerovo, the Fifty-seventh toward Kalach, and the Sixty-fourth advanced from Ivanovka toward Gavrilovka and Varvarovka in conjunction with the right flank of the Fifty-seventh Army.

After Soviet forces had smashed through the defenses of the Rumanian 1st, 2nd, 18th and 20th divisions and the German 29th Motorized Division, the Stalingrad Front threw General Volsky's 4th Mechanized Corps into the gap opened up by the Fifty-first Army and Major General T. I. Tanaschishin's 13th Mechanized Corps into the Fifty-seventh Army sector. General Shapkin's 4th Cavalry Corps also joined the action and seized the railroad station of Abganerovo on that same day.

The enemy attempted to halt the advance of the Fifty-seventh

Army toward Kalach by diverting his 16th and 24th tank divisions from Stalingrad. But they were moved too late, and in any case they lacked the strength to stop the powerful thrusts of the Southwest and Stalingrad fronts, which reached the area of Sovetsky with their tank units during the day of November 23.

The Southwest Front's 4th Tank Corps crossed the Don River, linked up with the 4th Mechanized Corps of the Stalingrad Front at Sovetsky and closed the ring around German forces trapped between the Volga and the Don.

Meanwhile, the First Guards Army and the Fifth Tank Army of the Southwest Front and the Fifty-first Army of the Stalingrad Front, reinforced by tank units, were pursuing the retreating enemy in an attempt to throw him back as far to the west as possible from the encircled Stalingrad group and so create the firm outer front needed for the liquidation of the trapped enemy.

This completed the first phase of the counteroffensive. By the first few days of December the noose had been tightly drawn around the German forces, and our troops proceeded to the next phase, the liquidation of the trapped groups.[20]

All this time Vasilevsky and the General Staff kept me up to date. The counteroffensive had reached its most crucial moment with the encirclement of the German Sixth Army and elements of the Fourth Tank Army, and our task was now to keep the enemy from breaking out.

On November 28 I was at Kalinin Front headquarters discussing the proposed offensive west of Moscow. Late in the

---

[20] An unusual problem developed when the Soviet forces attempted to mop up the Paulus grouping. They met far more resistance than had been expected, and Vasilevsky's calculations were thrown badly out of balance. Later he discovered the reason. His intelligence had estimated that between 85,000 and 90,000 troops had been caught in the trap. The actual number was close to 300,000. (Vasilevsky, *Voyenno-Istoricheskii Zhurnal*, January, 1966, pp. 15–16.)   H.E.S.

evening Stalin called me and asked whether I was familiar with the latest reports from Stalingrad. I told him I was. He then asked me to give some thought to how we were to proceed with the liquidation of the trapped German forces.

The next morning I sent Stalin the following telegram:

The trapped German forces are not likely to try to break out without help from a relief force from the direction of Nizhne-Chirskaya and Kotelnikovo.

The German command will evidently attempt to hold its positions at Stalingrad, Vertyachi, Marinovka, Karpovka, and the state farm of Gornaya Polyana; and it will mass a relief force around Nizhne-Chirskaya and Kotelnikovo for a thrust through our forces in the direction of Karpovka to form a corridor to supply and eventually evacuate the trapped forces.

If the enemy succeeds, such a corridor could be formed between a line running through Marinovka, Lyapichev and Verkhne-Chirsky on the north and a line running through Tsebenko, Zety, Gnilovskaya and Shabalin on the southeast.

The following steps will be necessary to prevent the Nizhne-Chirskaya and Kotelnikovo groups from linking up with the Stalingrad group and forming the corridor:

The Nizhne-Chirskaya and Kotelnikovo groups must be thrown back as soon as possible and a strong defense line must be set up from Oblivskaya through Tormosin to Kotelnikovo. Two tank groups of at least one hundred tanks each should be held in reserve in the Nizhne-Chirskaya and Kotelnikovo areas.

The trapped Stalingrad group should be cut in half. This will require a thrust in the direction of Bolshaya Rossoshka and a counterthrust in the direction of Dubininsky and Hill 135. On all other sectors our forces should take up defensive positions and operate only in detachment strength to wear down and exhaust the enemy.

After the trapped group has been cut in half, the weaker part should be eliminated first, and only then should we strike with all forces against the Stalingrad group.

ZHUKOV

No. 02
November 29, 1942

After I had sent this message to Stalin, I discussed my proposals with Vasilevsky, who expressed agreement. We also discussed future operations on the Southwest Front. Vasilevsky agreed to postpone "Operation Great Saturn" for the time being, and to throw the forces of the Southwest Front against the flank of the enemy's Tormosin grouping. The General Staff also concurred.

The Southwest Front was given the assignment, under the code name "Little Saturn," of striking with the First Guards and Third Guards field armies and the Fifth Tank Army in the general direction of Morozovsk to smash the enemy forces in that area. The thrust was to be supported by the Sixth Army of the Voronezh Front, which would attack in the direction of Kantemirovka.

By this time the Nazi command was in acute need of reserves to rectify the catastrophic situation of its troops at Stalingrad and in the Caucasus.

To prevent the Germans from shifting forces from Army Group Center, Supreme Headquarters had decided to launch an offensive on the Western and Kalinin fronts against the Rzhev salient (as I stated earlier). Planning and preparations for the offensive were completed in the period from November 20 to December 8.

The following directive was issued to the fronts on December 8:

Enemy positions in the area of Rzhev, Sychevka, Olenino and Bely are to be crushed by January 1, 1943, by a joint offensive of the Kalinin and Western fronts, and their troops are to reach a new defense line running through Yarygino, Sychevka, Andreyevskoye, Lenino, Novoye Azhevo, Dentelevo and Svity.

The Western Front should be guided in its operations by the following:

(a) On December 10 and 11 enemy defenses are to be broken through between Bolshoye Kropotovo and Yarygino; Sychevka is to be seized December 15 at the latest. By December 20 at least two rifle divisions should be moved up into the area of Andreyevskoye and, with the Forty-first Army of the Kalinin Front, close a trap around the enemy.

(b) After our forces have broken through the enemy defenses and reached the railroad, the mobile forces of the front and at least four rifle divisions should turn northward to strike at the rear of the enemy group in the Rzhev-Chertolino area.

The Thirtieth Army should break through enemy defenses in the Koshkino sector, seize the road junction northeast of Burgovo and reach the railroad at Chertolino no later than December 15. There it should coordinate operations with the front's mobile forces, striking along the railroad toward Rzhev with the objective of seizing the town on December 23.

The Kalinin Front should be guided in its operations by the following:

(a) The Thirty-ninth and Twenty-second armies are to continue their offensive in the general direction of Olenino with the objective of destroying the enemy group at Olenino no later than December 16.

Part of the Twenty-second Army is to launch an auxiliary attack in the direction of Yegory with the objective of assisting the Forty-first Army in the elimination of the enemy grouping at Bely.

(b) The Forty-first Army is expected to stop the enemy breakthrough at Tsytsyno by December 10 and restore its initial positions near Okolitsa.

By December 20 at the latest, elements of the Forty-first Army should reach a line through Molnya, Vladimirskoye and Lenino to link up with elements of the Western Front and trap an enemy force from the south. Bely should be in our hands no later than December 20. . . .

SUPREME HEADQUARTERS
J. STALIN
G. ZHUKOV

No. 170700

This operation, to be conducted jointly by two fronts, was crucial in our attempt to eliminate the Rzhev salient, and I would like to dwell on it here.

The command of the Kalinin Front, headed by Lieutenant General M. A. Purkayev, handled its assignment well. Attacking south of Bely, its troops achieved a breakthrough and advanced in the direction of Sychevka. Troops of the Western Front were, in turn, supposed to break through and join up with the Kalinin Front to trap the enemy's forces at Rzhev. But the Western Front was unable to breach the enemy's defenses.

Stalin asked me to drive immediately to General Konev's headquarters, see what the problem was and, if possible, rectify the situation. When I reached the command center of the Western Front, I soon realized there was no point in repeating the operation. The enemy had evidently guessed our intentions and had massed substantial forces from other sectors in the threatened area.

At the same time the Kalinin Front forces that had achieved their breakthrough were also in trouble. The enemy had succeeded, by a strong thrust against the flanks of our forces, in cutting off and trapping a mechanized corps commanded by Major General M. D. Solomatin.

We called on the Supreme Headquarters reserve for an additional rifle corps to relieve the trapped forces. General Solomatin's corps held out for more than three days until on the fourth night the relief force of Siberian troops was able to reach his men and lead them back to our lines. The soldiers and officers of the trapped corps were so exhausted that they had to be sent to the rear for rest.

Even though our troops failed to eliminate the Rzhev salient, their offensive prevented the German command from moving large reinforcements from this sector to Stalingrad. In fact, the Nazi command had to bring up four additional tank divisions and one motorized division to hold its positions in the Rzhev-Vyazma area.

In reviewing the failure of our offensive on the Western

Front, we realized that we had underestimated the problems of the terrain chosen for our main thrust.

Experience tells us that if the enemy holds positions on easily observable terrain without natural cover against artillery fire, such positions can be readily smashed by artillery and mortar fire and a successful offensive can be assured.

But if enemy defenses are located on terrain that makes observation difficult and that provides good cover on the reverse sides of hills and in gullies running parallel to the front line, the defenses are not easily smashed by artillery and an offensive is likely to fail, especially when the use of tanks is restricted.

In this particular case we ignored the influence of the terrain, which provided excellent cover for the German defense on the reverse slopes of a highly dissected topography.

Another reason for our failure to achieve a breakthrough was an inadequate supply of tanks, artillery, mortars and air support.

However, let us go back to our operations around Stalingrad. Those operations, designed to liquidate the trapped forces, proceeded very slowly during the first half of December. The enemy, hoping for the relief that Hitler had promised, fought stubbornly for every position. Our troops around the ring, weakened by the diversion of some units to counter the relief force from Kotelnikovo, made little progress.

For the Germans, the defeat at Stalingrad threatened to grow into a catastrophe of great strategic magnitude. To save the situation, the Nazi command tried, first of all, to stabilize the front around Stalingrad so that Army Group A could be pulled out of the Caucasus.

With this objective in mind, the Germans formed a new Army Group Don under the command of Field Marshal Erich von Manstein. In the view of the Nazi leadership, he was the most suitable man for the task and one of the ablest of the German commanders. The new army group was formed out of units shifted from other sectors of the Soviet-German front as well as from France and Germany.

As we have now learned, Manstein planned to form two shock forces to try to relieve the forces trapped at Stalingrad. One force was to be assembled at Kotelnikovo and the other at Tormosin.

But fate did not smile upon either Manstein or the trapped forces. The Wehrmacht was suffering from an acute shortage of reserves, and whatever forces could be mobilized moved very slowly along the overextended communication lines. Moreover, our guerrillas were aware of the destination of the German troops that were being rushed southward, and they did their utmost to sabotage the enemy's movements. In spite of the Nazis' reprisals and their precautions, valiant patriots succeeded in derailing dozens of trains loaded with German troops.

Time passed and the massing of the German forces that were supposed to go to the relief of Stalingrad continued to be delayed. With a foreboding of impending catastrophe, Hitler ordered Manstein to start the operation without waiting for all his troops to arrive.

Manstein launched the offensive on December 12, driving along the railroad from Kotelnikovo. His striking force included the 6th and 23rd tank divisions, later joined by the 17th Tank Division, as well as a separate battalion of heavy Tiger tanks, four infantry divisions, several reinforcement units and two Rumanian cavalry divisions. Within three days the enemy succeeded in advancing twenty-five miles toward Stalingrad and forcing the Aksai-Yesaulovsky River.

Fierce fighting broke out near Verkhne-Kumsky, and both sides suffered heavy losses. The enemy kept pressing forward regardless of cost. But the Soviet forces, hardened by previous battles, stood fast on their defense lines. Only after the Germans had thrown their 17th Tank Division into the battle and sharply stepped up aerial bombings did elements of the Fifty-first Army and General Shapkin's cavalry corps retreat behind the Myshkova River.

At that point the enemy relief force was twenty-five miles from Stalingrad and victory evidently seemed quite real to the Germans. But their hopes were premature. On orders from Supreme Headquarters, Vasilevsky reinforced the Soviet troops on December 19 with General Malinovsky's Second Guards Army. This army, well equipped with tanks and artillery, finally tipped the balance in favor of the Soviet side.[21]

[21] The problem of coping with Manstein's attempt to rescue the beleaguered Paulus was not so simple as Zhukov makes it appear. General Vasilevsky heard of the Manstein offensive on the morning of December 12. He happened to be at headquarters of the Fifty-first Army at Verkhne-Tsaritsynsk with Nikita S. Khrushchev. He immediately perceived the danger. Unable to get through to Stalin, he telephoned Marshal Konstantin Rokossovsky at the Don Front and told him that he intended to divert the crack Second Guards Army of General Rodion Ya. Malinovsky from the Don Front to the Stalingrad Front to cope with Manstein. Rokossovsky protested bitterly, but Vasilevsky insisted that Malinovsky be prepared to move to meet Manstein as soon as the orders could be cleared with Stalin. Vasilevsky was unable to reach Stalin until the evening of December 12. Stalin was not at all pleased. He refused to authorize the transfer immediately, and the best Vasilevsky could get was a promise to "examine the question at a meeting of the State Defense Committee." Meanwhile, Stalin telephoned Rokossovsky, who continued to protest violently at being deprived of Malinovsky's crack forces. The argument apparently went on all night. Vasilevsky was on pins and needles. He feared that Manstein would develop enough momentum to break through and that the Stalingrad encirclement might fail. Finally at 5 A.M. on the morning of December 13 Stalin telephoned and agreed to shift the Second Guards Army over to the Stalingrad Front as of December 15 and let it be used to halt Manstein. It went into action December 19 and within two days had brought Manstein's effort to a halt. (Vasilevsky and Rokossovsky in *Stalingradskaya Epopeya,* Moscow, 1968, pp. 103–107, 172–173.) While Russian memoirists and historians do not mention the fact, the Soviets were greatly aided in coping with Manstein's thrust by Hitler's continued refusal to permit Paulus to attempt to break out or retreat. Thus Paulus did not strike westward to make contact with Manstein but remained fighting defensively inside the circle.   H.E.S.

Meanwhile, the Southwest Front, reinforced by the Sixth Army transferred from the Voronezh Front, had started its offensive on December 16, with the objective of smashing the German forces on the middle Don and driving into the rear of the enemy's Tormosin grouping. The attacking forces included the First Guards Army under General Kuznetsov, the Third Guards Army under General Lelyushenko (by that time the First Guards had been divided into two armies: the First Guards and the Third Guards), and the Sixth Army under Major General F. M. Kharitonov.

These forces overcame the Italian Eighth Army and developed a rapid advance in the direction of Morozovsk. The advance was led by the 24th and 25th tank corps and the 1st Guards Mechanized Corps. On the right the 17th and 18th tank corps drove in the direction of Millerovo.

Manstein intended to use his forces in the Tormosin area for a thrust toward Stalingrad, but the rapid advance of the Southwest Front compelled him to use them to counter the threat to the flank and rear of the entire Army Group Don.

In a telegraphic report to Supreme Headquarters on December 28, General Vatutin described the offensive as follows:

Everything that faced our front, i.e., about seventeen divisions, has been completely crushed and their stores have been seized by our forces. We have taken 60,000 prisoners and about the same number of the enemy have been killed, so that, with a few rare exceptions, the pitiful remains of these forces are not putting up any resistance. The enemy continues to stand fast along the line from Oblivskaya to Verkhne-Chirsky. In the area of Morozovsk we took prisoners of the 11th Tank Division and the 8th Airborne Division, which previously faced Romanenko's army. Lelyushenko's army and the mobile forces of our front are encountering the stiffest resistance from enemy units that crossed the Don River from the area of Kotelnikovo and moved up to a line running through Chernyshkovsky, Morozovsk, Skosyrskaya and Tatsinskaya. These enemy forces are attempting to hold that line to halt the further advance of our mobile forces and thus to enable other German forces to pull back; or the enemy may, under favorable circumstances, try to hold on to that salient altogether for a later thrust aimed at relieving the encircled group at Stalingrad. But it won't work. We will do everything in our power to cut off that salient.

General Vatutin's report continued:

Our aerial reconnaissance is reporting daily enemy troop arrivals in the areas of Rossosh, Starobelsk, Voroshilovgrad, Chebotovka, Kamensk, Likhaya and Zverevo. It is hard to judge the enemy's intentions, but he seems to be preparing the Northern Donets as the main line of defense. The enemy will first have to close the two-hundred-mile-wide gap torn in his defenses by our forces. . . . It would be good if we could maintain continuous pressure, but that would require reinforcements. Our present forces are all busy completing Operation Little Saturn, and additional forces would be required for Great Saturn.

Stalin and I replied:

Your first task is to get Badanov out of trouble and to rush Pavlov and Rusiyanov to his assistance. You were right in allowing Badanov to give up Tatsinskaya in an emergency. It would be well if your thrust against Tormosin with the 8th Cavalry Corps were supported by an additional infantry unit. As for the 3rd Cavalry Corps and one rifle division that have been sent through Suvorovsky toward Tormosin, that was very timely. We have already given you the 2nd and 23rd tank corps to convert Little Saturn into Great Saturn. In a week you will be getting two more tank corps and three or four rifle divisions. . . . We have some doubts about the 18th Tank Corps, which you want to send to Skosyrskaya . . . you'd better leave it and the 17th Tank Corps around Millerovo and Verkhne-Tarasovsky. You should bear in mind that over long distances tank corps are best launched in pairs rather than alone; otherwise they risk falling into a situation like Badanov's.

"Where is the 18th Tank Corps now?" Vatutin was asked.
"The 18th Tank Corps is just east of Millerovo. . . . The 18th won't be cut off."

"Just remember Badanov, don't forget Badanov, get him out at any cost."

"I will do everything possible to get Badanov out," Vatutin assured us.

The 24th Tank Corps under General V. M. Badanov distinguished itself particularly during the offensive of the Southwest Front. It advanced 125 miles in five days and seized Tatsinskaya, cutting the Likhaya-Stalingrad railroad. Badanov's corps was then cut off by superior enemy forces that had been shifted from Kotelnikovo and Tormosin. But his men kept their heads. They put up a stubborn defense, inflicting heavy losses on the enemy, and under their commander's skillful leadership they ultimately broke out of the trap. In view of its great contribution to the defeat of the enemy in the Volga-Don area, the 24th Corps was converted into the 2nd Guards Tank Corps, and its commander was the first in the country to be awarded the Order of Suvorov Second Class. Many of his soldiers, commanders and political commissars also received decorations.

The successful strikes of the Southwest and Stalingrad fronts against the enemy forces in the areas of Kotelnikovo and Morozovsk finally sealed the fate of Paulus' forces encircled at Stalingrad. Our troops, in a brilliant execution of their assignment, broke up Manstein's attempt to reach the trapped Germans.

By the beginning of January, Vatutin's forces had reached a line running through Novaya Kalitva, Krizskoye, Chertkovo, Voloshino, Millerovo and Morozovsk, thus posing a direct threat to all the German forces in the Caucasus.

By the end of December the German troops around Kotelnikovo pulled back to a line running through Tsimlyanskaya, Zhukovskaya, Dubovskoye and Zimovniki. The enemy's Tormosin group pulled back to a line through Chernyshkovsky, Loznoy and Tsimlyanskaya.

Manstein's attempt to break through our outer front and free the encircled forces at Stalingrad had thus failed. This was now clear to both the command and the soldiers of the trapped units. Despair and a desire to save themselves from inevitable catastrophe were widespread. Now that their hopes for relief had been frustrated, deep disappointment set in.

After the collapse of the breakout attempt, the Nazi military and political leadership ceased further efforts to save the trapped forces, and instead ordered them to hold out as long as possible so as to tie down Soviet forces. The Germans needed as much time as they could get to pull their forces out of the Caucasus and to shift troops from other areas in order to create a new front capable of halting our counteroffensive.

Supreme Headquarters in turn took measures to liquidate the encircled German troops as rapidly as possible and thus make additional Soviet forces available to move against the retreating enemy in the Caucasus and elsewhere in the south.

Stalin constantly prodded the front commanders. At the end of December in a meeting of the State Defense Committee, he proposed that operations to liquidate the trapped Germans be headed by a single commander. The two front commanders were beginning to get in each other's way. The other members of the Defense Committee agreed.

"Whom should we entrust with the final liquidation of the enemy?" Stalin asked.

Someone suggested Rokossovsky.

"Why aren't you saying anything?" Stalin asked me.

"In my opinion, either commander is capable of doing the job," I replied. "Yeremenko's feelings would be hurt, of course, if you transferred his Stalingrad Front to Rokossovsky."

"This is not the time to worry about hurt feelings," Stalin interjected. "Telephone Yeremenko and tell him about the decision of the State Defense Committee."

That same evening I called Yeremenko on the high-security line and said, "Andrei Ivanovich, the State Defense Committee has decided to charge Rokossovsky with the final liquidation of the enemy's Stalingrad group, and you are to transfer the Fifty-seventh, Sixty-fourth and Sixty-second armies from the Stalingrad Front to the Don Front."

"What brought this on?" Yeremenko asked.

I explained the considerations that had led to the decision.[22]

The headquarters of the Stalingrad Front was supposed to continue to head the forces operating in the direction of Kotelnikovo. Shortly thereafter the Stalingrad Front was renamed the Southern Front and went into operations against German forces in the Rostov area.

By a Supreme Headquarters directive dated December 30, the three armies of the Stalingrad Front were transferred to the Don Front. As of January 1 the Don Front thus had a total of 212,000 men, 6,500 guns and mortars, 250 tanks and 300 planes.

At the end of December Vasilevsky was mainly concerned with operations against German forces at Kotelnikovo, Tormosin and Morozovsk. General Voronov was appointed representative of Supreme Headquarters at the Don Front, and with the Front Military Council he drew up a plan for the final liquidation of the trapped enemy forces. After the plan had been submitted to Supreme Headquarters and the General Staff, the following directive was sent to General Voronov:

In the view of Supreme Headquarters, your main task in the first phase of the operation should be the cutting off and destruction of the western enemy grouping around Kravtsov, Baburkino, Marinovka and Karpovka. This should be achieved by directing the main thrust of our forces southward from the area of Dmitriyevka, State Farm No. 1 and Baburkino toward Karpovka station, and an auxil-

[22] Yeremenko was justly incensed at the decision. "It was completely unexpected," he recalled later. "Ordinarily such a decision (to change the basic task of a front or to reorganize it) is carried out with the agreement of the front commander; or in any case the opinion of the commander and his Military Council is requested. In this instance we were simply suddenly ordered to fulfill the order of the Supreme Commander." (A. I. Yeremenko, *Stalingrad*, Moscow, 1961, p. 426.)   H.E.S.

iary thrust by the Fifty-seventh Army out of the area of Kravtsov and Sklyarov for a link-up of the two thrusts around Karpovka station.

In addition, the Sixty-sixth Army should strike through Orlovka in the direction of the settlement of Krasny Oktyabr and join up with a thrust of the Sixty-second Army that would cut off enemy forces in the factory district from the main grouping in the city.

Supreme Headquarters instructs you to revise the plan accordingly. The time set by you for the start of the operation is herewith approved. The first phase should be completed within five or six days.

Submit an operations plan for the second phase through the General Staff by January 9, taking account of the results of the first phase.

J. STALIN
G. ZHUKOV

No. 170718
December 28, 1942

In January the troops of the Southwest and Stalingrad fronts rolled back the outer front in the Don area by 125 to 150 miles to the west. The situation of the enemy forces caught in the ring greatly deteriorated. They had no prospects of being relieved. Their supplies were nearing exhaustion. Soldiers were put on a hunger ration. Their field hospitals were filled to capacity. Mortality from wounds and disease rose sharply. The inevitable catastrophe was at hand.

In an effort to put an end to the bloodletting, Supreme Headquarters ordered the Don Front commander to give the Sixth Army an ultimatum to surrender under generally accepted conditions. The Nazi command rejected our ultimatum and ordered the soldiers to fight to the last bullet while promising relief that the German troops knew would not come.

On January 10, after a powerful artillery softening-up, the Don Front began an offensive to cut up and destroy the enemy grouping piecemeal, but our forces did not achieve complete success.

A second offensive began on January 22 after additional preparation. This time the enemy was unable to withstand the blow and began to pull back.

In his memoirs, an intelligence officer of Paulus' Sixth Army gives the following description of the retreat of the German forces: "We were compelled to pull back along the entire front. . . . However, the retreat turned into flight. . . . In some places panic broke out. . . . Our route was strewn with corpses that the snow soon covered as if in compassion. . . . By now we were retreating without orders."

And he goes on:

"In a race with death, which had no trouble catching up with us and was wrenching its victims out of our ranks in great batches, the army was increasingly pressed into a narrow corner of hell."[23]

On January 31 the southern group of German forces finally gave up, and its remnants, led by Field Marshal Paulus, the Sixth Army commander, surrendered to our forces.[24] Remnants

---

[23] Wieder, *Stalingrad*.

[24] Rokossovsky described Paulus' surrender as follows:

"Troops of the Sixty-fourth, Fifty-seventh and Twenty-first armies proceeded to the liquidation of the southern [Nazi] group, delivering blows from the southwest and northwest and compelling the enemy to lay down his arms on January 31. Field Marshal Paulus was taken prisoner with his staff, and he was at once brought to us at staff headquarters.

"Marshal N. N. Voronov and an interpreter and I were in the building to which von Paulus was brought. The room was lighted by electricity, and we were sitting at a small table. I awaited this meeting with interest. At last the door opened and the duty officer reported the arrival of the Field Marshal and ushered him into the room. We saw a tall, thin, well-knit man in the field uniform of a general standing stiffly before us.

"His manner betrayed great tension which he could not conceal. A tic contorted his face, and he was obviously upset. It was apparent he was expecting something frightful to happen. This was painful to observe, and, glancing at Marshal Voronov, I invited Paulus with a quiet gesture to sit at the table. Looking to right and left, he timidly sat down. There were cigars and cigarettes on the table. I was smoking, and I invited Paulus

of the northern group followed on February 2. This marked the end of the great battle on the Volga, which had such a disastrous conclusion for this huge grouping of Nazi and satellite forces.

The Battle for Stalingrad was extremely fierce, and I personally can compare it only with the Battle for Moscow. From November 19 to February 2 we destroyed 32 divisions and 3 brigades, and the remaining 16 divisions in the German forces lost 50 to 75 percent of their strength.

Total enemy losses in the entire region of the Don, the Volga and Stalingrad amounted to 1.5 million men, 3,500 tanks and self-propelled guns, 12,000 guns and mortars, 3,000 planes and large amounts of other equipment. Losses of such magnitude had a disastrous effect on the general strategic situation and shook the entire military machine of Nazi Germany to its foundations.

Our victory at Stalingrad marked a turning point in the war in favor of the Soviet Union and the beginning of the expulsion of enemy forces from our territory.

It was a long-awaited and glorious victory not only for our forces, who had taken direct part in the defeat of the enemy, but for the entire Soviet people, who had labored day and night to provide the front with everything it needed. The loyal sons of Russia, the Ukraine, Byelorussia, the Baltic, the Caucasus, Kazakhstan and Central Asia won immortal glory by their steadfastness and mass heroism.

Officers and generals of the German forces as well as the German people themselves began to display increasingly hostile feelings toward both Hitler and the entire Nazi leadership. The

---

to do the same. He promptly did so and just as promptly drank a glass of strong hot tea, but because of his feverish state the twitching of his face and the shaking of his hands did not stop. To the very end of our conversation he was unable to bring himself fully under control." (Rokossovsky in *Stalingradskaya Epopeya*, Moscow, 1968, p. 186.)   H.E.S.

German people began to realize that Hitler and his associates had drawn the nation into an obvious adventure and that the promised victories had expired with their forces in the disaster on the Don and the Volga and in the Northern Caucasus.

"The defeat at Stalingrad threw a scare into both the German people and its army," General Westphal wrote. "Never before in the history of Germany had such a large number of troops suffered such a terrible fate."

The crushing of the German, Italian, Hungarian and Rumanian forces on the Volga and the Don also greatly reduced Germany's prestige among her allies. It gave rise to arguments and friction, a loss of confidence in the Nazi leadership, and a desire on the part of the satellites to extricate themselves from the war into which Hitler had drawn them.

The Soviet victory also had a sobering effect on neutral countries and on countries that had adopted waiting tactics and compelled them to acknowledge the great power of the Soviet Union and the inevitable defeat of Nazi Germany.

Everyone recalls the wave of delight that swept over the world at the news of the German defeat at Stalingrad, inspiring the occupied nations to continued resistance.

The defense of Stalingrad, the preparation of the counteroffensive and my contribution to the other operations in the south also meant a great deal to me. They represented much broader experience in the organization of a counteroffensive than I had had in 1941 during the Battle of Moscow, where the forces at our disposal were inadequate to trap the enemy forces.

For general supervision of the counteroffensive at Stalingrad and its results, I was among those awarded the Order of Suvorov First Class. The award of the first of these orders signified not only a great honor for me but was a symbol of the country's expectation that I would do even more to bring the hour of complete victory nearer. Vasilevsky received the second of the orders, and others who were awarded the Order of Suvorov

First Class were Voronov, Vatutin, Yeremenko and Rokossovsky. A large number of generals, officers, sergeants and soldiers also received high decorations.[25]

The defeat of the German forces at Stalingrad, on the Don and in the Caucasus created conditions favorable for expanding our offensive on all fronts in the southwest.

Operations in the Don-Volga area were followed by the successful Ostrogozhsk-Rossosh and Voronezh-Kastornoye operations. Soviet forces, pressing on toward the west with their winter offensive, captured Rostov, Novocherkassk, Kursk, Kharkov and several other key places. The over-all operational and strategic situation of the Nazi troops deteriorated along the entire Soviet-German front. The Soviet people, inspired by these historic victories of our forces, took energetic measures to provide the Red Army with even better arms and equipment for complete victory over Nazi Germany.

[25] On February 4 Rokossovsky and Voronov were called back to Moscow. When they arrived at the Moscow airport, Rokossovsky looked out the window and saw a group of generals and officers assembled to greet them. "On their shoulders shone dazzling gold epaulets," Rokossovsky recalled. "It was quite a surprise to us. I turned to Voronov and said, 'Look! What have we stumbled into?' He was equally surprised, but we soon recognized the familiar faces and figures of our fellow workers on the General Staff and Supreme Command. Everything became clear. Epaulets had been introduced into the Red Army, and we hadn't heard about it." The two officers went to the Kremlin and were ushered into Stalin's office. "We saw him standing on the other side of the room behind his desk," Rokossovsky said. "He came forward quickly to meet us. Before we could begin our report on developments he shook our hands and congratulated us on the successful completion of the operation to liquidate the enemy groupings. It was evident that Stalin was satisfied with the course of events and didn't hesitate to show it." (Rokossovsky in *Stalingradskaya Epopeya*, Moscow, 1968, pp. 189–190.)   H.E.S.

The Battle of

KURSK

JULY–AUGUST, 1943

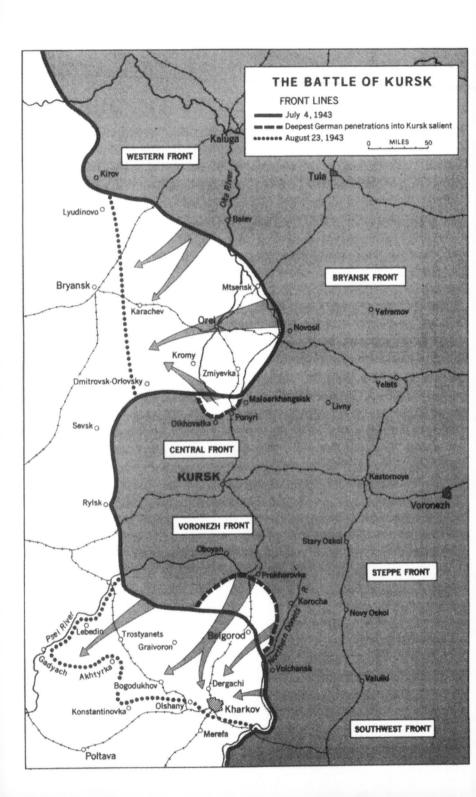

THE BATTLE OF KURSK

FRONT LINES
July 4, 1943
Deepest German penetrations into Kursk salient
August 23, 1943

0   MILES   50

WESTERN FRONT

Kaluga

Tula

Kirov

Lyudinovo

Ofa River

Belev

BRYANSK FRONT

Yefremov

Bryansk

Mtsensk

Novosil

Karachev

Orel

Kromy

Zmiyevka

Yelets

Dmitrovsk-Orlovsky

Maloarkhangelsk

Livny

Olkhovatka

Ponyri

Sevsk

CENTRAL FRONT

KURSK

Kastornoye

Rylsk

Voronezh

VORONEZH FRONT

Stary Oskol

Oboyan

STEPPE FRONT

Prokhorovka

Korocha

Novy Oskol

Psel River

Lebedin

Trostyanets

Belgorod

Graivoron

Gadyach

Akhtyrka

Volchansk

Valuiki

Bogodukhov

Dergachi

Konstantinovka

Olshany

Kharkov

Merefa

SOUTHWEST FRONT

Poltava

Editor's Note

After Stalingrad everything was different. After Stalingrad the Russians knew they were going to win the war and the Germans (except for Hitler) strongly suspected they might lose.

It was different for Zhukov, too. His relations with Stalin had stabilized into a state of as nearly mutual confidence as was ever likely to be possible with the suspicion-prone dictator. By this time Stalin himself had evolved an orderly, self-confident style of conducting the war. He was relying, more and more, on the experienced and brilliant pleiad of military commanders which the war itself had produced. The erratic interference of police generals like Kulik and Mekhlis was much less apparent. The General Staff under Vasilevsky's expert leadership was working very efficiently, particularly with the arrival in December, 1942, of General A. I. Antonov as Vasilevsky's deputy.

As Zhukov had foreseen, the staggering defeat of the Germans at Stalingrad had compelled them to pull back sharply. But the German strength, while dented, was still massive. They held firmly to the Ukraine, the Crimea, the important Donets industrial basin, most of Central Russia, the northeastern regions and the Baltic states. Their armies still stood within cannon range of Leningrad, and they possessed deep and valuable salients thrusting toward Moscow. The year was 1943, and the fighting in North Africa had not yet been concluded. The Germans stood astride all Europe, with the industries, resources and manpower of the whole continent at their disposal. The United States had turned the tide in the Pacific, but the defeat of Japan would require thousands of miles of fighting and thousands of casualties.

The war, in a word, was in mid-course. The outcome might be

predictable, but the Germans were far from beaten. They were a resolute, powerful, dangerous foe.

Zhukov had emerged from Stalingrad in the role of Stalin's deputy in the conduct of the war. He was now constantly on the move in his capacity of Deputy Supreme Commander in Chief, traveling from front to front, then back to Moscow, hammering out the strategy and tactics of the major phases of the conflict.

The question that was posed in the spring of 1943 was where the next great battle would take place and under what conditions. Zhukov became convinced very early in the spring—indeed, possibly as early as late winter—that the next major engagement would be fought on the Central Front and almost certainly in the area of Kursk and Voronezh. He came to this conclusion on the basis of the staggering losses suffered by the Germans at Stalingrad. They no longer, in his opinion, possessed the means to mount a major offensive at the far reaches of the Soviet front, that is, in the lower Don, Volga and North Caucasus area. They did not have groupings of armies sufficient to carry on a major offensive in the north around Leningrad, nor would this, in his view, offer them the military and political advantages which they needed to counteract the effects of Stalingrad.

Thus, all signs pointed to the Kursk area. Here were the main Nazi concentrations. Here a success would not only secure the German hold on the Soviet areas to the south, but might even once again open the way to Moscow. It would defeat major Soviet forces; and here alone the Germans might regain the strategic initiative lost with von Paulus' defeat on the lower Volga.

Zhukov's assessment of German plans and intentions proved remarkably exact. As the spring wore on, it became apparent that the Germans were preparing an offensive almost precisely as Zhukov had divined. The question on the Soviet side was how to react: should the Russians strike first or should they wait for the Nazi blow and strike back once the German force was spent?

Zhukov, following the principles of his battles of Moscow and Stalingrad, proposed to let the Germans strike first. Then he would grind them down and with powerful, previously concentrated forces strike back, inflicting a defeat of such magnitude that Germany's future ability to regain the initiative in the east would be destroyed.

Zhukov's arguments won the day—but not without much discussion. Stalin was still fearful of the Nazi striking power. As the moment of engagement neared, he became even more fearful. But Zhukov's strategy was victorious. The battle opened as he had anticipated, and he won it in his own way. It was probably the greatest battle of World War II—certainly the greatest armored engagement. More than six thousand tanks on both sides were brought into action. The defeat of the Germans was so appalling that never again were they able to seize the strategic initiative on the Eastern Front. It was the first time the Nazis used their powerful Tiger tanks and Ferdinand self-propelled guns on a mass scale. The Russian armor proved superior. There were more than two million men involved in the engagement on both sides. The Nazi losses were estimated by the Russians at half a million men. Probably the Soviet losses were close to that figure, but by this time the Russians could take this kind of loss and go forward. The Germans could not.

As a battle the Kursk engagement was enormously complex, but in principle it followed the well-known Zhukov lines.

He permitted the Germans to open the attack on July 5. Soviet intelligence was excellent. The Germans were allowed to tip their hand and move forward, and then, with characteristic swiftness, the Russians went over to the attack on July 12. This offensive differed from those at Moscow and Stalingrad. It had been prepared in advance. Everything was ready to go. When the Russians hit, it was with sledge-hammer force.

The results were devastating. The Germans staggered back with crippling losses. Within a few days it was apparent that they had been dealt a blow so savage that they would never be able completely to recover.

So confident were the Russians of their success that Zhukov had already begun to plan the offensives to follow—drives to free Kharkov, to liberate the Donets Basin, to begin the massive task of expelling the Germans finally from Soviet territory. It all went as Zhukov had foreseen.

Not that the engagement did not give rise to controversy and dispute. No battle of this magnitude could fail to produce arguments. There were those who held that the Russians suffered losses not commensurate with their gains, that a strategy different from Zhukov's could have defeated the Germans and spared Russian lives. But Zhukov was never a commander who questioned the cost in human lives if his military aim could be achieved.

Remarkably, this tremendous battle, which irrevocably turned the tide of war against the Germans, is almost unknown in the West. Its significance, however, was clear to Stalin from the beginning. When the official Order of the Day hailing the Kursk victory was submitted to him for signature July 24, 1943, he personally revised the last sentence of the draft communiqué, which read: "Thus the German plan for a summer offensive must be considered fully disrupted."

Stalin dictated this substitute: "Thus has been exploded the legend that the German summer offensives are always successful and that the Soviet forces are always compelled to retreat."

"We must say this," he added, "because the Germans, headed by Goebbels, have been making such a claim ever since their winter defeat at Moscow."

Then, twelve days later, when the advancing Soviet forces recaptured Orel and Belgorod, Stalin had another idea.

"Do you remember how in ancient times when troops won victories they rang the church bells in honor of the soldiers and their leaders?" he said. He proposed a modern substitute—

artillery salutes. That night for the first time there rang out over the Kremlin twelve salvos from 124 guns. The number was fixed by the fact that there happened to be 124 guns in firing order on the Kremlin grounds that night. The end of the war was marked by the firing of the 355th victory salute, of which that in honor of Orel and Belgorod, August 5, 1943, had been the first.

Some Soviet military historians call Kursk "the Nazi Waterloo." The designation does not seem inappropriate.

H.E.S.

11

Spring, 1943

The battle of the Kursk salient was one of the biggest and most decisive events of World War II. A major result of that battle was the final assumption of the strategic initiative by the Soviet armed forces. In the fighting for Orel, Belgorod and Kharkov, devastating blows were inflicted on the Nazi military machine, forcing the German Fascist command to give up its offensive strategy and go over to a strategic defense once and for all.

Interest in the battle of the Kursk salient continues to be strong. What was the situation in the summer of 1943 and how did it figure in the plans of the two sides? What did the Kursk battle contribute to the science of Soviet military art? These and other aspects require thorough study. In my capacity of first deputy to the Supreme Commander in Chief (a post I assumed in August, 1942), I took direct part in the planning of the battle and in the coordination of front operations in the area of the Kursk salient both during the period of defense and during our counteroffensive.

In the following account, I have concentrated on those aspects that have not been adequately discussed in the literature thus far.

After the defeat of the German, Rumanian, Italian and Hungarian forces on the Volga River, the Don River and in the Northern Caucasus, in the middle of March the enemy, suffering tremendous losses, pulled back to a line running through Sevsk, Rylsk, Sumy, Akhtyrka, Krasnograd, Slavyansk, Lisichansk and Taganrog. By March 15 a quiet period had set in on most fronts, with fierce fighting continuing only in some sectors of the Voronezh, Southwest and Southern fronts and in the Kuban Plain.

To prevent further deterioration of the position of its troops on the southern wing of the front, the German High Command, after regrouping its forces, had launched a counteroffensive against the Southwest Front in the second half of February. Its objectives were to throw the Soviet forces back beyond the Northern Donets River, set up a defense line along the Donets, and then strike at the forces of the Voronezh Front with the aim of seizing Kharkov and Belgorod. As we now know from captured documents, the Nazi command hoped that, under favorable conditions, it would be able to expand the operation and eliminate the Kursk salient.

In the early spring of 1943 I was on the Northwest Front, which was then commanded by Marshal S. K. Timoshenko. The troops of that front were engaged in fierce fighting in an attempt to eliminate the Demyansk bridgehead east of Staraya Russa. Our forces had reached the Lovat River and were preparing to cross it.

I don't recall the exact date, though I think it was March 13 or 14, when Stalin telephoned me at Northwest Front headquarters.

I reported to him about the situation on the Lovat line, and then explained that because the unusually early spring had made it difficult to cross the river the troops of the Northwest Front might have to halt their offensive temporarily. Stalin agreed with this assessment. He asked me a few other questions about future prospects on the Northwest Front, and then concluded: "Come back to Supreme Headquarters. We have to discuss the situation on the Southwest and Voronezh fronts. You may have to visit the Kharkov area."

I got back to Moscow late that evening. When I telephoned the Kremlin, I learned that Stalin had assembled a large group to discuss problems of fuel for the iron and steel industry, electric power, and aircraft and tank production. The Chief had left orders for me to join the conference as soon as I reached Moscow. After grabbing a quick bite, I drove to the Kremlin.

In Stalin's office I found members of the Politburo, ministers and the designers and directors of several major plants. It was clear from the reports that were being made that industry was still operating under great difficulties, including problems in the crucial aircraft, tank, artillery and munitions plants. The promised Lend-Lease aid from the United States was slow arriving.

The meeting lasted until three in the morning. After everyone had left, Stalin asked me, "Have you had dinner?"

"No," I said.

"In that case, come over to my place, and we can discuss the bad Kharkov situation immediately."

While we were having dinner, an officer from the General Staff brought us a situation map of the Voronezh and Southwest fronts. The staff officer, who was responsible for the Voronezh Front, reported that the situation had greatly deteriorated, especially southwest of Kharkov. Enemy forces had also launched an offensive near Poltava and Krasnograd, pressing our forces and producing a serious situation at the junction of two of our fronts.

We finished our dinner, or rather breakfast, around 5 A.M. Two hours later I was at the Central Airport ready to board a plane for the command center of the Voronezh Front. I was supposed to find out what the situation was and take appropriate measures on the spot. As soon as I had taken my seat in the plane, I fell asleep and did not wake up until we landed.

That same day I spoke with the Supreme Commander in Chief over the high-security line and described the situation on the Voronezh Front. After having seized Kharkov, enemy forces were continuing to advance without any particular opposition in the direction of Belgorod. They had already taken Kazachya Lopan.

"It is essential," I told Stalin, "that we move up all we can from the Supreme Headquarters reserve and from neighboring fronts. Otherwise the Germans will take Belgorod and push on toward Kursk."

An hour later I learned from a conversation with A. M. Vasilevsky, Chief of the General Staff, that Stalin had already issued orders to transfer the Twenty-first and Sixty-fourth armies and the First Tank Army to the Belgorod area. The tank army was to be held in reserve.

On March 18 German tanks tore into Belgorod, but they were unable to advance farther to the north. General N. D. Kozin, commander of the 52nd Guards Division, informed me that General I. M. Chistyakov, Twenty-first Army commander, had sent an advanced detachment under Lieutenant Colonel G. G. Pentyukhov, commander of the 155th Guards Rifle Regiment, toward Belgorod with the objective of engaging the enemy and capturing prisoners. The detachment ambushed the enemy's Death's Head Tank Division near Shapino, north of Belgorod, and took prisoners. We thus learned that the Germans were heading toward Oboyan.

By late that day we had positioned the main force of the 52nd Guards Rifle Division north of Belgorod, and the enemy was totally unable to dislodge the guardsmen from their defense line.

By March 20–21 the main forces of the Twenty-first Army had organized a strong defense north of Belgorod, and parts of the First Tank Army were massed in reserve south of Oboyan. At the end of March the enemy made repeated, unsuccessful attempts to break through our defenses near Belgorod and along the Northern Donets River, where the Sixty-fourth Army was deployed. After suffering heavy losses, the German troops began to fortify their lines. From that time on, the situation in the Kursk salient stabilized as both sides prepared for the decisive battle.

In an effort to strengthen the command of the Voronezh Front, Stalin appointed General N. F. Vatutin the new front commander. With his characteristic energy Vatutin immediately got to work creating a deep defense system.

He and I visited almost all the front units at the end of March and in early April, assisting commanders in assessing the situation, explaining their objectives and how best they could achieve them if the enemy launched an offensive. I was especially concerned about the situation in the 52nd Guards Rifle Division, whose sector I visited twice during this period. I felt that this division would have to take the main brunt of an attack. Vatutin and the army commander, General Chistyakov, agreed with me, and we decided to strengthen that sector with artillery as much as we could.

By agreement with Marshal Vasilevsky and the front commanders, the General Staff took a number of steps to obtain excellent intelligence on the sectors of the Central, Voronezh and Southwest fronts. Vasilevsky issued appropriate orders to front headquarters and other agencies to obtain information on the availability and location of reserves in the enemy's rear and on troop concentration areas where forces transferred from France, Germany and other countries were being massed.

Each of the front commands also undertook systematic aerial and ground reconnaissance. By early April we had obtained rather full information on enemy forces near Orel, Sumy, Belgorod and Kharkov. Having analyzed and discussed the intelligence with the commanders of the Voronezh and Central fronts, and then with Vasilevsky over the direct line, I sent the Supreme Commander in Chief the following report on April 8:

COMRADE VASILYEV [Stalin's code name]:
5:30 A.M., April 8, 1943

Herewith is my report on possible enemy operations in the spring and summer of 1943 and my conclusions about our defensive operations during the immediate future:

1. Having suffered heavy losses during the winter campaign of 1942–43, the enemy will apparently not be able to assemble sufficiently large reserves by spring to renew his advance into the Caucasus and toward the Volga River in an attempt to outflank Moscow in a deep-ranging maneuver.

In view of the lack of large reserves, the enemy will have to limit his offensive in the spring and first half of summer of 1943 to a narrower front. He will have to make his plans as he moves, stage by stage, with the ultimate objective of seizing Moscow in 1943.

Given the enemy's present disposition of forces opposite our Central, Voronezh and Southwest fronts, I hold that he will direct his principal offensive operations against these three fronts, hoping to defeat our forces in this area and thus achieve enough room for maneuver to outflank Moscow closer to the city.

2. In the first stage the enemy will apparently attempt to mass maximum force, including up to thirteen or fifteen tank divisions with a great amount of air support, and strike with his Orel-Kromy group to by-pass Kursk on the northeast and with his Belgorod-Kharkov group to by-pass Kursk on the southeast. An auxiliary strike, aimed at cutting up our front, may be expected from the west near Vorozhba, between the Seim and Psel rivers, directed against Kursk from the southwest.

With this attack the enemy would try to surround our Thirteenth, Seventieth, Sixty-fifth, Sixtieth, Thirty-Eighth, Fortieth and Twenty-first armies. The ultimate objective of this stage would be a line running through the Korocha River, the town of Korocha, the town of Tim, the Tim River and Droskovo.

3. In the second stage, the enemy is likely to strike against the

flank and rear of the Southwest Front in the general direction of Valuiki and Urazovo. He may try to join this drive with another strike from the area of Lisichansk northward toward Svatovo and Urazovo. Elsewhere the enemy may be expected to drive toward a line through Livny, Kastornoye, Stary Oskol and Novy Oskol.

4. In the third stage, after appropriate regrouping, the enemy may attempt to reach a line running through Liski, Voronezh and Yelets and, having covered his southeast flank, he may try to outflank Moscow through Ranenburg, Ryazhsk and Ryazan.

5. We can expect the enemy to put greatest reliance in this year's offensive operations on his tank divisions and air force since his infantry appears to be far less prepared for offensive operations than last year. Opposite the Central and Voronezh fronts, the enemy has now up to 12 tank divisions, so that, by moving 3 or 4 additional tank divisions from other sectors, he may throw as many as 15 or 16 tank divisions with a combined strength of 2,500 tanks against our Kursk grouping.

6. In view of this threat, we should strengthen the antitank defenses of the Central and Voronezh fronts, assemble as soon as possible 30 antitank artillery regiments in the Supreme Headquarters reserve for use in threatened sectors, concentrate all self-propelled artillery regiments along the line through Livny, Kastornoye and Stary Oskol [in the rear], placing some of the regiments immediately at the disposal of Rokossovsky and Vatutin, and concentrate as much air strength as possible in the Supreme Headquarters reserve so that massed air attacks in conjunction with tanks and rifle units can strike at the enemy's shock forces and thus disrupt his offensive plans.

I am not familiar with the final disposition of our operational reserves, but in my view they should be assembled in the areas of Yefremov, Livny, Kastornoye, Novy Oskol, Valuiki, Rossosh, Liski, Voronezh and Yelets, with most of the reserves concentrated around Yelets and Voronezh. Deeper reserves should be positioned at Ryazhsk, Ranenburg, Michurinsk and Tambov. One reserve army should be stationed in the area of Tula and Stalinogorsk.

I consider it unwise to launch a preventive attack in the next few days. It would be better if we first wore the enemy down with our defenses and destroyed his tanks, and only then, after having moved up fresh reserves, went over to a general offensive and finally destroyed his main force.

KONSTANTINOV [my code name]

On April 9 or 10, I do not recall exactly which, Marshal Vasilevsky arrived at Voronezh Front headquarters. He and I went over the details of my report and discussed the disposition of operational and strategic reserves and the character of the impending operations. There were no differences of opinion between us. We drafted a Supreme Headquarters directive about the disposition of reserves and the creation of a new Steppe Front [in the rear of the Kursk salient], and sent it to the Supreme Commander in Chief for his signature. The document specified the location of armies and front reinforcements. Headquarters of the new Steppe Front was to be established at Novy Oskol, the front's command center at Korocha and its auxiliary control center at Veliki Burluk. The commanders and headquarters staffs of all fronts were requested to give the General Staff their views about the impending operations. These recommendations soon started coming in.

On April 10 the following report was addressed to the General Staff by General Malinin, Chief of Staff of the Central Front:

FROM THE CENTRAL FRONT   April 10, 1943
To COL. GEN. ANTONOV, CHIEF OF OPERATIONS
   OF THE GENERAL STAFF OF THE RED ARMY
   In reply to No. 11,990:
   . . . 4. Objective and most likely directions of an enemy offensive in the spring-summer period of 1943:
   (a) In view of the distribution of forces and especially in view of the results of the offensive operations of 1941–42, we can expect the enemy to limit his offensive in the spring and summer of 1943 to the Kursk-Voronezh operational direction. Enemy offensives on other sectors are unlikely. In view of the general strategic situation at this stage of the war, the Germans would find it to their ad-

vantage to consolidate their hold over the Crimea, the Donets Basin and the Ukraine, and this would require advancing their line to Shterovka, Starobelsk, Rovenki, Liski, Voronezh, Livny and Novosil. To achieve this objective, the enemy will require at least sixty infantry divisions with air, tank and artillery support. The enemy has these forces at his disposal in this particular direction. That is why the Kursk-Voronezh operational direction assumes such importance.

(b) Based on these operational suppositions, we can expect the enemy to strike with his main force simultaneously along outer and inner operational radii:

(1) Along the inner radius from Orel through Livny toward Kastornoye and from Belgorod through Oboyan toward Kursk.

(2) Along the outer radius from Orel through Kromy toward Kursk and from Belgorod through Stary Oskol toward Kastornoye.

(c) Unless we take counteraction, the enemy's success in these operations may result in the defeat of the forces of the Central and Voronezh fronts and the seizure of the Orel-Kursk-Kharkov railroad and put him along the line required to insure firm control over the Crimea, the Donets Basin and the Ukraine.

(d) Soon after the end of the spring thaw and floods the enemy may start to regroup his forces and concentrate them for an offensive in these directions and create the needed reserves. The offensive can therefore be expected roughly in the second half of May.

5. In view of this operational situation, I would recommend the following steps:

(a) The combined forces of the Western, Bryansk and Central fronts should strike at the enemy's grouping around Orel and thus prevent his offensive from Orel through Livny toward Kastornoye, seize the Mtsensk–Orel–Kursk railroad, which is so essential to us, and deprive the enemy of the use of the Bryansk rail and road junction;

(b) this will require reinforcing the Central and Voronezh fronts with air support, especially fighters, and with at least ten antitank artillery regiments per front;

(c) for that purpose strong Supreme Headquarters reserves should also be located in the areas of Livny, Kastornoye, Liski, Voronezh and Yelets.

LIEUTENANT GENERAL MALININ,
Chief of Staff, Central Front

No. 4203

The Voronezh Front command also made its recommendations to the General Staff:

TO THE CHIEF OF GENERAL STAFF   April 12, 1943
OF THE RED ARMY

The forces now facing the Voronezh Front are as follows:

1. Nine front-line infantry divisions (26th, 68th, 323rd, 75th, 255th, 57th, 332nd, 167th and one unidentified division). These divisions hold a line through Krasno-Oktyabrskoye, Bolshaya Chernetchina, Krasnopolye and Kazatskoye. According to prisoner interrogations the unidentified division is moving toward Soldatskoye and is supposed to replace the 332nd. This information is being checked. According to unverified information, the second echelon is made up of six infantry divisions. Their location has not been established, and this information is being checked. Our radio intelligence has detected the headquarters of a Hungarian division near Kharkov, and this division may be moved up to a secondary sector.

2. Six tank divisions (the Greater Germany, the Adolf Hitler, the Death's Head, the Reich, the 6th and 11th), including three front-line divisions and three (Greater Germany, 6th and 11th) in the second line. According to our radio intelligence, headquarters of the 17th Tank Division is being moved from Alekseyevskoye to Taranovka, suggesting a northward shift of the entire division. Judging from the disposition of forces, the enemy would be able to move up three additional tank divisions from the Southwest Front sector to the Belgorod area.

3. We can thus expect the enemy along the Voronezh Front to mass a striking force of as many as 10 tank divisions and at least 6 infantry divisions, or a total of 1,500 tanks, with concentrations around Borisovka, Belgorod, Murom, and Kazachya Lopan. That strike force may have strong air support by roughly 500 bombers and at least 300 fighters.

The enemy's intentions would be to strike concentric blows from the Belgorod area toward the northeast and from the Orel area toward the southeast with the objective of encircling our forces west of the Belgorod-Kursk line. Subsequently we can expect the enemy to strike southeast at the flank and rear of the Southwest Front to be able to move northward later.

However, there is a possibility that the enemy may not move southeastward this year and will instead adopt another plan calling for an offensive northeastward to by-pass Moscow after the concentric strikes out of the areas of Belgorod and Orel. We must keep this possibility in mind and prepare reserves accordingly.

To sum up, the enemy along the Voronezh Front is most likely to strike his main blow out of the area of Borisovka and Belgorod toward Stary Oskol, directing part of his forces toward Oboyan and Kursk. The enemy is not yet ready for a major offensive. The start of such an offensive should not be expected before April 20, and is more likely in the first few days of May. However, isolated attacks can be expected at any time, and our troops must be constantly on the alert.

> FEDOROV [Vatutin's code name]
> NIKITIN [Khrushchev's code name]
> FEDOTOV [code name of F. K. Kor-
> zhenevich, Chief of Staff]

No. 55/k.

In other words, as of April 8–12 Supreme Headquarters had not yet arrived at a concrete plan of action for our forces in the area of the Kursk salient for the spring-summer period of 1943. No offensive out of the Kursk area was being planned at that time because our strategic reserves were still in the process of being formed and the Voronezh and Central fronts, having suffered losses in previous fighting, required reinforcements in manpower, arms and equipment. In accordance with that situation, the front commanders received orders from Supreme Headquarters to prepare their fronts for defense.

12

The Plans for Kursk

Stalin telephoned me April 10 at Bobyshevo (Voronezh Front headquarters) and asked me to return to Moscow the following day to discuss plans for the spring-summer campaign of 1943, especially in the Kursk salient.

I was back in Moscow on the evening of April 11.

Vasilevsky told me that Stalin had asked that we have ready a situation map and the necessary calculations and recommendations by the following evening.

All day on April 12, Vasilevsky, Antonov and I worked on the materials for the conference. We got to work early in the morning and, since we were in complete agreement, we were ready by evening. General Antonov was a master at presenting material, and while Vasilevsky and I drafted the report for Stalin, Antonov prepared the situation map and a map of the plan of operations in the Kursk salient.

We all agreed that Germany was capable of supplying the forces and preparing for a major offensive in only one of the strategic sectors. The greatest threat seemed to be posed to the Kursk salient. We concluded that, because of political, economic and military strategic considerations, the Nazis would seek to hold their front from the Gulf of Finland to the Sea of Azov at any price and would launch a major offensive in the Kursk salient with the objective of smashing the troops of the Central and Voronezh fronts. This could change the strategic situation in the Germans' favor, while the elimination of the salient would straighten the front and increase the general operational density of the German defense. The situation in the salient enabled the Germans to strike against Kursk from two directions: southward from the Orel area and northward from the Belgorod area. We assumed that the German armies would remain on the defensive elsewhere along the German-Soviet front since, according to the General Staff's information, they lacked the forces for other offensives.

In the evening of April 12 we drove to Supreme Headquarters. Stalin listened more attentively than ever before to all we had to say. He agreed that we concentrate our main forces around Kursk, but he was still worried about the Moscow sector.

Having discussed the plan of action, we decided to provide for a defense in depth in all threatened sectors, particularly in the Kursk salient. Appropriate orders were to be issued to the front commanders. The troops were to dig in deeply. Supreme Headquarters reserves in the process of being formed or yet to be prepared were not to be moved up to the front for the time being, but to be concentrated near threatened sectors.

Supreme Headquarters thus adopted a preliminary decision on the proposed defense plan as early as mid-April. To be sure, we reverted to this question repeatedly, and a final decision was made by Supreme Headquarters at the end of May and the beginning of June, when we knew virtually all the details of the enemy's plan to strike against the Voronezh and Central fronts with major tank forces, using the new Tiger tanks and Ferdinand self-propelled guns.

The Voronezh, Central, Southwest and Bryansk fronts were

regarded by Supreme Headquarters as the principal sectors in the first stage of the impending campaign. It was there that the main action was expected to unfold. The plan was to meet the expected German offensive with a powerful defense, to wear down the enemy and then to go over to the counteroffensive and final victory. At the same time, we worked out a plan for offensive operations in case the enemy offensive were to be prolonged.

The plan for our defense was thus not forced upon us by events but was prepared well in advance, while the timing of our offensive was to depend on the situation at the given moment. We did not intend to be slow beginning the offensive, nor on the other hand did we intend to rush into it. We also established the basic concentration area for the Supreme Headquarters reserves. These were to be massed around Livny, Stary Oskol and Korocha, ready to form a defense line in case the enemy succeeded in breaking through in the Kursk salient. Other reserves were to be located on the right flank of the Bryansk Front around Kaluga, Tula and Yefremov. At the junction of the Voronezh and Southwest fronts, around Liski, the Fifth Guards Tank Army and several other units were to get ready for operations.

Vasilevsky and Antonov were instructed to start working out the supporting documentation for these plans in time for another discussion at the beginning of May.

The Party's Central Committee, the State Defense Committee, Supreme Headquarters and the General Staff did tremendous amounts of work preparing the Soviet Army for the spring-summer campaign of 1943.

The preparation for large-scale action required a number of improvements in the organization of the forces and in the provision of modern equipment. The General Staff took steps to improve the army command structure. The organization table of fronts and armies was reviewed and improved. They were reinforced with additional artillery, antitank and mortar units. The troops were also strengthened in the communications field. Rifle divisions were equipped with improved automatic and antitank weapons and combined into corps to give greater efficiency to the command structure and more power to the armies. New artillery and mortar units were formed and equipped with weapons of higher quality. Artillery brigades, divisions and corps were formed within the Supreme Command reserve to provide a high firing density on the principal sectors. Antiaircraft divisions began to join the various fronts and the nation's air defense forces, greatly enhancing our over-all air defense.

The Central Committee and the State Defense Committee gave particular attention to tank production. The front also received the first self-propelled guns designed and produced by Soviet industry.

By the summer of 1943 we had, in addition to individual mechanized and tank corps, five well-equipped tank armies, each consisting of two tank corps and one mechanized corps. In addition, eighteen heavy-tank regiments were formed to strengthen the field armies and ensure breakthroughs in the enemy defenses.

Much was also done to reorganize the air force, which was beginning to be equipped with planes of improved design, including the modified LA-5 and the Yak-9. In addition to new equipment for the entire air force, new units, including eight air corps of the long-range bomber force, were formed as part of the Supreme Headquarters reserve. The Soviet air force now exceeded the Germans' in number of planes. Each front had its own air army of 700 to 800 planes.

Artillery was converted to motorized traction. Trucks were also supplied to the army engineers and signal troops, and a large motor pool was provided for the support units of all the major fronts. Dozens of new motor battalions and regiments were placed at the disposal of the Administration of Rear Services in the Supreme Command, increasing the maneuverability and capability of all support services.

Much attention was given to the training of new manpower. In 1943 hundreds of thousands of soldiers were schooled and equipped at various training centers and organized into major strategic reserves. As of July 1, the Supreme Headquarters reserve contained several field armies, two tank armies and one air army. The tremendous amount of work done by the Party and the State Defense Committee in strengthening and retraining the Soviet forces on the basis of accumulated experience greatly enhanced the fighting capacity of the troops on all fronts.

Particular attention was devoted to improving the caliber of Party political work. Additional thousands of Party members were introduced into the forces, further raising the already high morale of the soldiers. In 1943 the armed forces included 2.7 million Party members and a roughly equal number of Young Communist League members.

Army political agencies and Party and Young Communist organizations made every effort to increase morale and the political awareness of the troops. A decree of the Central Committee, dated May 24, 1943, on the reorganization of the structure of Party and Young Communist organizations in the Red Army, and giving a greater role to the army newspapers, facilitated this work. According to the decree, Party organizations were to be established at the battalion rather than the regimental level. Regimental Party bureaus were to become equivalent to Party committees. This structure made possible more effective control of Party members in the lower units. The political work of commanders, political commissars, Party and Young Communist organizations in implementing the May decree was a major factor in raising the military preparedness level of the Soviet armed forces on the eve of the large-scale fighting with the enemy in the spring-summer campaign of 1943.

More than 200,000 guerrillas were operating in the rear of the enemy. These were directed by the Central Headquarters of the Guerrilla Movement and by underground committees in cities, districts and provinces.

By the summer of 1943, before the Battle of Kursk, the Soviet armed forces were superior to the German Fascist forces both quantitatively and qualitatively.

The Soviet Supreme Command now had at its disposal all the necessary means to hold the strategic initiative in all sectors and to dictate its will to the enemy.

The German command, realizing that its armed strength had lost its superiority over the Soviet Army, undertook a series of "total" measures to shift all available forces to the Soviet-German front.

Taking advantage of the West's failure to open a second front, the Nazi command moved its best forces to the east. The German war industry, working twenty-four hours a day, rushed to provide the troops with new Tiger and Panther tanks and Ferdinand self-propelled guns. The German Air Force received new Focke-Wulf-190A and Henschel-129 planes. German ground forces were given additional manpower and supplies.

Germany's strength on the Soviet front included 232 German and satellite divisions with a total of 5.3 million men, 56,000 guns and mortars, 5,850 tanks and self-propelled guns and 3,000 planes. Headquarters at all levels were intensely busy with plans for the coming offensive.

For the operations against the Kursk salient, the German command intended to use at least 50 divisions, including 16 tank and motorized divisions, 10,000 guns, 2,700 tanks and 2,000 planes. Hitler and his clique had no doubt about their success. Nazi propaganda did all it could to instill confidence in the troops and promised that the impending battle would yield the certain victory that Hitler wanted to achieve at all cost. But once again the adventurist plans of German imperialism were to be frustrated.

In early May I returned to Supreme Headquarters from a trip to the North Caucasus Front. By that time the General Staff had completed its basic plans for the spring-summer campaign. Intensive intelligence-gathering in the enemy rear and by air had clearly established that the main flow of enemy troops and matériel was in the direction of Orel, Kromy, Bryansk, Kharkov, Krasnograd and Poltava. This confirmed our April forecast. Both the Supreme Command and the General Staff began to suspect that the Germans might begin their offensive within the next few days.

Stalin demanded that the Central, Bryansk, Voronezh and Southwest fronts be warned to hold their forces in complete readiness to meet the expected onslaught, and the relevant directive was issued by Supreme Headquarters on May 8. Upon receipt of the directive, the front commands took additional measures to strengthen their firing systems, antitank defenses and engineering obstacles.

One report of the Central Front command in response to this directive read as follows:

1. After receipt of the Supreme Headquarters directive, orders were issued to all armies and independent corps of the Central Front to get their troops into battle readiness by the morning of May 10.

2. The following steps were taken on May 9 and 10:

(a) The troops were informed about a possible offensive action by the enemy in the immediate future.

(b) Units in the first and second echelons and the reserves were brought up to complete readiness. Unit commands and headquarters staffs are verifying troop readiness on the spot.

(c) Field intelligence and artillery harassment of the enemy have been intensified in the various sectors, especially in the Orel direction. The reliability of fire controls is being verified in practice by the first-line units. Second-line units and reserves are carrying out additional reconnaissance in the direction of probable operations and are coordinating plans with front-line units. Additional supplies of ammunition are being moved up to firing positions. Field obstacles have been reinforced, especially in sectors open to likely tank attacks. Defense zones are being mined in depth. Communications have been checked and they are working without fault.

3. The Sixteenth Air Army has intensified its reconnaissance and is carefully observing the enemy in the areas of Glazunovka, Orel, Kromy and Komarichi. Air units and army troops are in complete readiness to repulse enemy air strikes and to break up any offensive operations.

4. To break up any enemy offensive in the Orel-Kursk direction, the entire artillery of the Thirteenth Army and the planes of the Sixteenth Air Army have been alerted for possible counterpreparation.

Similar reports were received from other fronts.

Although they did not deny the need for defensive measures, General Vatutin, the commander of the Voronezh Front, and his political officer, N. S. Khrushchev, in their report to the Supreme Commander in Chief proposed that a preventive strike be launched against the enemy's Belgorod-Kharkov grouping. Vasilevsky, Antonov and the other officers in the General Staff did not support the idea. I agreed with the General Staff and so reported to Stalin.

But the Chief was still questioning whether to await the enemy offensive or to strike a preventive blow. Stalin was afraid that our defenses might not be able to withstand the enemy onslaught, as in 1941 and 1942. At the same time, he was not sure our troops would be able to smash through the strong enemy defenses. This doubt continued, as I recall, until almost mid-May.

As a result of repeated discussion and the evidence we supplied him, Stalin finally firmly decided to meet the German attack with artillery fire, with air strikes and with counterattacks by our operational and strategic reserves. Then, having worn down the enemy, we were to launch our own powerful counteroffensive in the Belgorod-Kharkov and Orel directions, followed by deep-ranging offensive operations in all major directions. After the defeat of the Germans in the Kursk salient, Supreme Headquarters proposed to liberate the Donets Basin and the entire Ukraine east of the Dnieper River, eliminate the enemy bridgehead on the Taman Peninsula in the Northern Caucasus, reach the eastern part of Byelorussia and thus prepare the way for the complete expulsion of the enemy from Soviet territory.

The main German forces in the Kursk salient were to be defeated according to the following plan of Supreme Headquarters:

As soon as the enemy's main concentrations in the jumping-off areas for the offensive were identified, all artillery and mortar units were to open fire in coordination with aerial strikes. While assisting defensive operations on the ground, our air force was to win complete mastery in the air. This objective was to be achieved with the help of air units from neighboring fronts and the long-range force of the Supreme Command.

When the enemy launched his ground offensive, the troops of the Voronezh and Central fronts were to defend every position, every firing line, and launch counterattacks with available reserves, including individual tank corps and entire tank armies. And as soon as the enemy was weakened and brought to a halt, a major Soviet counteroffensive was to be launched by the forces of the Voronezh, Central, Steppe and Bryansk fronts, the left wing of the Western Front and the right wing of the Southwest Front.

In accordance with this general plan of action, a Supreme Headquarters directive to the individual fronts made the following specific assignments:

The Central Front was to defend the northern part of the Kursk salient, wearing down the enemy in defensive operations, and then, in conjunction with the Bryansk and Western fronts, to launch a counteroffensive to defeat the German forces around Orel.

The Voronezh Front, defending the southern part of the Kursk salient, was to inflict maximum losses on the enemy in defensive operations and then go over to the counteroffensive, in coordination with the Steppe Front and the right wing of the Southwest Front, to smash the enemy forces around Belgorod and Kharkov. The main effort of the front was to be concentrated on the left wing in the sector of the Sixth and Seventh Guards armies.

The Steppe Front, situated behind the Central and Bryansk fronts along a line running through Izmalkovo, Livny, the Kshen River and Bely Kolodez, was to prepare for defense along that line in case of a breakthrough on those fronts as well as to make ready to take part in counteroffensive operations.

Troops of the Bryansk Front and the left wing of the Western Front were to operate in conjunction with the Central Front to blunt the enemy offensive and be ready to go over to the counteroffensive in the Orel direction.

Central Headquarters of the Guerrilla Movement was instructed to organize massive diversive actions in the enemy rear against all the major transport lines of Orel, Bryansk, Kharkov and other oblasts and to collect and deliver intelligence information.

In a number of sectors of the south and the northwest isolated offensive operations were planned to tie down enemy troops and prevent shifts of reserves.

Our troops began to prepare for the Battle of Kursk in the second half of April. I spent all that period with the troops of the Voronezh and Central fronts, studying the situation and preparations for the anticipated operations.

On May 22 I sent the following report to Stalin, addressing him by the code name of Ivanov:

Comrade Ivanov, herewith is my report on the situation at the Central Front as of May 21.

1. Our intelligence has established that as of May 21 the enemy has 15 infantry divisions in the front line, and 13 divisions, including 3 tank divisions, in the second line facing the Central Front. In addition, we have information that the 2nd Tank Division and the 36th Motorized Division are assembling south of Orel. The information about these two divisions still requires checking. The enemy's 4th Tank Division, which was previously west of Sevsk, has been moved elsewhere. There are also 3 divisions, including 2 tank divisions, in the areas of Bryansk and Karachev. Consequently, the enemy has at his disposal, as of May 21, a total of 33 divisions, including 6 tank divisions.

Instrumental and visual reconnaissance has identified 800 guns, mainly 105-mm and 150-mm. Most of the artillery faces our Thirteenth Army, the left flank of the Forty-eighth Army and the right flank of the Seventieth Army, i.e., along a line through Trosno, Pervoye and Pozdeyevo. Behind that main artillery zone are 600 to 700 tanks between Zmiyevka and Krasnaya Roshcha, with most of the armor concentrated east of the Oka River.

The enemy has concentrated 600 to 650 planes around Orel, Bryansk and Smolensk, with most of the air power concentrated around Orel.

In the last few days, the enemy has been passive on the ground and in the air, limiting himself to light aerial reconnaissance and occasional small strafing raids. He has been digging in both along the front line and in depth, especially opposite the Thirteenth Army sector between Krasnaya Slobodka and Senkovo; a second defense line has already been observed beyond the Neruch River and a third line is being dug two or three miles north of the Neruch.

Prisoner interrogations indicate that the German command is aware of our grouping south of Orel and of our preparations for an offensive and that the German units have been forewarned. Captured pilots say that the German command is planning an offensive of its own and has been massing air power for that purpose.

I have personally visited the front line of the Thirteenth Army, observed enemy activities from various points and, after discussions with division commanders of the Seventieth and Thirteenth armies and, with the army commanders Galanin, Pukhov and Romanenko, have concluded that there is no evidence of preparations for an immediate offensive along the enemy's front line. I may be wrong and the enemy may be skillfully concealing his preparations, but on the basis of an analysis of his disposition of tank units, the low density of infantry units, the absence of heavy artillery and the scattered disposition of reserves, I feel that he will be unable to launch an offensive before the end of May.

2. The defenses of the Thirteenth and Seventieth armies are well prepared and echeloned in depth. The Forty-eighth Army's defense is more liquid and provided with a low density of artillery. Thus if the enemy strikes at Romanenko's army [the Forty-eighth] and tries to by-pass Maloarkhangelsk on the east with the objective of by-passing Kostin's [Rokossovsky's code name] main grouping, Romanenko may not be able to stop the enemy advance, and the front's reserves, disposed mainly behind Pukhov [the Thirteenth Army] and Galanin [the Seventieth Army], may not be able to reach Romanenko in time to help. It seems to me that Romanenko should be reinforced with 2 rifle divisions, 3 T-34 tank regiments, 2 antitank artillery regiments and 2 mortar regiments or artillery regiments from the Supreme Headquarters reserve. With these additional forces, Romanenko would be able to improve his defenses and, when necessary, go over to the offensive with a dense grouping.

The main shortcoming in the defenses of Pukhov and Galanin and the other armies of the front is a shortage of antitank artillery regiments. As of today, the front has a total of four such regiments, two of which are in rear positions without traction vehicles. In view of the acute shortage of 45-mm guns in battalions and regiments, the front-line antitank defenses are weak. It seems to me that Kostin should be supplied as soon as possible with four more antitank artillery regiments (with Romanenko's two that would make six altogether) and three regiments of self-propelled 152-mm artillery.

3. Kostin's preparations for an offensive are still incomplete. After discussing this matter, Kostin, Pukhov and I decided that the proposed breakthrough sector should be moved one or two miles to the west of the originally planned sector, i.e., to Arkhangelskoye inclusive, and that a reinforced corps with a tank corps be positioned in the front line west of the railroad. The breakthrough should not be attempted with the artillery now available to Kostin because the enemy has greatly strengthened his defenses in depth in that direction. If we want to be sure of achieving the breakthrough, one more artillery corps will have to be assigned to Kostin. The front's ammunition supply amounts to one and a half complements on the average. Please see to it that Yakovlev [Soviet artillery chief] supplies the front with three additional complements for the basic calibers in the next two weeks.

4. Pukhov now has 12 divisions, 6 of them combined into 2 corps and the 6 others under Pukhov's personal command. It would help matters if you could immediately form and assign 2 corps commands to Pukhov as well as 1 corps command to Galanin, who also has 5 independent divisions in addition to a rifle corps.

Please make the necessary decisions.

YURYEV [Zhukov's code name]

I reported in a similar vein on the situation in the Voronezh Front.

Having observed firsthand the work of the front commands and lower headquarters as well as that of the General Staff, I should point out that their untiring activities played a key role in the battles of the summer period. Staffs worked day and night gathering and analyzing information on enemy forces, their capabilities and intentions. The processed information was then reported to the higher command, enabling them to take well-founded decisions.

Since we began well enough in advance, our forces were able to create a strong defense zone. The military councils of individual fronts and armies, the commanders, headquarters staffs and political commissars made a great effort to ensure the provision of a rigorous defense in depth and a flexible system of fire, to dispose troops as effectively as possible, to train the soldiers in skilled defensive and offensive fighting and to assure reliable control of troops in battle.

13

The Germans Attack

As I said earlier, the operations plan was being constantly corrected to accord with the changing situation. In working out a plan of action in the Kursk salient, Supreme Headquarters and the General Staff had to gather intelligence on the disposition of enemy troops, on movements of armored and artillery forces and bomber and fighter units and, most important, on the intentions of the enemy command.

To derive from all this the proper conclusions, the General Staff had to analyze thoroughly a vast mass of data, some of which was inevitably erroneous since information was being gathered by a great number of people in intelligence agencies as well as by guerrillas.

The enemy tried, of course, to conceal his intentions. He carried out spurious troop shifts and other misleading maneuvers. Our higher staffs were expected to distinguish between the false and the genuine. Proper procedures on a large scale could be ensured only through centralized directives and a coordination of effort rather than on the basis of individual ideas or assumptions. The Supreme Command had to rely on the collected intelligence for its own decisions concerning the enemy's capabilities and intentions in any particular strategic sector.

From their evaluation of the situation, Supreme Headquarters and the General Staff concluded that the enemy was massing its strongest forces against the Central Front around Orel. Actually, as we learned later, the forces facing the Voronezh Front proved stronger. The enemy had massed nine motorized and tank divisions (1,500 tanks) there, compared with seven divisions (1,200 tanks) along the Central Front. This explains to a large extent why the Central Front was more successful in fending off the enemy attack than the Voronezh Front.

A few words should be said at this point about our reserves. In planning the Kursk operation, Supreme Headquarters made a special effort to have large reserves at its disposal. Along the line from Livny to Stary Oskol [behind the Kursk salient] the Supreme Command concentrated the forces of the new Steppe Front (reorganized out of the Steppe Military District), which was intended either to parry the enemy in an emergency or to reinforce our striking forces in case of a general counteroffensive. The Steppe Front was made up of the Fifth Guards Field Army and the Twenty-seventh, Fifty-third and Forty-seventh field armies, the Fifth Guards Tank Army, the 1st Guards Mechanized Corps, the 4th Guards Tank Corps and the 10th Tank Corps, and the 3rd, 5th and 7th cavalry corps. It was supported by the Fifth Air Army. The front was under the command of General Konev, with Lieutenant General I. Z. Susaikov as a member of the Military Council, and Lieutenant General M. V. Zakharov as Chief of Staff.

The Steppe Front, which essentially represented the strategic reserve of Supreme Headquarters, was assigned an extremely important role in the impending battle. It was expected to stop any deep breakthrough by the enemy, and in our contemplated counteroffensive it was supposed to reinforce our striking power by coming up from the rear. The front's disposition at a substantial distance from the enemy was intended to provide room for maneuver.

The objective of the Steppe Front thus differed substantially from that of the Reserve Front that had operated on the approaches to Moscow in the autumn of 1941. The Reserve Front was basically a second operational defense line in the rear of the Western Front.

Toward the end of June the situation finally became quite clear: it was obvious that the enemy would launch an offensive in the Kursk region within the next few days.

At the time I was at the Central Front with Rokossovsky, visiting the Thirteenth Army, the Second Tank Army and the reserve corps. On June 30 I had a call from the Supreme Commander in Chief. He instructed me to remain in the Orel sector to coordinate the operations of the Central, Bryansk and Western fronts. "A. M. Vasilevsky will be in charge on the Voronezh Front," Stalin said.

We had provided for an extremely high artillery density in the Thirteenth Army sector, where we expected the main enemy blow: up to 148 guns and mortars per mile of front line.

In an effort to stop a massed enemy tank strike, we had deployed our antitank defense in great depth, with a maximum of artillery, tanks, mines and other engineering obstacles, on the Central and Voronezh fronts.

The most powerful antitank defenses on the Central Front were concentrated in the sector of the Thirteenth Army and the adjoining flanks of the Forty-eighth and Seventieth armies, and on the Voronezh Front in the sector of the Sixth and Seventh Guards armies. There the density was 25 guns per mile and, counting the second line of defense, as many as 48 guns per mile. The antitank defenses in this sector were further reinforced by two tank regiments and one tank brigade. The density of antitank artillery in the Thirteenth Army sector was more than 48 guns per mile.

Antitank strongpoints and areas had been established in all sectors open to tank attack. In addition to artillery and tanks, our antitank defenses included large mine fields, antitank ditches, scarps and other engineering obstacles. We also prepared mobile-obstacle detachments and antitank reserves. All these measures proved quite effective, and the major defeat suffered by the enemy's tank forces in the course of the battle contributed greatly to the over-all defeat of the enemy troops.

Our intelligence established that the enemy's 1st, 4th and 8th air corps, with a total of two thousand planes under the command of Field Marshal Richthofen, were operating against the Central and Voronezh fronts. Beginning in March, enemy planes had steadily intensified raids against our rail junctions, highways, cities and key objectives in the rear; in early June the air attacks concentrated increasingly on our troops and support units along the front. Cover for our forces in the Kursk salient was provided by the Second, Fifth and Sixteenth air armies and by two fighter divisions of the Soviet air defense forces. Our antiaircraft defenses were greatly reinforced in view of the expected enemy offensive. By July the Central Front had deployed 5 antiaircraft divisions from the Supreme Headquarters reserve, 5 regiments of medium-caliber and 23 regiments of small-caliber artillery. The Voronezh Front had 4 antiaircraft divisions from the Supreme Headquarters reserve, 25 antiaircraft regiments, 3 antiaircraft divisions and 5 antiaircraft batteries. These forces enabled the fronts to cover a large number of objectives with double, triple, quadruple and even quintuple fire. The antiaircraft units were closely tied in with fighter aircraft and observation, early-warning and communications services. This carefully prepared air-defense system in the Kursk salient enabled us to provide good cover for our forces and to inflict heavy losses on the enemy's air force.

Our fortifications zone was more than a hundred miles deep —including the national defense line along the Don River, as deep as 150 to 175 miles. Thus the fronts were well prepared to provide the cover for our troops that enabled them to counter the enemy's offensive with great effectiveness.

A great deal of work was also done by the rear services of fronts, armies and smaller units. Very little has been written about the members of support services who by their labor and creative initiative greatly aided the troops and commands at all levels and contributed so much to the defeat of the enemy and our ultimate victory.

The Central Front's rear services were headed by General N. A. Antipenko, those of the Voronezh Front by General N. P. Anisimov. I knew both generals well. Antipenko had commanded the rear services of the Forty-ninth Army on the Western Front during the Battle of Moscow, and had proved himself an able organizer. And I was to get to be familiar with Anisimov during my service as commander of the First Ukrainian Front.

Supplying more than 1.3 million soldiers, 3,600 tanks, 20,000 guns and 3,130 planes (including long-range bombers) for the Battle of Kursk required a tremendous amount of work. Despite the difficult conditions, the rear services handled their task brilliantly and ensured a steady flow of provisions during both the defensive phase of the battle and the rapid shift to a counteroffensive.

The local residents of the Kursk salient were also of great help to the rear services and the troops. Industrial plants near the front line repaired tanks, planes, trucks, artillery and other equipment and sewed uniforms and hospital garments. Residents contributed enormously to the work of building fortifications and constructing and repairing roads. It can truly be said that the front and rear worked as one. Everyone did his utmost for victory over the enemy—irrefutable evidence of the common goals of our people and the armed forces in the struggle for their Socialist homeland.

I should add that Generals Vatutin and Rokossovsky dealt personally with many rear services problems, and this explains to a large extent the excellent supply situation at the start of the battle.

Through May and June intensive military and political training was conducted in all ground and air units as each soldier and commander prepared to meet the enemy. They did not have to wait long. Through intelligence Supreme Headquarters and the individual fronts were able to establish the exact time of the enemy offensive. On July 2 Supreme Headquarters warned the front commanders that the enemy could be expected to move between July 3 and 6.[1]

On July 4 I was at Central Front headquarters. In a telephone conversation over a high-security line with Marshal Vasilevsky, who was at Vatutin's headquarters, I learned about the outcome of an engagement with advanced enemy detachments near Belgorod. I was also told that information received earlier that day from a captured soldier of the 168th Infantry Division —to the effect that the enemy offensive would be launched at dawn on July 5—had been confirmed and that, in accordance with the plan of Supreme Headquarters, the Voronezh Front was ready to open fire with its artillery and air units preliminary to the counterattack.

I passed this information on to Rokossovsky and Malinin. After 2 A.M. on July 5 General Pukhov, the Thirteenth Army commander, called Rokossovsky to report that a captured sapper of the 6th Infantry Division had said the German forces would launch their offensive at about 3 A.M.

Rokossovsky asked me, "What shall we do? Inform Supreme Headquarters or issue orders for the preliminary bombardment ourselves?"

"We can't waste time," I told him. "Give the order according to plan, and I will call Stalin and report the information."

I was put through to the Supreme Commander in Chief at

[1] The code name of the German offensive was Operation Citadel. H.E.S.

once. He was at Supreme Headquarters and had just finished talking with Vasilevsky by telephone. I told him about the prisoner's information and the decision to open the preliminary counterattack bombardment. Stalin approved of the decision and asked me to keep him informed. He would be at Supreme Headquarters waiting for events to unfold.

I got the impression that he was tense. In fact, all of us, despite our long-prepared defenses in depth, despite our powerful striking potential, were in a state of high excitement. It was night, but none of us felt like sleeping.

As is usual in such situations, Rokossovsky and I were in the office of the Chief of Staff, General Malinin. I knew him from the Battle of Moscow, where he had served as Chief of Staff of the Sixteenth Army. He was a thoroughly trained staff man of superior ability. He and his superbly organized associates handled their functions brilliantly. One of his most efficient colleagues was his right-hand man, the operations chief, General I. V. Boikov, a modest, hard-working, creative officer.

The front's artillery Chief of Staff, Colonel G. S. Nadysev, was also present. Every now and then he would disappear for telephone conferences with commanders of the artillery units from Supreme Headquarters reserve and with General V. I. Kazakov, the front's artillery commander, who was with the 4th Artillery Corps. It should be said that the artillery staffs and all the artillery commanders of the front, armies and lower units did an excellent job in coordinating artillery fire during both the defensive phase and the bombardment preliminary to the counteroffensive.

At 2:20 the ground shook as the mighty symphony of the battle of the Kursk salient began. The boom of heavy artillery and the explosions of M-31 rockets were clearly audible.

In the midst of the preliminary bombardment, Stalin called.

"Well, have you begun?"

"Yes, we have."

"What's the enemy doing?"

I said that the enemy was attempting to reply with fire from a few batteries.

"All right, I'll call again," Stalin said.

We could not yet fully assess the result of our preliminary bombardment, but the mere fact that the Germans' offensive, launched at 5:30 A.M., was not well organized or fully coordinated suggested that they had taken heavy losses. Prisoners later reported that our softening-up bombardment had been unexpected, that the German artillery had suffered greatly and that communications and observation and control systems had been disrupted almost everywhere.

It should be noted, however, that our plan for preliminary bombardment had not been completed in every detail by the start of the enemy offensive. Our artillery lacked exact information on troop concentrations in jumping-off areas and on the precise location of targets during the night of July 4–5. It was not, of course, an easy task to establish the location of targets with the intelligence we had available at that time, but a great deal more could have been done. As a result, our fire was aimed at areas rather than at specific targets. And this enabled the enemy to avoid excessive losses. He was able to launch his offensive within two to two and a half hours and, despite the tremendous fire density in our defenses, advanced two to four miles on the first day. This could have been prevented by better preliminary counterattack fire.

We should also remember that, because the preliminary bombardment took place at night, aerial support was insignificant and, to be frank, ineffective. Our strikes at the enemy's airfields at dawn were too late; by that time German planes were already in the air in support of their ground forces. Our air strikes were much more effective against tactical military units and enemy columns attempting to regroup in the course of the battle.

Even though our preliminary bombardment inflicted heavy losses on the enemy and disorganized his control of the offensive, there is no denying that we had expected better results. After observing the course of the battle and interrogating prisoners, I came to the conclusion that both the Central Front and the Voronezh Front had started firing too soon, when the Germans were still asleep in the trenches, dugouts and foxholes and their tanks were still under cover in waiting areas. German losses in tanks and manpower could have been greater if the preliminary counterattack bombardment had begun somewhat later—say, a half-hour before the beginning of the offensive.

Between 4:30 and 5 A.M. the enemy's planes took to the air, and simultaneously artillery fire opened up against the positions of the Central Front, especially in the Thirteenth Army sector. A few minutes later the enemy began his offensive, with three tank divisions and five infantry divisions in his first line of attack. These forces struck at the Thirteenth Army and the adjoining flanks of the Forty-eighth and Seventieth armies. The attack was met by the powerful fire of our entire defense system and repulsed with heavy enemy losses.

Throughout the day of July 5 the Germans carried out five fierce attacks in an attempt to break through our forces, but without substantial results. On almost all sectors of the front Soviet troops stood fast; it seemed that nothing could budge them. Only toward the end of the day did enemy units succeed in driving wedges into our defenses for a distance of two to four miles in the area of Olkhovatka and in one or two other sectors.

An especially courageous fight was put up by soldiers of the Thirteenth Army, particularly the 81st Division under General A. B. Barinov, the 15th Division under Colonel V. N. Dzhanzhgava, the 307th Division under General M. A. Yenshin and the 3rd Antitank Brigade under Colonel V. N. Rukosuyev. A battery commanded by Captain G. I. Igishev took the brunt of the attack and destroyed nineteen tanks during the day. All the men of the battery died heroically in battle, but did not let the Fascists pass. A good fight was also put up by General Galanin's Seventieth Army, which had been formed by frontier guards from the Far East, Transbaikalia and Central Asia. That evening a decision was taken to move up the Second Tank Army and the 19th Tank Corps from the reserve the next morning for a counterattack in conjunction with the Thirteenth Army. They were to throw the enemy back to his original positions and to restore the entire defense system in the Thirteenth Army sector.

Despite the thoroughly prepared defenses, the magnificent courage and mass heroism of our troops, the enemy succeeded, at the cost of heavy losses, in advancing up to six miles on July 5 and 6. On both days German planes spread havoc, but the enemy was unable to break through our tactical defense.

After regrouping his shock tank forces, the enemy began a fierce attack against Ponyri on the morning of July 7. All day the roar of battle on the ground and in the air engulfed the area. Although the enemy kept pouring new tank units into the battle, here again he was unable to achieve a breakthrough.

The following day the German attack intensified in the direction of Olkhovatka, and again the enemy was frustrated by the heroic stand of the Soviet troops. The artillerymen of the 3rd Antitank Brigade under the command of Colonel Rukosuyev particularly distinguished themselves, in an uneven battle against three hundred enemy tanks.

Subsequent enemy attempts to smash through the Soviet defense were equally unsuccessful. The Germans lost a large proportion of their tanks—on which Hitler had counted heavily for success—and were unable to advance even one additional mile by July 10.

During the battle, on July 9, Stalin called me at the Central Front command center and, discussing the situation, suggested,

"Isn't it about time to throw the Bryansk Front and the left wing of the Western Front into action as we planned?"

I said that the enemy no longer had the strength to break through our defenses on the Central Front and, unless we wanted to give him time to organize the defensive positions we were forcing him into, we should promptly go over to the offensive with all the forces of the Bryansk Front and the left wing of the Western Front. Without these the Central Front would be unable to carry out the planned counteroffensive.

After hearing me out, Stalin said, "Well, in that case, go see Popov and throw the Bryansk Front into action. . . . When do you think the Bryansk Front will be able to start its offensive?"

"On the twelfth," I replied.

"All right," Stalin said.

I did not need to ask him about the situation on the Voronezh Front since I was in direct contact with both Vasilevsky and the General Staff, and I knew that a fierce battle was under way there, too.

14

Zhukov Strikes

On July 9, following Stalin's instructions, I was at Bryansk Front headquarters, where I met the front commander, General M. M. Popov; his Military Council member, L. Z. Mekhlis; and his Chief of Staff, General L. M. Sandalov. They had already received orders from Supreme Headquarters to go over to the offensive.

I must mention here General Sandalov's extraordinary operational skill and his ability to plan offensive operations and organize a system of control over the troops. I knew him from the Battle of Moscow, in which he served as Chief of Staff of the Twentieth Army. He was an exceptionally able chief of staff, thoroughly familiar with operational and strategic problems.

The offensive had been planned beforehand. The armies of the Bryansk Front were commanded by extraordinarily skilled and experienced generals. The Third Army was under General A. V. Gorbatov, the Sixty-first under General P. A. Belov and the Sixty-third under General V. Ya. Kolpakchi. The Eleventh Guards Army of the Western Front, which was supposed to join the offensive, was commanded by General I. Kh. Bagramyan. I visited every one of these armies and, so far as I was able, assisted them with my advice.

As it happened, I became particularly involved in the operations of Bagramyan's army. He and I had long enjoyed good, comradely relations. The Western Front commander, Lieutenant General V. D. Sokolovsky, and a representative from Supreme Headquarters, N. N. Voronov, who was concerned with artillery matters, were also with the Guards Army at the time.

Following a report on artillery preparations by the army's artillery chief, General P. S. Semenov, the question was raised whether we should not use some new technique that was unfamiliar to the enemy. After long discussion, we decided to start the offensive, not after the artillery barrage, as was usual and as the enemy was likely to expect, but during the barrage, at a time when its rate of fire and power were on the increase. It should be noted that the method fully proved itself.

Troops of the Bryansk Front and the Eleventh Guards Army of the Western Front began their offensive on July 12. On the very first day our forces broke through the German defenses, which had been thoroughly prepared in depth, and began to advance toward Orel.

As expected, the enemy scrambled to keep control of the Orel bridgehead and started moving forces from the Central Front against the Bryansk Front and the Eleventh Guards Army. The Central Front used the respite to begin its own counteroffensive on July 15.

And so the long-prepared German offensive in the Orel area finally collapsed. The German forces were to experience the anguish of severe defeat and to feel the might of Soviet arms which had been forged for the explicit purpose of victory over this strong, experienced and hated enemy.

On July 12 Stalin called me at the Bryansk command center and ordered me to fly to the Prokhorovka sector, north of Belgorod, where a fierce tank battle was in progress.[2] I was supposed to study the situation and take over the coordination of the Voronezh and Steppe fronts.

On July 13 I reached General Vatutin's command center, where I met Marshal Vasilevsky. After familiarizing myself with the operations of both the enemy and our own troops, I expressed my complete agreement with the steps Vasilevsky had already taken. Stalin had instructed him to drive to the Southwest Front to organize the offensive that was supposed to coincide with the counteroffensive planned by the Voronezh and Steppe fronts.

We decided to intensify the counterattack then under way to seize the German defense lines near Belgorod on the heels of the retreating enemy and thus pave the way for the general counteroffensive of all the fronts.

That day marked the turning point of the battle in the Belgorod sector. The German forces, having suffered heavy losses, had lost hope of a victory and had decided to take up defensive positions. On July 16 they ceased attacking and began to pull back their rear echelons toward Belgorod. The following day their advance elements also retreated, putting up stubborn resistance against our advance.

On July 18 Vasilevsky and I visited the Sixty-ninth Army under Lieutenant General V. D. Kryuchenkin, the Fifth Guards Field Army under Lieutenant General A. S. Zhadov and the Fifth Guards Tank Army under Lieutenant General P. A. Rotmistrov. We watched the fierce fighting near the Komsomolets State Farm and the village of Ivanovskiye Vyselki, where the 29th and 18th tank corps were in action. There the enemy put up stiff resistance and even launched counterattacks. Throughout the day the armies of Rotmistrov and Zhadov were

---

[2] Most military authorities believe this was the greatest armored engagement ever fought. More than 1,500 tanks and self-propelled armored guns took part.   H.E.S.

able to push the Germans back only by about two and a half to three miles, and the Sixth Guards Army under General I. M. Chistyakov succeeded only in occupying a height near Verkhopenye. Chistyakov's troops were visibly exhausted, having been in battle without sleep or rest since July 4. We needed additional forces to block the enemy's planned retreat, and called on the 18th Tank Corps under Major General B. S. Bakharov, the 29th Tank Corps under Major General I. F. Kirichenko and parts of the Fifty-third Army under General I. M. Managarov.

Here I want to reply to assertions that, unlike the Central Front, the command of the Voronezh Front had been unable to determine the precise direction of the main enemy strike and had therefore scattered its forces over a sector a hundred miles long instead of massing them in front of the major German attack. It has also been asserted, in the one-volume *Velikaya Otechestvennaya Voina Sovetskogo Soyuza 1941–45* [*The Great Patriotic War of the Soviet Union 1941–45*], published in Moscow in 1965, that the Sixth Guards Army, which bore the brunt of the main German strike toward Kursk from the south, had a longer sector to defend (forty miles) than its neighbors (which had about thirty miles), and that the average artillery density in the sector of the Sixth Guards Army was 41 guns and 4 tanks per mile compared with an average of 57 guns and 11 tanks for the Voronezh Front as a whole.

In their analysis of the situation before the attack, Supreme Headquarters, the General Staff and the Voronezh Front command expected the main enemy strike to be launched not only against the Sixth Guards Army but against both it and the Seventh Guards Army. As for the length of sectors, the Sixth and Seventh Guards armies were defending a combined seventy-mile sector compared with a combined eighty-mile sector defended by the two other armies of the front, the Thirty-eighth and Fortieth.

The average density of artillery and tanks has also been calculated incorrectly. The Thirty-eighth and Fortieth armies had an insignificant artillery density with only a few tanks in their sectors. Almost all the artillery units from the Supreme Headquarters reserve and all the tank units and front reserves were concentrated in the sector of the Sixth and Seventh Guards armies. Moreover, the Sixth Guards Field Army was backed up by the First Tank Army, which had prepared its own defense line, and behind the junction of the Sixth and Seventh Guards armies stood the Sixty-ninth Army, also on a prepared defense line. Finally, we had the front reserves, consisting of the 35th Guards Rifle Corps and the 2nd and 5th Guards tank corps, in the operational zone behind the Sixth and Seventh Guards armies.

In other words, the criticism directed against General Vatutin, the Voronezh Front commander, is based on a miscalculation of the density of forces under the specific conditions of that operational and strategic situation. It is a calculation based on the tactical density of the armies alone and does not include the artillery of the Supreme Headquarters reserve in the Sixth Guards Army sector. As for tank density, the front command was relying mainly on the First Tank Army and the 2nd and 5th Guards tank corps. Any calculation of forces needed in major battles must include not only the tactical defenses but also the forces positioned in depth. Otherwise errors will arise.

As far as the outcome of the defensive phase of the Kursk battle is concerned, it must be remembered that on the first day the enemy threw almost five corps (the 2nd Tank Corps of the SS, the 3rd Tank Corps, the 48th Tank Corps, the 52nd Army Corps and part of the Raus Corps) against the Sixth and Seventh Guards armies, compared with three corps against the Central Front. There was a significant difference, therefore, in the strengths of the German thrusts near Orel and near Belgorod.

With regard to General Vatutin's personal ability in operational and strategic matters, I must state in all objectivity that he was a highly erudite and courageous military leader.[3]

As I said earlier, we prepared our counteroffensive in the Kursk salient long before the enemy began his offensive. The operations plan considered at Supreme Headquarters in May contemplated a counteroffensive in the Orel direction, code-named "Kutuzov." Its objective was to strike at the enemy's forces around Orel from three converging directions with the forces of the Central and Bryansk fronts and the left wing of the Western Front.

I stated previously that the Bryansk and Western front offensives began on July 12 and that of the Central Front on July 15, thus unfolding a powerful three-front offensive with the immediate objective of smashing the enemy's forces in the region of Orel.

This counteroffensive and the exhaustion of enemy forces around Belgorod forced the German command to acknowledge that its Operation Citadel had failed. In an effort to save its troops from complete defeat, the German command decided to pull Field Marshal Manstein's forces back to the defense lines from which they had launched their offensive.

Because of the exhaustion of our own First Tank Army and the Sixth and Seventh Guards field armies, the enemy was able to pull his main forces back to the Belgorod defense line by July 23.

When they reached the front edge of the German defense line on that date, the troops of the Voronezh and Steppe fronts

[3] The criticism of the Voronezh Front and its commander, General Vatutin, who was killed in action less than a year later, appeared in Soviet works published after the downfall of Nikita S. Khrushchev, who was Vatutin's Military Council member. It would seem that Soviet critics launched their attack because of Khrushchev's association with Vatutin. Zhukov, who had no love for Khrushchev after the latter removed him from office, nevertheless springs to the defense of his fellow commander, General Vatutin.   H.E.S.

were not immediately able to go over to the counteroffensive as ordered. Before they could do so, fuel stores, ammunition and other supplies had to be replenished, coordination of all the services had to be organized, reconnaissance had to be carried out, and a certain amount of regrouping was essential, especially in artillery and tanks. All this required at least eight days, even on the tightest schedule.

After repeated discussion and with the greatest reluctance, the Chief finally approved our decision since there was no other way out. The forthcoming operation was projected in great depth and required careful preparation and assured supplies; otherwise it might fail. A properly prepared offensive must not only guarantee a breakthrough in the enemy's tactical and operational defense in depth, but must also establish a new line to provide proper support of subsequent offensive operations. However, Stalin kept pressing us. Vasilevsky and I had a hard time convincing him of the necessity of avoiding excessive haste and of not starting the operation until it was fully prepared from every point of view. Stalin finally agreed with our arguments.

Since his death it has been said that Stalin never listened to anyone and made military and political decisions by himself. This is not true. If arguments were presented to him in convincing fashion, he listened. And I know of cases where he gave up his own views and decisions, as, for instance, with the starting dates of proposed offensives.[4]

[4] Stalin was by no means as reasonable as Zhukov suggests. For instance, on May 22–23, 1944, a violent argument occurred in Stalin's Kremlin office over plans for a major offensive in Byelorussia. General Rokossovsky, then commander of the First Byelorussian Front, insisted that a two-pronged blow be struck at the German positions at Bobruisk. Stalin wanted a single blow. The argument grew hotter and hotter, and finally Stalin ordered Rokossovsky to leave the room and think it over. Rokossovsky was kept in the waiting room for two hours, then brought back. Rokossovsky stuck to his position. Stalin looked daggers at him and sent

The basic plan for the counteroffensive, which had been worked out and approved by the Supreme Commander in Chief in May, was repeatedly corrected and discussed anew at Supreme Headquarters during the defensive phase of the battle of the Kursk salient. This was a plan for the second stage of the defeat of the German forces in the areas of Orel, Belgorod and Kharkov and, as such, was part of the over-all plan for the summer-autumn campaign of 1943.

The first phase—the defensive phase—was completed by Soviet forces on the Central Front on July 12 and on the Voronezh Front on July 23.

The discrepancy in time between these operations stems from differences in the scale of fighting and from the fact that the Central Front received the support of the Bryansk and Western fronts, which went over to the offensive against enemy forces around Orel on July 12 and forced the Germans to pull back seven divisions that had been operating against the Central Front.

Nor did the second phase of the battle—the counteroffensive—begin simultaneously on both fronts. Troops near Belgorod did not start their offensive until August 3, twenty days after the Central, Bryansk and Western fronts.

These three fronts required less time for preparation because their offensives had been planned and all supplies provided during the defensive stage of the battle. The forces near Belgorod required more time because the troops of the Steppe

---

him out again. While Rokossovsky was waiting outside Stalin's office, Molotov and Malenkov appeared. They warned him that he had better give in to Stalin. Rokossovsky told them he would ask to be relieved of his command if the single-blow plan was accepted. At that point the door opened and he was again asked to join the council. For a third time he presented his arguments, and finally Stalin with great reluctance agreed to Rokossovsky's view. Such stubbornness in defending opinions was seldom encountered at the Kremlin. (Rokossovsky, *Voyenno-Istoricheskii Zhurnal*, June, 1964.)   H.E.S.

Front lacked a fully worked-out plan when they were drawn into the counteroffensive. Having been kept in the Supreme Headquarters reserve, they were not familiar with their precise objectives, their jumping-off areas or the specific enemy forces they were supposed to engage.

While the counteroffensive was being prepared, I spent most of my time with the Voronezh and Steppe fronts, except on July 30 and 31, when I visited the Fourth Tank Army of the Western Front at Stalin's request.

According to the operations plan for the Voronezh and Steppe fronts, which had been code-named "Rumyantsev," the main thrust from the Belgorod area was to be carried out by the adjoining flanks of the two fronts in the general direction of Bogodukhov, Valki and Novaya Vodolaga, by-passing Kharkov on the west. As soon as our forces reached the Kharkov area, the Southwest Front was to go over to the offensive. Its Fifty-seventh Army, commanded by General N. A. Gagen, had the task of by-passing Kharkov on the southwest.

The counteroffensive of the Voronezh Front forces was launched under more difficult conditions than the attack around Orel. They had suffered heavy losses in manpower, matériel and supplies during the defensive fighting. The enemy had been able to retreat to his previously prepared defense lines and thus was better prepared to meet our offensive. All indications were that heavy fighting was in the offing, especially for the troops of the Steppe Front, who had to attack the fortified Belgorod defense line.

I would like to make a small digression at this point. I am sometimes asked by Soviet historians whether the Steppe Front was used properly during the Battle of Kursk. On the surface such a question seems quite legitimate. It is a fact that a large part of the Steppe Front was used in scattered units during the defensive fighting and that the front joined the counteroffensive in weakened condition.

Actually, there are no grounds for doubt. Supreme Head-quarters did make proper use of the Steppe Front. If its forces had not been used to support the Voronezh Front during the defensive phase, the latter might have been in an extremely serious situation. We obviously could not have tolerated such an outcome; it is not difficult to guess where it might have led.

As for the alternative of throwing all the forces of the Steppe Front into the counteroffensive at once, it should be pointed out that conditions were not yet ripe for putting it to this use. At the time, some of its armies were still needed to reinforce the Voronezh Front. The outlook for a successful counteroffensive on the Belgorod-Kharkov sector did not become clear until July 20–23, and then extensive preparations were still needed before the actual counteroffensive could begin. But let us get back to our narrative.[5]

On July 23 the Soviet forces, in pursuit of the enemy, reached the lines north of Belgorod and essentially restored the defensive positions that the Voronezh Front had held up to July 5.

After discussing the situation with the front commands, the General Staff and Stalin, we decided to halt the advance and to begin thorough preparations for the forthcoming operations.

Before we could go over to the offensive, the fronts had to regroup their forces and equipment; organize thorough target reconnaissance for artillery and air support; replace the losses suffered by the various units, especially the Sixth and Seventh Guards field armies and the First Tank Army and several artillery units; and replenish fuel stores, ammunition reserves and the other supplies essential for an offensive in depth. In addition, the Steppe Front had to work out its own plan for the

---

[5] This "digression" is part of the continued feud between Zhukov and Marshal Konev, who happened to be commander of the Steppe Front, a fact Zhukov barely manages to mention. Konev did not play a major role at Kursk, and the "historians" are obviously seeking evidence that Zhukov deliberately kept Konev out of the field of major action. H.E.S.

counteroffensive and assure the necessary flow of supplies.

The general plan for the counteroffensive was as follows:

The Voronezh Front was to strike its main blow with the Fifth and Sixth Guards field armies, the Fifth Guards Tank Army and the First Tank Army in the general direction of Akhtyrka. The density of artillery in the proposed breakthrough sector of the Fifth and Sixth Guards field armies was to be raised to 350 guns and mortars per mile of front line, and the number of tanks to 70. The divisional sectors were cut down to two miles each.

Such a massed concentration was required for a breakthrough because we planned to drive two entire tank armies through the gap on the first day of the offensive. To the right of this sector, the Fortieth and Thirty-eighth armies were to advance in the general direction of Graivoron and then toward Trostyanets. Air support would be provided by the Second Air Army under General S. A. Krasovsky.

The Steppe Front under General Konev, consisting of the Fifty-third and Sixty-ninth armies, the Seventh Guards Army and the 1st Mechanized Corps, had as its immediate objective the seizure of Belgorod, with a subsequent advance toward Kharkov in coordination with the main force of the Voronezh Front. The Steppe Front was to be supported by the Fifth Air Army under General S. K. Goryunov.

In the course of preparations for the Steppe Front offensive, I had occasion to meet General I. M. Managarov, the commander of the Fifty-third Army. He made a very good impression on me even though I had to spend a lot of time explaining the operations plan to him. But when the work was done, he took an accordion and beautifully played some very lively things that immediately made us feel a great deal fresher. I looked at him and thought to myself: soldiers love such merry commanders and will follow them through fire and water.

I thanked Managarov for his fine playing and expressed the

hope that he would play the artillery overture for the Germans on August 3 just as well.

He smiled and said, "We will do our best. We've got some good instruments to play with."

I also liked the army's artillery chief, Lieutenant General N. S. Fomin, who was an expert at using large amounts of artillery in an offensive. He worked with Colonel General M. N. Chistyakov, a representative of Supreme Headquarters, in properly distributing the artillery and in providing all the munitions and information needed for an effective artillery offensive.

15

The Battle Assessed

The counteroffensive at Belgorod began on the morning of August 3. Reconnaissance had established that the enemy was rushing motorized and tank divisions and other reinforcements from various sectors to strengthen his forces in the Belgorod-Kharkov area.

The heavier artillery and air strikes were launched by the Voronezh Front to open the way for a quick breakthrough by the Fifth and Sixth Guards armies, reinforced by large numbers of tanks. In the second half of the day the First Tank Army and the Fifth Guards Tank Army were thrown into the battle, and their advanced units drove as far as twenty miles by the end of the day, completing a breakthrough in the Germans' entire tactical defense.

The Steppe Front did not have the powerful artillery and air support of the Voronezh Front, and its offensive proceeded more slowly. By the end of the first day the leading units of the Steppe Front had advanced almost ten miles. We regarded this as a great achievement because the Steppe Front faced a much stronger and more deeply echeloned defense than the Voronezh Front.

The following day the German defense stiffened and the Steppe Front offensive slowed down. But that did not disturb us because the shock forces of the Voronezh Front were advancing swiftly, threatening to outflank Belgorod on the west. Toward the end of the day on August 4 the enemy, sensing a trap, began to pull back his forces, enabling the Steppe Front to speed up its advance.

At six o'clock in the morning of August 5 the 270th Guards Rifle Regiment of the 89th Guards Rifle Division was the first to break into the city of Belgorod, along with elements of the 305th and 375th rifle divisions. Other units that distinguished themselves in the capture of the city were the 93rd, 94th Guards and 111th rifle divisions. After clearing enemy remnants from the city, the troops of the Steppe Front resumed their advance in coordination with the Voronezh Front.

That evening Moscow fired a salute honoring the troops of the Bryansk, Western and Central fronts for the capture of Orel and the troops of the Steppe and Voronezh fronts for the seizure of Belgorod. It was the war's first artillery salute in honor of a Red Army victory. The morale of the soldiers rose sharply as a result, and their faces radiated joy, gallantry and confidence in their own strength.

After reviewing the situation, the command of the Steppe Front and I drafted a report for Stalin on August 6, recommending future operations against the Germans in the Belgorod-Kharkov sector:

From the Front   August 6, 1943

FOR COMRADE IVANOV [Stalin's code name]

In connection with the successful breakthrough in the front and our offensive in the Belgorod-Kharkov sector, we propose the following future operations:

1. The Fifty-third Army and Lieutenant General M. D. Solomatin's 1st Mechanized Corps will attack along the Belgorod-Kharkov highway, with the main thrust in the direction of Dergachi.

This army should reach a line running from Olshany to Dergachi, relieving elements of Zhadov's army on that line.

The Sixty-ninth Army will attack on the left of the Fifty-third in the direction of Cheremoshnoye. Having attained that objective, the Sixty-ninth will transfer a couple of its best divisions to the Fifty-third Army and will join the front reserves for reconstitution in the area of Mikoyanovka, Cheremoshnoye and Gryaznoye. The Sixty-ninth should be reinforced with 20,000 men as soon as possible.

The Seventh Guards Army will attack from the area of Pushkarnoye in the direction of Brodok and then toward Bochkovka, moving the enemy lines back from north to south. In addition, elements of the Seventh Guards Army will strike from the Cheremoshnoye-Zaborovka sector in the direction of Tsirkuny to reach a line running through Cherkasskaya, Lozovaya, Tsirkuny and Klyuchkin. Some of its forces from Zaborovka will attack toward Murom and then toward Ternovaya to help the Fifty-seventh Army cross the Northern Donets between Rubezhnoye and Stary Saltov.

2. The Fifty-seventh Army of the Southwest Front should be transferred to the Steppe Front for a thrust from the sector of Rubezhnoye and Stary Saltov in the general direction of Nepokrytaya and then the Frunze State Farm. The Fifty-seventh Army would thus reach a line running through the Kutuzovka State Farm, the Frunze State Farm and Rogan Severnaya. If the Fifty-seventh were to remain under the jurisdiction of the Steppe Front, it should be instructed to go over to the offensive in the stated direction as soon as the Seventh Guards Army reaches the Murom area.

3. For the second phase, i.e., the Kharkov operation, the Fifth Guards Tank Army holding a line through Olshany, Stary Merchik and Ogultsy should be transferred to the Steppe Front.

The Kharkov operation could be organized roughly as follows:

(a) The Fifty-third Army and the Fifth Guards Tank Army would seize Kharkov from the west and southwest.

(b) The Seventh Guards Army would attack southward from the Tsirkuny-Dergachi line.

(c) The Fifty-seventh Army would attack westward from the line between the Frunze State Farm and Rogan and seize Kharkov from the south.

(d) The Sixty-ninth Army (provided it will have been reinforced by that time) would take up positions at Olshany between the Fifth Guards Army and the Fifty-third Army and would drive southward to support the Kharkov operation from the south. The Sixty-ninth should reach a line running through Snezhkov-Kut, Minkovka, Prosyanoye and Novoselovka.

(e) The left flank of the Voronezh Front should be advanced to a line running through Otrada, Kolomak, and Snezhkov-Kut. That task should be entrusted to the Fifth Guards Army and the left flank of the Twenty-seventh Army. The First Tank Army should reach a line running through Kovyagi, Alekseyevka and Murafa. The Southwest Front should attack from Zamostye in the general direction of Merefa along both banks of the Mzha River, with some of its elements driving through Chuguyev toward Osnova, and other elements clearing the enemy from the forest south of Zamostye and reaching a line through Novoselovka, Okhochaye, Verkhni Bishkin and Geyevka.

4. In addition to the 20,000-man reinforcements for the Sixty-ninth Army, the Kharkov operation will require 15,000 more men to reinforce the Fifty-third and Seventh Guards armies and 200 T-34, 100 T-70 and 35 KV tanks to strengthen the front tank forces. In addition, 4 regiments of self-propelled artillery and 2 sapper brigades will be required. The air power of the front will also have to be reinforced with 90 fighters, 40 PE-2 light bombers and 60 IL-2 ground attack aircraft.

Please confirm.

ZHUKOV
KONEV
ZAKHAROV

No. 64

Having gained control of Belgorod, the Soviet forces began to develop their offensive in the direction of Kharkov. To avoid entrapment, the enemy began pulling his troops out of Kharkov on August 22. The following morning, after engagements with the enemy's rear guard, troops of the Steppe Front entered the city to an excited reception by its residents.

A city-wide rally was promptly held, with representatives of the Soviet Army and the government and Party organizations of the Ukraine on the speakers' stand. The rally proceeded with a great show of enthusiasm as the working people of Kharkov celebrated their liberation. Moscow fired a salute in honor of the valiant troops that had freed Kharkov, that glorious city of the Ukraine. The rally was followed by a dinner at which I. S. Kozlovsky, the noted concert artist, sang Russian and Ukrainian songs. His heartfelt performance moved everyone present to tears. He sang for a long time, and all of us who had missed good vocalists for so many months were very grateful to him.

Meanwhile, the troops of the Steppe Front had engaged the enemy south of Kharkov in the direction of Merefa. The Voronezh Front, in turn, repulsed German counterattacks at Bogodukhov and Akhtyrka and, on August 25, gained firm control of a line running through Sumy, Gadyach, Akhtyrka and Konstantinovka, where it began to prepare for an offensive toward the middle reaches of the Dnieper River. The same assignment was given to the Steppe Front.

Troops of the Western, Bryansk and Central fronts continued their offensive in the Orel area. By August 18 they had reached a line running east of Lyudinovo, fifteen miles east of Bryansk and through Dmitrovsk-Orlovsky.

This completed the great operations in the areas of Kursk, Orel, Belgorod, Kharkov, Bogodukhov and Akhtyrka. They ended with the complete defeat of the main force of the German Army, on which Hitler had been depending to achieve his major political and strategic objectives.

This tremendous confrontation of Soviet and German forces lasted fifty days. It ended with a Soviet victory over thirty picked German divisions, including seven tank divisions, who lost more than half their strength. During that battle the enemy's losses totaled 500,000 men, 2,000 tanks and self-propelled guns, including many Tigers, Panthers and Ferdinands, 3,000 guns and a large number of planes. Those losses could not be replaced by the Nazi leadership even with "total" measures.

The outstanding victory of our troops at Kursk demonstrated the growing power of the Soviet state and its armed forces. Both at the front and in the rear, the victory was forged by the efforts of all the Soviet peoples under the leadership of the Communist Party. In the fighting at Kursk the Soviet troops displayed exceptional courage, mass heroism and military mastery. In recognition of these achievements, the Communist Party and the government honored more than 100,000 soldiers, officers and generals with orders and medals, awarding many the title of Hero of the Soviet Union.

The victory at Kursk had great international significance and further enhanced the prestige of the Soviet Union.

The shadow of the coming catastrophe now fell over Nazi Germany. The showdown on the German-Soviet front in the summer of 1943 compelled the Nazis to transfer fourteen divisions and other reinforcements from other fronts, thus significantly weakening their forces in Italy and France.

Hitler's attempt to seize the strategic initiative from the Soviet command ended in total defeat, and henceforth until the war's end the German forces were compelled to limit themselves to defensive operations. This was evidence that Germany was weakening. Her ultimate defeat was now only a matter of time.

The Soviet strategic and operational-tactical commands matured enormously. The counteroffensive at Kursk involved far larger forces than previous offensive operations. For example, seventeen weakened field armies without special tank units took part in the defense of Moscow; fourteen field armies, one tank army and several mechanized corps were engaged in the Battle of Stalingrad; but in the Kursk operations twenty-two full-strength field armies, five tank armies and six air armies and large long-range bomber units participated.

In the Kursk counteroffensive we used special mechanized and tank units widely for the first time; and in several operational maneuvers they were the decisive factor, penetrating the enemy lines in depth and driving wedges into the rear of enemy groupings.

The tank armies, artillery divisions and corps, and powerful air armies essentially changed our capabilities—and, consequently, the character of front operations, not only in scale but also in objectives. In comparison with the first period of the war Soviet forces became far more mobile, and this increased the average daily rate of advance significantly. The density of artillery and tanks per mile of front line was sharply raised. In the summer offensive we found it possible to create a density of 250 to 300 guns and 25 to 30 tanks per mile of front.

One of the decisive factors in the victory at Kursk was the high morale and political conviction of our troops. This was achieved by intensive and painstaking political agitation carried out by commanders, political commissars, Party and Komsomol organizations, both in the preparatory period and during the battle itself.

Soviet guerrillas operating in the enemy's rear also contributed to the Soviet victory at Kursk, Orel and Kharkov. The "railroad war" carried out by the guerrillas of Byelorussia, Smolensk, and Orel oblasts and the Dnieper valley was especially effective in cutting enemy supply lines. The guerrillas blew up trains, stations and yards and provided the Soviet command with intelligence data that enabled it to assess the strategic situation and enemy intentions in the summer of 1943.

The Battle of

BERLIN

JANUARY–MAY, 1945

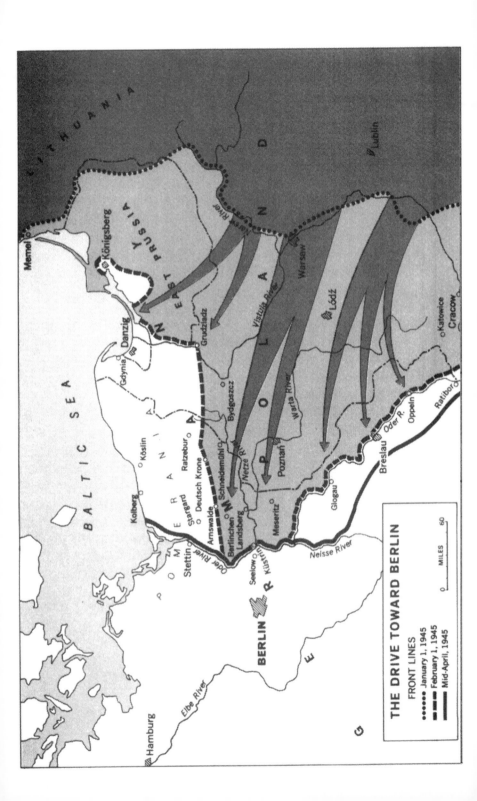

THE DRIVE TOWARD BERLIN

FRONT LINES

· · · · · · · January 1, 1945
▬ ▬ ▬ ▬ February 1, 1945
▬▬▬▬▬▬ Mid-April, 1945

0   60
MILES

Editor's Note

The Battle of Berlin was the culminating and conclusive engagement of the war. It was the war's most dramatic conflict, the Götterdämmerung of the Third Reich, climaxed by the melodramatic deaths of Adolf Hitler, Eva Braun, Goebbels and his family and others in the Führer bunker in the heart of Berlin.

This was the moment toward which Zhukov and the Russian commanders had been moving since the tide of war slowly began to turn with Zhukov's first great victory at Moscow in December, 1941. It was the moment of which the Russian people had dreamed.

The year 1944 was spent by the Red Army in remorseless operations which harassed, chivied and pounded the Nazis out of the Soviet Union. Zhukov began 1944 in the Ukraine. He and Vasilevsky directed a general offensive by four army fronts in a rolling sweep across the broad Ukrainian plains.

The Soviet military machine was moving very smoothly now and when the brilliant General N. F. Vatutin, commander of the First Ukrainian Front, was fatally wounded at the end of February Zhukov took his place on March 1, assuming a direct operational post for the first time since early in the war.

By late spring Zhukov had shifted back to the role of Supreme Headquarters coordinator, this time in the Byelorussian sector, where another powerful four-front offensive, Operation Bagration, got under way in June. Zhukov coordinated two fronts and Vasilevsky two.

Soviet troops were moving up to and beyond Russia's western frontiers. By autumn the Germans had been expelled from almost the last segments of Soviet territory. The end was near. Stalin was turning his mind, more and more, to grandiose political questions: Who would dominate Eastern Europe at the end of the war? What kind of Germany would emerge? What about the Balkans and the eastern Mediterranean? The Polish question became more acute. Stalin wanted a Polish government subservient to him. The Polish government-in-exile in London strove valiantly to cling to hopes of a postwar future.

And what of the balance of political force within the Soviet Union itself, between the Party and the army, between the Politburo and the generals? By the autumn of 1944 politics was becoming a major factor in Soviet military planning. Before this, survival and vanquishment of the Nazis had been the prime consideration.

Politics was becoming even more important in the Soviet High Command. The brilliant Soviet commanders aggressively competed against one another, none more ruggedly than Zhukov. During the push into Byelorussia Zhukov's anger boiled over. He fired a corps commander and ordered a division commander into a penal company in a race to win a big victory (the capture of Baranovichi) before Vasilevsky's forces could capture Vilnius.

In October the planning for the final battle, the Berlin battle, was well under way in the General Staff. General Antonov, Acting Chief of Staff, and his associates completed the detailed scheme of operations in the last three days of October and the first days of November. Their plan provided for a rapid advance on the German capital with no halts. It was to be carried out in a forty-five-day period. The first stage—a strike 150 to 180 miles into German territory to the Bydgoszcz-Poznań-Breslau-Vienna line—was to take fifteen days. Another thirty days were allotted to the final extinction of the Nazi forces and the capture of Berlin.

During the November 7 holiday period the great Soviet commanders came into Moscow. Operational halts were imposed on the western armies, particularly the three Byelorussian army groups, while positioning took place for the final advance. The commanders—Marshals Zhukov, Vasilevsky, Rokossovsky, Konev, F. I. Tolbukhin and Army General I. D. Chernyakhovsky—consulted with Stalin and the General Staff on the grand finale. It was agreed that the last offensive would be launched January 20, 1945, although final orders and confirmations were not issued until late in December.

The November holiday period came to an end. The marshals had conferred. The plans for taking Berlin seemed complete. They returned to their commands. Then Stalin made a decision which was certain to affect history. He decided that Berlin would be captured by Marshal Zhukov, commanding the First Byelorussian Front. The fact that the First Byelorussian Front was headed by Marshal Rokossovsky, an equally brilliant commander, was a minor problem, easily disposed of. Stalin telephoned Rokossovsky and informed him that the "Supreme Command" (meaning himself) had decided to name Rokossovsky commander of the Second Byelorussian Front.

"The decision," Rokossovsky recalled, "was very unexpected. I had just been at Supreme Headquarters discussing plans for the operations of the First Byelorussian Front toward Berlin. Our proposals had been accepted without comment, and now I was getting a new assignment. I could not help asking the Supreme Commander in Chief, 'Why am I being penalized?' Stalin answered that his deputy, Marshal Zhukov, was being named commander of the First Byelorussian Front and I would learn the other necessary information at Supreme Headquarters."

Zhukov took over command of the First Byelorussian Front on November 16. Rokossovsky replaced General G. F. Zakharov, commander of the Second Byelorussian Front, on the same day. Stalin announced that he personally would coordinate the four army groups that would participate in the Berlin operation.

This left Vasilevsky without a function until he was given command of the Third Byelorussian Front after the death of General Chernyakhovsky in February, 1945.

The stage was now set for the race to Berlin. But there was one more contender for honors: Marshal Konev, commander of the First Ukrainian Front, operating just south of Marshal Zhukov's First Byelorussian Front. Stalin's explicit decision was that Zhukov was to capture Berlin. He laid down operational zones which restricted the approaches to Berlin to Zhukov's forces and ruled Konev out of competition. But Konev was a powerful and ambitious rival. He was not going to be shouldered out of a chance at the greatest prize of the war easily.

December, 1944, came to an end. There was a cheerful New Year's celebration in Moscow for the first time since the start of war, and when January opened, the huge Soviet armies were poised for the lunge at Berlin. Enormous quantities of supplies, ammunition, matériel and manpower had been accumulated. Among them, Zhukov, Rokossovsky and Konev mustered 2,500,-000 men, 41,000 guns, more than 6,000 tanks and 6,500 planes. The Germans faced them with possibly one million men and a quarter to one-third of the Soviet resources in guns, tanks and planes.

These vast forces roared into action January 12, 1945—a week ahead of schedule. The speed-up was at Stalin's instruction, a response to Winston Churchill's ardent plea for Soviet action to counter the dangerous and unexpectedly successful Nazi western offensive in the Ardennes.

The Soviet armies rammed forward, Zhukov's troops in the vanguard, smashing through the Nazi defense lines. By the end of January they were ready for the final thrust to Berlin. But then the attack ground to a halt, and was not renewed until April 16. Why? This is one of the major enigmas of the last days of the war—one which finds Zhukov pitted in virulent argument against his fellow marshal, Chuikov. Stalin made the decision not to press for Berlin in February. The suspicion is strong that he was politically rather than militarily motivated. The controversy still rages twenty-five years later, and Marshal Zhukov's account of the Battle of Berlin is basically designed to answer his critics on this point.

Stalin made another move as the war neared its end. He deliberately changed the ground rules to give Konev a chance at capturing Berlin. Whether this was related to the delay in the final assault on the Nazi capital or to his own personal political calculations may never be known. Whatever his motivation, he knowingly exacerbated the tense relationships between his military proconsuls and set the stage for a quarter-century of acrimonious argument and hard feelings.

Berlin finally fell to the combined blows of Zhukov's First Byelorussians and Konev's First Ukrainians. Marshal Zhukov's forces were in the vanguard and won the prime honor of seizing the Reichschancellery and the Hitler bunker.

Ominously, the war ended in a blaze of rumor and suspicion. The Soviet commanders, Zhukov among them, felt they were racing the Americans and the English to Berlin. Indeed, Stalin fixed the mood by posing the question to his commanders: "Who is to capture Berlin, we or the Allies?"

The competition was not only between Zhukov and Konev, but between the rival Allied forces. Or so the Russians thought. Thus, in a sense, Zhukov's victory in the Battle of Berlin might be considered—at least from the Soviet side—the opening and successful first act in the cold war which succeeded the hot war.

Small wonder that the military and political controversies over the Battle of Berlin still echo. They will be argued for another hundred years. For a long time Marshal Zhukov was not able, because of the restrictions imposed upon him when he was removed from office by Nikita Khrushchev, to tell his own story. His version of what happened in the final days of the war, whether accurate or not (and it must be considered an eloquent piece of special pleading), was published immediately after Khrushchev fell from power. It is Zhukov's personal bid for his role in history as the conqueror of Berlin and the victor over Hitler.

H.E.S.

The Berlin operation was part of the final assault against Nazi Germany. The participation of most of the Soviet armed forces in that assault speeded the end of the war and Germany's unconditional capitulation.

As the concluding operation of World War II in Europe, Berlin has a special strategic significance since it provided the final solution to key military and political problems on which the postwar organization of Germany and her place in the political life of Europe depended.

In preparing for the final fight with Fascism and the storming of Berlin, the Soviet armed forces strictly followed the policy that had been agreed upon and proclaimed by the Allies— the policy of unconditional surrender by Germany, militarily, economically and politically. The Soviet Union consistently pursued the objective of a complete liquidation of Germany's Fascist social and political system and of calling to account all the major Nazi criminals for their vile deeds, atrocities, mass murders, destruction and outrages upon the peoples of the occupied countries, including our own long-suffering land.

Supreme Headquarters' strategic plan for the final operations of the war had largely taken shape by November, 1944, after Soviet troops had reached the boundary of East Prussia and the Narew and Vistula rivers on a broad front. The early formulation of the strategic aspects of the plan enabled the military councils of the individual fronts to give careful consideration to all operational, political and supply problems. According to the strategic plan, the final assault against Berlin was to be preceded by two major offensive operations: one in East Prussia by the forces of the Third and Second Byelorussian fronts, and the other—subsequently named the Vistula-Oder operation— in the direction of Warsaw and Berlin by forces of the First Byelorussian and First Ukrainian fronts.

According to the plan, the First Byelorussian Front was to strike in the general direction of Poznań, and the Second Ukrainian Front had as its objective the Oder River northwest of Glogau, at Breslau and at Ratibor. The Second Byelorussian Front would be concerned entirely with enemy troops in East Prussia. Its main forces, which were supposed to cut off the enemy's East Prussian group, were to be fighting in East Prussia before the beginning of February, and its left wing, after reaching the lower reaches of the Vistula north of Bydgoszcz (Bromberg), was to assume defensive positions.

The immediate objective of the First Byelorussian Front was to break through the enemy defenses in two sectors and, having defeated the German forces around Warsaw and Radom, to advance to a line running through Lódź. Subsequently, the front was to advance toward Poznań and reach a line running from Bydgoszcz through Poznań to the south, where it would connect with the First Ukrainian Front.

There was no way for Supreme Headquarters to predict the situation beyond that point. The advance of the Second Byelorussian Front could be delayed, in which case Soviet forces would be unable to cut off East Prussia as planned. The First Byelorussian Front would then be obliged to divert a substantial part of its forces, or even its main thrust, to the north. All these eventualities were envisaged in the planning and execution of the operation.[1]

As for our neighbor on the south, we were confident that he would not lag behind. In strength the First Ukrainian Front was almost up to the level of the First Byelorussian Front. Moreover, the two fronts were to carry out adjoining thrusts. We assumed therefore that there would be no need for the First Byelorussian Front to be concerned about its southern flank. Nor did Supreme Headquarters anticipate any need for a diversion of troops of the First Byelorussian Front to the southwest and south. In fact, there was no way in which Supreme Headquarters could have anticipated such a shift in an operation that extended several hundred miles in depth and in which the enemy command had room for maneuver with reserves. The enemy was in a position to move additional forces from the Western front, to remove troops from his isolated Baltic grouping and, by maneuvering along the entire front, to mass his forces wherever necessary and thus slow our advance. However, the Nazi command was unable to make full use of these opportunities, and this was to cost them dearly. At the critical moment they lacked the necessary reserves to stem our advance.

Supreme Headquarters felt that the future operations of the First Byelorussian Front, once it had reached the Bydgoszcz-Poznań line, should be decided on the basis of the situation

---

[1] Zhukov is misleading here. While it is true that "all eventualities" were no doubt envisaged in the plan, the fact remains that on November 15 Stalin specifically ruled that Zhukov and the First Byelorussian Front were to make the drive on Berlin. The operational areas of the Second Byelorussian Front and the First Ukrainian Front were deliberately devised to assure Zhukov a clear thrust to Berlin and to prevent Konev or Rokossovsky from getting in his way. Konev was well aware of this and was most unhappy about it. H.E.S.

existing at that time. In the actual course of the offensive, however, the forces of the First Byelorussian Front achieved their objective ahead of schedule. As early as January 23 they had seized Bydgoszcz with their right wing and advanced northwestward toward Schneidemühl and Deutsch Krone. On January 25 the center of the front trapped an enemy group at Poznań, and the left wing, operating in close coordination with the First Ukrainian Front, reached Jarocin.

Around noon on January 25 I had a telephone call from Stalin. I briefed him on the situation, and he inquired about our next moves. I said that since the enemy was demoralized and unable to put up serious resistance, we would continue our drive toward the Oder River and attempt to seize a bridgehead at Küstrin. The right wing of our front would advance to the north and northwest against the enemy forces in eastern Pomerania, which did not seem to pose any serious threat to us.

Stalin replied, "When you reach the Oder, you will have placed your advanced units almost a hundred miles from the flank of the Second Byelorussian Front. You cannot do that. You must wait until the Second Byelorussian Front completes its operation in East Prussia and regroups its forces on the Vistula."

I asked when that would be. Stalin said, "In ten to fifteen days. Also bear in mind that the First Ukrainian Front cannot advance in order to assure your left flank because it will be busy mopping up the enemy around Oppeln and Katowice."

Nevertheless, I asked Stalin not to stop our offensive now because it would be more difficult to overcome the enemy's fortified zone at Meseritz later. I also requested one more army to secure our right flank. He promised to think about it, but I had no further word from him that day.[2]

---

[2] As is apparent from Zhukov's recommendation to Stalin, the Marshal was preparing for a breakneck race to the Oder River and on to Berlin. So, it turned out, was Konev. It was at this point that the first signs of

On January 26 reconnaissance units of the First Guards Tank Army reached the Meseritz fortified zone and took a large number of prisoners. Interrogation established that the fortified zone was not yet fully manned in several sectors, and that German forces were still being moved up.

On the basis of this information I issued orders to accelerate our advance toward the Oder River with our main forces and to try and seize bridgeheads on the west bank. To secure the right flank of the forces driving toward the Oder (the First and Second Guards tank armies, the Fifth Shock Army, the main force of the Eighth Guards Army and the Sixty-ninth and Thirty-third armies), I ordered the Third Shock Army, the Polish First Army,

---

Stalin's hesitations appeared. Here is how General Shtemenko described the situation as it appeared to the General Staff:

"The offensive of Soviet troops in East Prussia, on the Vistula and in Silesia had been so decisive and precipitous that within two weeks the First Byelorussian and First Ukrainian fronts had achieved their aims, reaching the Poznań-Breslau line.

"Since they had completed the first stage of the campaign, it was necessary to determine the next move immediately now that the attack on Berlin had become the order of the day and was, you might say, our immediate goal.

"On the twenty-sixth of January the General Staff learned of the decision made by the commander of the First Byelorussian Front to continue his offensive without halt until he captured the German capital. He proposed taking four days to move up his troops, particularly his artillery and rear services, to replenish his supplies, to get his mechanized units into order, to put the Third Shock Army and the First Polish Army into the first echelon, and on February 1–2 to renew the offensive with all his forces.

"His first objective was to force the Oder on the march, following up with a swift blow at Berlin, directing the chief force of his attack on the German capital from the northeast, the north and the northwest. To achieve this, the Second Guards Tank Army would strike from the northwest and the First Guards Tank Army from the northeast.

"The next day [January 27] the General Staff received the decision of the commander of the First Ukrainian Front to move on his front without measurable pause, launching an offensive on February 5–6 that would

the Forty-seventh and Sixty-first armies and the 2nd Cavalry Corps to swing to the north and northwest against enemy forces in eastern Pomerania. Parts of the Eighth Guards Army and the First Guards Tank Army were to mop up the trapped garrison at Poznań. At first we thought only twenty thousand men had been encircled there, but it turned out to be sixty thousand, and the liquidation of the forces in the fortified city took until February 23.

According to our estimates, the enemy troops in eastern Pomerania would not be able to strike at our forces before they reached the Oder, and if an enemy counterattack did occur, we would still have time to shift part of our forces from the

---

reach the Elbe by February 25–28, while his right wing, in cooperation with the First Byelorussian Front, captured Berlin.

"Thus both fronts aimed to take Berlin without any kind of pause. But how could Marshal Konev's plan be reconciled with Stalin's orders that Berlin was to be taken by the First Byelorussian Front and that front only? After heated debate in General Antonov's offices the General Staff decided to approve both plans, and Supreme Headquarters agreed to this. However, the demarcation line between the two fronts was to be the one recommended by Marshal Zhukov—that is, the line that had been previously approved was to stay in effect up to Smigiel. Beyond that the line was to be Unruhstadt–Obra River–Oder River–Ratzdorf–Friedland–Gross Köris–Michendorf. In fact, this line pushed thte troops of the First Ukrainian Front south of Berlin and gave them no opening for a direct blow from the south or southwest, compelling them to advance toward Guben and Brandenburg.

"The General Staff knew that this was absurd—on the one hand approving the plan of Marshal Konev for his right wing to attack Berlin and on the other establishing a demarcation line that would not permit him to carry out his plan. We had to find some way out of this situation, and we believed that either the situation itself would provide its own needed correction or that we would be able to correct this stupidity in some way in the course of the operation, particularly since we were still some distance from Berlin. But, as the evolution of events disclosed, it proved impossible to carry out the attack on Berlin in so short a time." (Shtemenko, *Voyenno-Istoricheskii Zhurnal*, May, 1965, pp. 65–68.)   H.E.S.

Oder line to attack the Pomeranian group. And that was what happened.

After several conversations, Stalin finally agreed with the front's estimates of the situation, but he insisted that we secure our right flank without the benefit of additional forces. His concern about the right flank turned out to be well founded. Developments showed that the enemy threat from eastern Pomerania was growing steadily.

Meanwhile, our offensive was forging rapidly ahead. The main forces of the First Byelorussian Front broke through the Meseritz fortified zone and on February 3 made a brilliant thrust to the Oder River, seizing one small bridgehead on the west bank near Küstrin.[3]

By that time enemy pressure against our right flank had greatly increased. Aerial reconnaissance established that large

---

[3] This Oder bridgehead, not much more than thirty miles from Berlin, was as far as Zhukov was to get until the resumption of the drive on Berlin on April 16. It is this delay and the argument over the reasons for it that have produced one of the greatest of Soviet postwar military controversies. Was the delay military or political? Shtemenko contends it was purely military:

"By the end of January it became known that the enemy had created a strong group in Pomerania. The General Staff viewed this as a threat to the right flank and rear of our forces advancing on Berlin. Moreover, a gap of more than sixty miles had been opened up between the First and Second Byelorussian fronts. It was covered only by cavalry, and our forces were experiencing acute shortages of ammunition and fuel because the supply bases were still on the Vistula. This situation compelled Supreme Headquarters and the General Staff to re-examine their original decision. It was impossible to make a dash for Berlin, ignoring the strong enemy forces on the flank as well as the rear and supply situation. Twenty years have now passed, the cards are all on the table and no one has to assume responsibility for these decisions. In their memoirs some comrades have ventured serious speculations about the possibilities of our having seized Berlin in February, 1945." (Shtemenko, *Voyenno-Istoricheskii Zhurnal,* May, 1965, pp. 67-68.)   H.E.S.

enemy forces had been massed in Pomerania. Quick action was needed to meet the threat from the north. The First and Second Guards tank armies were ordered to transfer their Oder River sectors to neighboring units and to move by forced marches northward toward Arnswalde. The reinforced 7th Cavalry Corps, with artillery, sapper units and supplies, was also moved toward Arnswalde from the left flank.

To our right, north of Bydgoszcz, troops of the Second Byelorussian Front were to implement a Supreme Headquarters directive dated February 8, calling for an offensive to start February 10 along a line from Grudziadz to Ratzebur, with the objective of clearing the enemy from all of eastern Pomerania between Danzig and Stettin and reaching the coast of the Baltic Sea.

The offensive began on schedule, but was unable to achieve its objectives. After the fresh Nineteenth Army had been moved up from Supreme Headquarters reserves, the Second Byelorussian Front resumed its offensive on February 24. The First Byelorussian Front joined the offensive against eastern Pomerania on March 1 with the First and Second Guards tank armies. This helped the left flank of the Second Byelorussian Front to speed up its advance. It reached the Baltic coast and captured Köslin on March 5 and then swung all its armies eastward toward Gdynia and Danzig. The First Tank Army of the First Byelorussian Front, which was operating near Kolberg at that time, was temporarily transferred to the Second Byelorussian Front by Supreme Headquarters to assist in operations against Gdynia. The other forces on the right wing of the First Byelorussian Front went on to clear the rest of the Baltic coast and the lower east bank of the Oder River.

This seems to be a good place to deal with one question that has been raised by some memoirists, particularly Marshal Chuikov: Why didn't the command of the First Byelorussian Front, after reaching the Oder at the beginning of February,

obtain authorization from Supreme Headquarters to drive on
toward Berlin without a stop?

In his memoirs, published in the magazine *Oktyabr*,[4] and
in the historical journal *Novaya i Noveishaya Istoriya*, Marshal
Chuikov asserts that "Berlin could have been taken in February
and this would, of course, have brought an earlier end to the
war."[5]

Chuikov's assessment has been challenged by several comrades
in articles in the journal *Voyenno-Istoricheskii Zhurnal*.[6] The
Marshal has replied that "these objections come not from active
participants in the Vistula-Oder operation, but from those who
had a hand in drafting the orders of Supreme Headquarters and
of the [First Byelorussian] front ordering a halt in the drive
toward Berlin and execution of the east Pomeranian operation
or from authors of certain historical works."[7]

I must say that the advance toward Berlin was not so simple
as Chuikov thinks.

On January 26, when it became clear that the enemy would
be unable to stem our offensive on the fortified approaches to
the Oder River, we made a recommendation to Supreme Headquarters along the following lines: By January 30 our troops
were to reach a front running through Berlinchen, Landsberg
and Grätz, move up support units, replenish supplies, and on
the morning of February 1 or 2 resume our offensive in an effort
to force the Oder without stopping and drive on toward Berlin
with by-pass movements on the northeast, north and northwest.
That recommendation was approved by Supreme Headquarters
on January 27. The following day Marshal Konev, the commander of the First Ukrainian Front, submitted his recommendation calling for liquidation of the Breslau grouping and

[4] March–May, 1964.
[5] February, 1965, p. 6.
[6] March and April, 1965.
[7] *Novaya i Noveishaya Istoriya*, February, 1965.

a continued advance that would reach the Elbe River by February 25–28, while the right wing would operate in conjunction with the First Byelorussian Front in an effort to capture Berlin. That recommendation was also approved by Supreme Headquarters on January 29.

It is a fact, as Chuikov asserts, that the enemy had only limited forces on the approaches to Berlin and that his defenses were quite weak. But, as I noted earlier, it was at this time that the enemy grouping in eastern Pomerania began to pose a serious threat to the flank and rear of the forces driving toward the Oder. Here is what Field Marshal Keitel had to say after the end of the war: "In February and March of 1945 we planned to carry out a counteroffensive against the forces that were advancing toward Berlin and we intended to use the Pomeranian bridgehead for that purpose. The plan was that troops of Army Group Vistula, covering their flanks around Grudziadz, would break through the Russian front and advance along the valleys of the Warta and Netze rivers toward Küstrin from the rear." This plan has also been confirmed by General Guderian, the former Chief of Staff of German ground forces. In his book *A Soldier's Memoirs* he wrote that the German command intended to strike a powerful counterattack with the troops of Army Group Vistula "with lightning speed, before the Russians were able to move up large forces or to guess our intentions."

This testimony by German military leaders leaves no doubt about the reality of the threat posed by the enemy forces in Pomerania. However, the Soviet command anticipated the enemy's intentions and took the necessary steps against them.

At the beginning of February the Germans had their Second and Eleventh armies between the Oder and the Vistula—a total of 16 infantry, 4 tank and 3 motorized divisions, 4 brigades and 8 battle groups. Our intelligence reported a continuing flow of troops into the area. Moreover, the Germans had their Third Tank Army near Stettin for possible use either around Berlin or to reinforce the east Pomeranian forces (which is what actually happened). Could the Soviet command risk a continued drive toward Berlin in view of this threat from the north?

Chuikov says: ". . . as for risk, it is often needed in war. And in this particular case the risk was well founded. Our forces had already advanced three hundred miles in the Vistula-Oder operation and from the Oder had only thirty-five to fifty miles to go to reach Berlin."[8]

Of course, we could have ignored the threat and launched both tank armies and three or four field armies straight toward Berlin. But with a thrust from the north the enemy would have been able to break through our flanks, cut us off at the Oder River and thus place the troops around Berlin in a precarious situation.

History shows that risks should be taken, but not blindly. A useful lesson in this connection is offered by the Red Army's drive against Warsaw in 1920, when a reckless, unsecured advance turned success into a serious defeat.[9]

"An objective assessment of the strength of the German forces in Pomerania would show that any threat to our troops from that direction could have been localized by the Second Byelorussian Front," Chuikov contends. The facts do not bear out that assertion. The task of eliminating the enemy threat in eastern Pomerania was originally assigned to the Second Byelorussian Front, but its forces turned out to be quite inadequate. The offensive launched by the Second Byelorussian Front on February 10 made very slow headway. In ten days its troops

---

[8] *Ibid.*, p. 7.

[9] Actually, in offering so many reasons against the immediate drive on Berlin and in emphasizing the risks, Zhukov is contradicting his own specific proposals to Stalin in late January and early February when he wanted permission to go directly into the attack. His reference to the 1920 catastrophe of the Red Army at Warsaw is a tangential dig at Stalin, who was a strong supporter of that ill-fated drive.   H.E.S.

advanced no more than thirty to forty miles. At the same time, in fact, German forces south of Stargard went over to the counteroffensive and pushed our troops southward five to eight miles. In view of that situation, Supreme Headquarters decided to move up four field armies and two tank armies of the First Byelorussian Front to cope with the east Pomeranian forces, which by then numbered forty divisions. The enemy's force in eastern Pomerania, indeed, was able to hold out against both Soviet fronts until the end of March. That is how hard a nut it proved to be.

Chuikov contends that the First Byelorussian and First Ukrainian fronts could have provided eight to ten armies, including three or four tank armies, for an offensive against Berlin in February, 1945.[10] I cannot agree with that either. At the beginning of February the First Byelorussian Front had only four understrength armies (the Fifth Shock Army, the Eighth Guards and the Sixty-ninth and Thirty-third armies) on the Oder River out of a total of eight field armies and two tank armies. The other forces of the front had been swung around to face the enemy in eastern Pomerania, and one corps each from the Eighth Guards and Sixty-ninth armies were still busy against the trapped German forces at Poznań. As for the First Ukrainian Front, between February 8 and 24, it was still conducting an offensive northwest of Breslau with four field armies, two tank armies and the Second Air Army. The enemy, having brought up substantial forces, was offering stubborn resistance. The First Ukrainian Front finally reached the Neisse River after having advanced sixty miles in a period of seventeen days. Its forces attempted to cross the river, but failed, and therefore took up defensive positions.

It must also be borne in mind that our forces suffered heavy losses during the Vistula-Oder operation, and that the average strength of the rifle divisions was down to 5,500 men by Feb-

[10] *Novaya i Noveishaya Istoriya*, 1965, No. 2, p. 7.

ruary 1, and as low as 3,800 to 4,800 in the Eighth Guards Army. The two tank armies had a total of 740 tanks, with an average of 40 per brigade and as few as 15 to 20 tanks in many brigades. The situation was roughly the same in the First Ukrainian Front.

In short, neither the First Ukrainian Front nor the First Byelorussian Front was in a condition to carry out the Berlin operation in February, 1945. To exaggerate the capabilities of one's forces is just as dangerous as to underestimate the strength of the enemy. This has been demonstrated by the experience of the war and should not be ignored.[11]

We must not forget, finally, about the supply situation of our forces, which had advanced three hundred miles in a period of twenty days. At such a high rate of advance it was natural for the support units to be lagging behind, and the troops were feeling the need of supplies, especially fuel. The air force did not have time to move its planes to more advanced bases either.

Without analyzing the problems of the support services under these conditions, Chuikov writes:

If Supreme Headquarters and the front headquarters had properly organized the flow of supplies and had been able to deliver the required amount of munitions, fuel and foodstuffs to the Oder in time, and if our air force had been able to rebase itself on airfields near the Oder and our pontoon and bridge-building units had as-

[11] Shtemenko points out that it was "extremely difficult" to work out plans for the final Berlin offensive because of Stalin's arbitrary decision that the German capital was to be captured by Zhukov. He also notes that during the delay on the Oder Soviet forces were extremely active in Hungary—where Budapest was captured and the bitter ten-day battle of Lake Balaton was fought—in driving on Vienna, in moving on Czechoslovakia and in gingerly mopping up Silesia without damaging mills and mines ("Gold," Stalin had called the area in a remark to Konev). This was also the period of the Yalta Conference and preparations for it. Thus there is substantial reason to believe that Stalin had some geopolitical considerations in mind in pausing before the final smash at Berlin. H.E.S.

sured river crossings for our forces, four of our armies—the Fifth
Shock Army, the Eighth Guards and the First and Second tank armies
—could have continued their offensive toward Berlin in early February, advanced another fifty to sixty miles and completed this
gigantic operation with the immediate capture of the German capital.[12]

Such "iffy" statements cannot be taken seriously, even coming
from a writer of memoirs. In fact, Chuikov's own acknowledg-
ment that support services, the air force and pontoon units were
lagging behind suggests that under such conditions a direct
drive against Berlin would have been the purest adventure.
Chuikov writes:

On February 4 the commander of the First Byelorussian Front
[Zhukov] convened a meeting at the headquarters of the Sixty-ninth
Army, including himself, Berzarin, Kolpakchi, Katukov, Bogdanov
and myself. We were sitting at map tables discussing the plan for
the offensive against Berlin when the direct telephone from Moscow
rang. I was sitting nearby and could hear everything. Stalin was
calling. He asked Zhukov where he was and what he was doing.
The Marshal replied that he had gathered his army commanders at
Kolpakchi's headquarters and was discussing the offensive against
Berlin. After Zhukov had finished his report, Stalin demanded, to
the surprise of the front commander, as it seemed to me, that he
stop this planning and get busy on the operation against the enemy
forces of Army Group Vistula in Pomerania.[13]

But there never was such a conference at Sixty-ninth Army
headquarters. On February 4 and 5 I was at the headquarters
of the Sixty-first Army, which was occupying the right wing of
the front preparatory to operations against the enemy's Pomeranian forces. So the talk with Stalin reported by Chuikov
could not have taken place.[14]

[12] *Oktyabr*, April, 1964, pp. 128–129.

[13] *Novaya i Noveishaya Istoriya*, February, 1965, pp. 6–7.

[14] It is extremely unlikely that Chuikov made up the story of the confer-

Chuikov also contends that the possibility that Berlin could have been seized in February, 1945, was later raised at a military-science conference in Berlin in 1945, but that the question was not discussed further because it would have implied criticism of Stalin's actions.[15] True, the question was posed at the conference, but by a representative of the General Staff, Major General S. M. Yenyukov, and not by Chuikov. As far as I remember and as the stenographic record of the proceedings shows, Chuikov did not comment on the question at all.[16] Now about the Berlin operation itself.

The original idea and plan for the Berlin operation were further developed at Supreme Headquarters throughout the entire period of the Vistula-Oder operation. At first Supreme Headquarters thought of starting the operation with three fronts simultaneously, but it developed that the Second Byelorussian Front, which after the East Prussian operation had to move its forces from the Danzig-Gdynia area to the lower reaches of the Oder, would not have been ready to force the Oder River before April 20.

In view of the existing military and political situation, Su-

---

ence attended by Zhukov, Berzarin, Kolpakchi, Katukov, Bogdanov and himself. What is more probable is that Chuikov has confused the place or date. This enables Zhukov to give a debater's answer to Chuikov while ignoring the substance of Chuikov's report.   H.E.S.

[15] *Op. cit.*, p. 7.

[16] This is another example of Zhukov's use of debating tactics. Chuikov did not contend that he himself raised the question of the Berlin operation at the December, 1945, military conference. What is important here is that the issue was regarded as striking enough to be discussed even though raising it implied criticism of Stalin's leadership. Only a major issue would have been brought up in such circumstances. It is obvious from Chuikov's statement, and from other statements about the December, 1945, conference which are to be found in the professional literature, that Soviet military men have been debating this issue from the very end of the war. H.E.S.

preme Headquarters decided to launch the Berlin operation with two fronts not later than April 16. At the beginning of April Marshal Konev, the commander of the First Ukrainian Front, and I were summoned to Supreme Headquarters for the last time to go over the final operations plans for our two fronts. The main thrust toward Berlin and the capture of the city were entrusted to the First Byelorussian Front. The First Ukrainian Front was to strike from the Neisse River against enemy forces south of Berlin and to cut off the main force of Army Group Center from the enemy forces at Berlin, thus securing the operations of the First Byelorussian Front on the south.

At this meeting Stalin also instructed Konev to be ready to strike at Berlin from the south if the enemy managed to put up stiff resistance on the eastern approaches to the city and slowed the advance of the First Byelorussian Front.[17]

[17] Shtemenko describes the meeting in these terms:

"On the 31st of March the General Staff and the front commanders examined the plans for all the fronts and reached agreement on all details. Marshal Konev was very disturbed over the demarcation line with his neighbor to the right [Zhukov] because it gave him no opportunity for a strike at Berlin. No one at General Staff, however, could remove this obstacle.

"On the next day, April 1, 1945, Supreme Headquarters discussed the plan for the Berlin operation. The front situation, the Allies' operations and their intentions were reviewed. Stalin observed that it was necessary to take Berlin in the shortest time possible, and because of this the period for preparation of the operation was extremely limited. It must begin not later than April 16 and must be finished in not more than twelve or fifteen days.

"The front commanders agreed with this conclusion and promised Supreme Headquarters that their troops would be ready in time. Then there was a discussion of the offensive plan which we had approved. In reporting on the plan, the Chief of the General Staff [Antonov] noted that the dividing line between the fronts excluded the troops of the First Ukrainian Front from direct participation in the Battle for Berlin and said that this might have a negative influence on carrying out the operation within the

Since the Second Byelorussian Front would not be able to cross the Oder before April 20, the First Byelorussian Front had to advance with an uncovered right flank in the first crucial days of the operation, and the enemy made an attempt to take advantage of this.

General Jodl made the following statement during an interrogation:

"The General Staff knew that the Battle for Berlin would be decided on the Oder, and therefore most of the Ninth Army, which was defending Berlin, had been moved to the front lines. Hurriedly formed reserves were to be concentrated north of Berlin for a strike against the flank of Marshal Zhukov's forces."

The unusual and highly complex offensive against Berlin required the most careful preparation at all front and army levels. Troops of the First Byelorussian Front were expected to break through a deeply echeloned defense zone extending from

---

designated period. Marshal Konev spoke against the dividing line and emphasized the usefulness of directing part of the First Ukrainian Front forces, especially its tank armies, to the southwest limits of Berlin.

"Evidently appreciating the inadequacy of the reasons for the existing demarcation line between the fronts and desiring to take Berlin swiftly, Stalin decided the question in his own way. He did not fully reject his original idea, nor did he express agreement with the General Staff and the First Ukrainian commander. On the map of the planned operation he simply erased that part of the demarcation line which cut the First Ukrainian Front off from Berlin. He brought the line up to Lübben, thirty-six miles southeast of the city, and stopped there. 'Whoever breaks into the city first—let him take Berlin,' he said to us later.

"That was the origin of the specific demarcation line between the First Byelorussian and the First Ukrainian fronts which did not continue to the full depth of the offensive but which halted on the southeast approaches to the city. The General Staff was satisfied with this solution because the cursed demarcation line had given us nothing but trouble for two months. Marshal Konev offered no objection. He was also satisfied. As things actually worked out, Berlin was taken by the two fronts." (Shtemenko, *Voyenno-Istoricheskii Zhurnal,* May, 1965, pp. 70–71.)   H.E.S.

the Oder River all the way to heavily fortified Berlin.

Never before in the experience of warfare had we been called upon to capture a city as large and as heavily fortified as Berlin. Its total area was almost 350 square miles. Its subway and other widespread underground engineering networks provided ample possibilities for troop movements. The city itself and its suburbs had been carefully prepared for defense. Every street, every square, every alley, building, canal and bridge represented an element in the city's defense system.

Soviet reconnaissance planes made six aerial surveys of Berlin and all its approaches and defense zones. The aerial photographs were used with captured documents and prisoner interrogations to compile detailed assault maps that were supplied to all commands down to company level. The army engineers constructed an exact model of the city and its suburbs for use in planning the final assault.

Army commanders, chiefs of staffs, members of military councils, the front's political commissar, the artillery chiefs of the front and of individual armies, all corps commanders and service chiefs of the front gathered at a conference April 5 to 7 for command games using maps and models. Also present was the front's commander of support services, who made a careful study of the problem of ensuring a steady flow of supplies. From April 8 to 14 more detailed games were played at the level of individual armies, corps, divisions and lower units of all services and the air force.

Because of the front's overextended communications and the expenditure of supplies on the unanticipated east Pomeranian operation, the First Byelorussian Front was still not fully provided with supplies by the start of the Berlin operation. Heroic efforts by our support services were required to move up the essential stores in time, but, as usual, they were up to their task.

In the course of the preparations, the question of reinforcing the shock effect on the enemy was considered. Since troops are ordinarily most impressionable during the night, we decided to launch the offensive two hours before dawn. To avoid accidents in the darkness, we planned to illuminate enemy positions with 140 searchlights. The effectiveness of searchlights was demonstrated during the preliminary war games, and all participants favored their use.[18]

The use of our tank forces was also thoroughly discussed. In view of the enemy's strong tactical defenses on the Seelow heights, we decided to introduce the two tank armies only after the heights had been seized. We did not expect the tank armies to break out into open operational terrain after our tactical breakthrough, as they had in the Vistula-Oder and east Pomeranian operations. However, in the actual course of the battle, when the thrust of the first echelon of our front proved inadequate to break through the enemy defenses, it was feared that the offensive would be held up. After a discussion with the army commanders, late on April 16 we decided to reinforce the thrust of the field armies with a powerful strike by all our planes and the tank armies.

The enemy threw everything he had into the battle, but toward evening on the seventeenth and on the morning of the eighteenth we succeeded in overcoming the defenses on the Seelow heights and resumed our advance. Then the Germans moved up from Berlin substantial forces, including antiaircraft artillery, which slowed the offensive to some extent. We would be delayed again unless we found some way to overcome the resistance of these additional forces.

[18] Zhukov's great "searchlight technique" was a flop. The searchlights were powerless to penetrate the smoke and fog of battle and actually blinded both troops and commanders. The lights were switched off and on, which further confused everyone. Chuikov was extremely critical of the device and complained that he was unable to follow the progress of battle from his observation point. (Chuikov, *Oktyabr*, 1964, pp. 144–145.) H.E.S.

During those days Stalin was very worried that our offensive would be held up. He therefore ordered the commander of the First Ukrainian Front to strike at Berlin from the south, in accordance with the operations plan approved on April 3. After heavy fighting the enemy's defenses on the approaches to Berlin finally gave way on April 20.[19]

General Weidling, commander of the Germans' 56th Tank Corps, said during an interrogation, "April 20 was the hardest day for my corps and probably for all the German troops. They had suffered tremendous losses in previous fighting; they were worn down and exhausted, and were no longer able to resist the tremendous thrust of the superior Russian forces."

At 1:50 P.M. on April 20 the long-range artillery of the 79th Rifle Corps of the Third Shock Army, under the command of Colonel General V. I. Kuznetsov, was the first to open fire against Berlin, thus laying the basis for the historic assault of the German capital. The following day elements of the Third Shock Army, the Second Guards Tank Army and the Forty-seventh Army broke into the outskirts of Berlin and engaged the battle in the city.

In addition to these three armies, we also decided to throw the First and Second Guards tank armies into the battle in an effort to crush the enemy's morale and will to fight, to render maximum support to our weakened field armies and thus speed the capture of Berlin. In any case, by that time we had no other

---

[19] What Zhukov obscures here is that Stalin's order unleashed Konev to drive on Berlin. The order resulted from Zhukov's difficulty in breaking through the Berlin defenses. No such thrust had been approved on April 3, as Zhukov attempts to insinuate. Zhukov does not mention it, but Stalin's worry—and this seems finally to have caused him to launch the Berlin offensive on April 16—was that the Western Allies might make a dash for Berlin in spite of the agreements which placed the German capital in the Russian operational zone. He was also concerned that the Germans might open their front to the Western armies while maintaining fierce opposition to the Russians in the east.   H.E.S.

operational assignments requiring the special maneuverability of tank forces.

The battle soon reached its culmination. We all wanted to finish it off by the May 1 holiday to give our people something extra to celebrate, but the enemy, in his agony, continued to cling to every building, every cellar, floor and roof. The Soviet forces inched forward, block by block, building by building. The troops of Generals Kuznetsov, Berzarin and Bogdanov moved closer and closer to the center of the city. And finally I received the long-awaited call from Kuznetsov: the Reichstag had been taken; our red banner had been planted on it and was waving from the building.

What a stream of thoughts raced through my mind at that joyous moment! I relived the crucial Battle for Moscow, where our troops had stood fast unto death, envisioned Stalingrad in ruins but unconquered, the glorious city of Leningrad holding out through its long blockade of hunger, the thousands of devastated villages and towns, the sacrifices of millions of Soviet people who had survived all those years, the celebration of the victory of the Kursk salient—and now, finally, the goal for which our nation had endured its great sufferings: the complete crushing of Nazi Germany, the smashing of Fascism, the triumph of our just cause.

Most of Hitler's associates, including Bormann, Göring, Himmler, Keitel and Jodl, managed to escape from Berlin, but Hitler and Goebbels, seeing no other way out, ended their lives by suicide.

Like passionate gamblers, up to the very last moment they had hoped for that lucky card that might save themselves and Nazi Germany. As late as April 30 and May 1 the Nazi leaders were still playing for time, opening talks for a cease-fire in Berlin and calling on Admiral Dönitz's newly proclaimed government to negotiate Germany's surrender. General Krebs, an experienced military diplomat, tried by every means to draw General

Chuikov into lengthy and disputatious discussions, but that trick did not work either. General Sokolovsky, who had been entrusted with the negotiations, told Krebs categorically that military activities could be halted only by the complete and unconditional surrender of the German forces to all the Allies. The Nazis refused to agree to an unconditional surrender, and the talks broke off.[20]

Our forces were given the order to finish off the enemy. They launched the final assault on the center of Berlin at 6:30 P.M. General Weidling, the commander of Berlin, surrendered with his generals and staff officers at six in the morning on May 2 and declared that his forces were ready to capitulate.

By three o'clock that afternoon the rest of the Berlin garrison, a total of seventy thousand men, had surrendered. It was all over. And from the Reichstag waved the red banner, symbol of the freedom and might of the Soviet people, of the land of the Soviets.

It had taken just sixteen days for the troops of three fronts —the First Byelorussian, the First Ukrainian and the Second Byelorussian—to crush enemy forces in the area of Berlin and to seize the German capital. The victory had been made possible by the fact that the Soviet Army neared the end of the war mightier than ever before, both materially and spiritually, surpassing the enemy substantially both in military mastery and in operational and strategic skill.[21]

[20] This is a rather distorted version of Krebs' mission. It was intended as a preliminary to negotiations for surrender by the government which Hitler designated as his official heir before committing suicide. It is true that Krebs, acting for Goebbels, was attempting to get formal negotiations going with a view to legitimatizing the successor government and that hopes of sowing disunity between the Allies and the Soviet forces were not entirely absent from the endeavor.   H.E.S.

[21] The cost of the final battle in Soviet casualties—killed, wounded and missing—was enormous: 305,000 from April 16 to May 8 in the First and Second Byelorussian and the First Ukrainian fronts alone. This reflected

For the Berlin operation the country had supplied the army with forces and supplies that would have been adequate for still another operation of the same magnitude. The Party of Lenin had done everything possible to inspire the fighting men in their difficult task and to instill in them faith in the success of our just cause. All the soldiers, commanders and political commissars had given their pledge to the Party and the nation to pursue the enemy to the victorious end, and all were driven by but a single desire: to reach Berlin as quickly as possible and make the enemy pay for the sufferings of the Soviet people. The Soviet soldier who had traveled the hard road to the approaches of Berlin was consumed with hatred for the enemy and wanted only to finish him off as quickly as possible and rid mankind of the threat of Fascist enslavement.

All the good people of the world who look back on those terrible days of the war when the fate of mankind hung in the balance will remember with respect and affection those who did not spare their lives fighting for the common cause, for the fate of their country, for the freedom and independence of all nations.

I find it difficult to single out for special commendation anyone in particular in that last engagement with the enemy. All who participated in the Berlin operation conducted themselves in a manner befitting Soviet soldiers and displayed a high degree of military skill and capacity for heroism. The Motherland fully appreciated their feats. And now they proudly wear on their breasts the medal that reads, "For the Capture of Berlin." Tens of thousands of soldiers, officers and generals were decorated with orders, while military units that took direct part in the assault of the enemy capital were awarded the honorary title of "Berlin."

---

the enormous pressure by Stalin to break through to Berlin for the kill —and the fanatic Nazi resistance. Both Allied and German casualties during this period in the Western fighting were far smaller.   H.E.S.

The fall of Berlin and the link-up between the Soviet Army and the troops of our allies led to the final collapse of Nazi Germany and its armed forces. The disorganized German Army was no longer capable of resistance. Everywhere in Italy and Western Europe, German troops began to capitulate. On May 8 representatives of the German command signed the Act of Unconditional Surrender, thus acknowledging their total defeat.

Index

OTHER
COOPER SQUARE PRESS
TITLES OF INTEREST

WITH THE ARMIES OF THE TSAR
A Nurse at the Russian Front,
1914–1918
Florence Farmborough
352 pp., 48 b/w photos,
4 maps
0-8154-1090-5
$19.95

THREE WHO MADE
A REVOLUTION
A Biographical History of
Lenin, Trotsky, and Stalin
Bertram D. Wolfe
680 pp., 54 b/w photos
and illustrations
0-8154-1177-4
$23.95

'44
In Combat from Normandy
to the Ardennes
Charles Whiting
With a new preface
240 pp.,
29 b/w illustrations
0-8154-1214-2
$17.95

HITLER'S SHADOW WAR
The Holocaust and World War II
Donald M. McKale
504 pp.,
39 b/w illustrations
0-8154-1211-8
$28.95 cloth

HITLER'S WAR
Edwin P. Hoyt
With a new preface
440 pp., 60 b/w photos,
4 maps
0-8154-1117-0
$18.95

JAPAN'S WAR
The Great Pacific Conflict
Edwin P. Hoyt
With a new preface
568 pp., 57 b/w photos,
6 maps
0-8154-1118-9
$19.95

THE GI'S WAR
American Soldiers in Europe during World War II
Edwin P. Hoyt
With a new preface
664 pp., 29 b/w photos,
6 maps
0-8154-1031-X
$19.95

WARLORD
Tojo against the World
Edwin P. Hoyt
With a new preface
280 pp., 10 b/w photos
0-8154-1171-5
$17.95

INFERNO
The Fire Bombing of Japan, March 9–August 15, 1945
Edwin P. Hoyt
170 pp., 10 b/w photos,
2 maps
1-56833-149-5
$24.95 cloth
Madison Books

THE INVASION BEFORE NORMANDY
The Secret Battle of Slapton Sands
Edwin P. Hoyt
212 pp., 22 b/w photos,
4 maps
0-8128-8562-7
$18.95
Scarborough House

GUADALCANAL
Edwin P. Hoyt
314 pp., 43 b/w photos,
10 maps, 1 diagram
0-8128-8563-5
$18.95
Scarborough House

TRAGIC FATE OF THE U.S.S. INDIANAPOLIS
The U.S. Navy's Worst Disaster at Sea
Raymond B. Lech
336 pp., 52 b/w photos,
2 maps
0-8154-1120-0
$18.95

HEROES NEVER DIE
Warriors and Warfare in World War II
Martin Blumenson
644 pp.
0-8154-1152-9
$32.00 cloth

KASSERINE PASS
Rommel's Bloody,
Climactic Battle for Tunisia
Martin Blumenson
358 pp., 18 b/w photos,
5 maps
0-8154-1099-9
$19.95

HITLER
The Survival Myth
Updated Edition
Donald M. McKale
304 pp., 12 b/w photos
0-8154-1128-6
$17.95

HITLER'S COMMANDERS
Officers of the *Wehrmacht*,
the *Luftwaffe*, the *Kriegsmarine*,
and the *Waffen-SS*
Samuel W. Mitcham Jr.
and Gene Mueller
384 pp., 52 b/w photos,
8 maps
0-8154-1131-6
$18.95

HITLER'S FIELD MARSHALS
And Their Battles
Samuel W. Mitcham Jr.
456 pp., 26 b/w photos,
9 tables, 22 maps
0-8154-1130-8
$18.95

HUNTERS FROM THE SKY
The German Parachute Corps,
1940–1945
Charles Whiting
With a new preface
240 pp., 12 b/w photos,
8 maps
0-8154-1145-6
$17.95

THE MEMOIRS OF FIELD-
MARSHAL WILHELM KEITEL
Chief of the German High
Command, 1938–1945
Edited by Walter Gorlitz
New introduction by
Earl Ziemke
296 pp., 4 maps
0-8154-1072-7
$18.95

ANZIO
The Battle That Failed
Martin Blumenson
224 pp., 4 maps
0-8154-1129-4
$17.95

DEFEAT INTO VICTORY
Battling Japan in Burma and
India, 1942–1945
Field-Marshal Viscount
William Slim
New introduction by
David W. Hogan Jr.
576 pp., 21 maps
0-8154-1022-0
$22.95

THE DESERT FOX IN NORMANDY
Rommel's Defense of
Fortress Europe
Samuel W. Mitcham, Jr.
248 pp., 8 maps, 9 tables
0-8154-1159-6
$17.95

TRIUMPHANT FOX
Erwin Rommel and the
Rise of the *Afrika Korps*
Samuel W. Mitcham, Jr.
376 pp., 26 b/w photos,
8 maps
0-8154-1055-7
$17.95

CORREGIDOR
The American Alamo of
World War II
Eric Morris
560 pp., 23 b/w photos,
4 maps
0-8154-1085-9
$19.95

OCCUPATION
The Ordeal of France,
1940–1944
Ian Ousby
384 pp., 16 b/w photos
0-8154-1043-3
$18.95

THE WEEK FRANCE FELL
June 10–June 16, 1940
Noel Barber
336 pp., 18 b/w photos
0-8154-1091-3
$18.95

CANARIS
Hitler's Master Spy
Heinz Höhne
736 pp., 29 b/w photos,
3 maps
0-8154-1007-7
$19.95

HITLER IN VIENNA, 1907–1913
Clues to the Future
J. Sydney Jones
344 pp., 54 b/w
illustrations, 16 maps
0-8154-1191-X
$24.95 cloth

THE HOUSE OF KRUPP
The Steel Dynasty That
Armed the Nazis
Update Edition
Peter Batty
With a new afterword
360 pp., 17 b/w photos
0-8154-1155-3
$18.95

HANGED AT AUSCHWITZ
An Extraordinary Memoir
of Survival
Sim Kessel
New introduction
by Walter Laqueur
192 pp.
0-8154-1162-6
$16.95

MENGELE
The Complete Story
Gerald L. Posner
and John Ware
New introduction
by Michael Berenbaum
400 pp., 41 b/w photos
0-8154-1006-9
$18.95

JULIUS STREICHER
Nazi Editor of the Notorious
Anti-Semitic Newspaper
Der Stürmer
Randall L. Bytwerk
With a new afterword
264 pp., 31 b/w photos
0-8154-1156-1
$17.95

THE JEHOVAH'S WITNESSES
AND THE NAZIS
Persecution, Deportation, and
Murder, 1933–1945
Michel Reynaud
and Sylvie Graffard
Introduction by
Michael Berenbaum
304 pp., 22 b/w photos
0-8154-1076-X
$27.95 cloth

SIEGFRIED
The Nazis' Last Stand
Charles Whiting
With a new preface
312 pp., 24 b/w photos,
6 maps
0-8154-1166-9
$17.95

THE HITLER YOUTH
Origins and Development,
1922–1945
H. W. Koch
382 pp., 40 b/w photos,
2 maps
0-8154-1084-0
$18.95

SWING UNDER THE NAZIS
Jazz as a Metaphor for Freedom
Mike Zwerin
With a new preface
232 pp., 45 b/w photos
0-8154-1075-1
$17.95

THE MEDICAL CASEBOOK OF
ADOLF HITLER
Leonard L. Heston, M.D.
& Renate Heston, R.N.
Introduction by
Albert Speer
192 pp., 3 b/w photos,
4 graphs
0-8154-1066-2
$17.95

MUSSOLINI
A Biography
Jasper Ridley
464 pp., 24 b/w photos,
3 maps
0-8154-1081-6
$19.95

GENERAL OF THE ARMY
George C. Marshall,
Soldier and Statesman
Ed Cray
876 pp., 24 b/w photos
0-8154-1042-5
$29.95

Available at bookstores
or call 1-800-462-6420

200 Park Avenue South ♦ Suite 1109♦ New York, New York 10003-1503
www.coopersquarepress.com